AME BY CHARABANC

teman

31 May 1933

SLOW ON THE
FEATHER

frontispiece: The author, 1951

Wilfrid Blunt

SLOW ON THE FEATHER

Further Autobiography
1938–1959

We may be slow on the feather
And seem to the boys old fools,
But we'll still swing together
And swear by the best of schools.

William Cory
'The Eton Boating Song'

MICHAEL RUSSELL

© Wilfrid Blunt 1986

First published in Great Britain 1986
by Michael Russell (Publishing) Ltd,
The Chantry, Wilton, Salisbury, Wiltshire

Designed by Humphrey Stone

Typeset at The Spartan Press Ltd, Lymington,
Printed and bound in Great Britain
by Biddles Ltd, Guildford and King's Lynn

Indexed by P. S. H. Lawrence

Also by Wilfrid Blunt

THE HAILEYBURY BUIILDINGS, 1936

DESERT HAWK (Abd el-Kader), 1947

THE ART OF BOTANICAL ILLUSTRATION, 1950

TULIPOMANIA, 1950, rev. ed., 1977

BLACK SUNRISE (Mulai Ismail), 1951

SWEET ROMAN HAND, 1952

PIETRO'S PILGRIMAGE (Pietro Della Valle), 1953

SEBASTIANO (Sebastiano Locatelli), 1956

A PERSIAN SPRING, 1957

LADY MURIEL (Lady Muriel Paget), 1962

OF FLOWERS AND A VILLAGE, 1963

COCKERELL (Sir Sydney Cockerell), 1964

OMAR, 1966

ISFAHAN, PEARL OF PERSIA, 1966

JOHN CHRISTIE OF GLYNDEBOURNE, 1968

THE DREAM KING (Ludwig II of Bavaria), 1970

THE COMPLEAT NATURALIST (Linnaeus), 1971

THE GOLDEN ROAD TO SAMARKAND, 1973

ON WINGS OF SONG (Mendelssohn), 1974

'ENGLAND'S MICHELANGELO' (G. F. Watts), 1975

SPLENDOURS OF ISLAM, 1976

THE ARK IN THE PARK (London Zoo), 1976

IN FOR A PENNY (Kew Gardens), 1978

THE ILLUSTRATED HERBAL (with Sandra Raphael), 1979

MARRIED TO A SINGLE LIFE, 1983

to
CHRISTOPHER
and to the memory of
ANTHONY
my two brothers
with undiminished affection
and gratitude

Contents

Acknowledgements

In writing this book I have received help from many friends. My first debt of gratitude must be to my former colleague at Eton, Mr Peter Lawrence – a leading authority on the history of the College and author of several books on this subject, two of which, *An Eton Camera 1850–1919* and *An Eton Camera 1920–1959*, published by Michael Russell, provide an admirable survey of this school over more than a century. He has also recently created a Museum of Eton Life to house a collection of Etoniana. Not only has he allowed me to use many of the photographs that he has assembled over the years, he has been endlessly helpful by reading what I had written, thus saving a non-Etonian from innumerable blunders and solecisms. He has also compiled the index.

My friend and literary executor Mr John Holmstrom has read and re-read my typescript and galleys, always providing me with extremely stimulating criticism. Sir Rupert Hart-Davis very kindly volunteered to go through the proofs, checking printers' errors while at the same time keeping a watchful eye on an author's stylistic quirks and foibles; as an Old Etonian and a literary figure of great distinction his advice has naturally been of particular value. The enthusiasm of Mr Michael Russell and his constant help with the text, the illustrations and the production of this book and its predecessor have been far in excess of what any author has a right in these days to expect of his publisher. To 'O', who has allowed me to quote at length from his letters which give a vivid account of the problems that face an aesthete in a philistine house, I am indebted for the substance of chapter 9.

As it is some thirty years since I first began to scribble the fragments from which *Slow on the Feather* has ultimately taken shape, I find it hard to recall all those who, over the years, have been kind enough to assist me in various ways. They include – and

I ask forgiveness for any inadvertent omissions – the following:

Mrs John Brasier, Mr Marcus Brasier (for photography), Mr John Coleby, Mrs Anthony Crosland, Mr Robert Cross, the late Mr Francis Cruso, Professor Stephen Frowen, Mr Cecil Gould, Mr Leonard Halcrow, Mrs Arthur Harrison, Mrs Hubert Hartley, the late Hon. George Lyttelton, Professor Karl Morrison, Mr Richard Ollard, Mr Raef Payne, Dr Kelsall Prescot, Mr Oliver Thomas, Miss Charmian Young (for typing), and – last but not least – my two brothers.

Mr John Christian has allowed me to reproduce his delightful watercolour of myself, surrounded by the themes of some of my books, which was presented to me when I retired from the curatorship of the Watts Gallery in October 1985, and Mr Humphrey Lyttelton kindly gave me permission to use his striking caricature of Lord Quickswood. I must also thank the Syndics of the Fitzwilliam Museum, Cambridge, for permitting me to include a photograph of the Poussin formerly belonging to my brother Anthony.

I have made use of, and quoted brief extracts from, a number of books, my debt to their authors and publishers being, I hope, adequately acknowledged in the footnotes.

W.J.W.B.

Foreword

> In these days a man is nobody unless his biography
> is kept so far posted up that it may be ready for the national
> breakfast table on the morning after his demise.
>
> ANTHONY TROLLOPE, *Dr Thorne*

'Biography is one of the new terrors of death.' So wrote Dr John Arbuthnot nearly three hundred years ago, and for the famous it is certainly still true today.

Admittedly death comes to us all, but a man of distinction is particularly vulnerable. While he lives, and provided he is reasonably discreet, our laws of libel protect him to a considerable extent from the public exposure of certain aspects of his private life which he may have tried to keep hidden. But when the death-rattle is heard the vultures gather and, sooner or later, the world hears that its hero had, like the rest of us, feet of clay. It was Lytton Strachey who first began to topple the 'great Victorians' from their pedestals, and now it is the turn of their successors – Strachey amongst them – to be toppled, and then stripped naked. To change the metaphor yet again, there seem to be few cupboards without skeletons.

Robert Skidelsky, in the first volume of his admirable and frank biography of John Maynard Keynes,[1] reminds us how the kindly biographer may, even after the death of his subject and in the freer climate that exists today, feel that he still has his hands tied for a considerable time by what Virginia Woolf called 'the widow and the friends' syndrome. She wrote:

> Suppose, for example, that the man of genius was immoral, ill-tempered, and threw the boots at the maid's head. The widow would say, 'Still I loved him – he was the father of my children; and the

[1] *Hopes Betrayed, 1883–1920*, Macmillan, 1983.

public, who love his books, must on no account be disillusioned. Cover up; omit!' The biographer obeys. And thus the majority of Victorian biographies are like the wax effigies now preserved in Westminster Abbey . . . effigies which have only a smooth likeness to the body in the coffin.'[2]

Though Roy Harrod's biography of Keynes[3] was written after his subject's death in 1946, it was too soon after and Harrod had to tread warily. Friends who were also involved – many of them, of course, still alive – might sue for libel: a risk that remains today. But Harrod's reticence stemmed principally from his spinsterish attitude with regard to what he considered fitting to be disclosed. There was certainly no shortage of material, for even in the twentieth century, when lack of storage space and the use of the telephone have robbed us of so much, the most casual scribbles of the famous or expected-to-become-famous tend to be preserved; and

> Lives of great men all remind us,
> As we through their pages turn,
> That we too may leave behind us
> Letters that we ought to burn.

Letters inscribed 'Read and then destroy' are guaranteed immortality.

In fact, it was not until more than twenty years after Keynes's death that Michael Holroyd[4] publicly disclosed the full story of Keynes's homosexuality during the first thirty-seven years of his life – something of such vital importance that without it half of the man is missing. This is, incidentally, the precise time-span covered in my *Married to a Single Life* (1983).[5]

It might reasonably be supposed that one advantage at least of being a 'man of no importance' would be that nobody will bother to write your biography. I could easily have slipped silently into presumed respectable oblivion; yet, strange though it may seem to many people, I did not want to do that, and I would have felt ashamed had I produced a bowdlerised self-portrait. I shall leave

---

[2] Quoted in Skidelsky, *op. cit.*, p. xx.
[3] *The Life of John Maynard Keynes*, Heinemann, 1951.
[4] In his *Lytton Strachey*, Heinemann, vol. 1, 1967.
[5] In subsequent footnotes referred to as *M.S.L.*

behind me no children, and no visible memorial beyond about thirty books. As Samuel Butler wrote in his *Notebooks*:

> Bodily offspring I do not leave, but mental offspring I do. Well, my books do not have to be sent to school and college, and then insist on going into the church, or take to drinking, or marry their mother's maid.

In particular, I felt that some account of the problems that face a homosexual schoolmaster could possibly be of help to others similarly handicapped through no fault of their own.

My brother Christopher described *Married to a Single Life* as 'undressing in public'[6] – which might have served as a good title, its sequel then being *Naked but Unashamed*. Like my mother I am by nature a truthful person; but, unlike her, I am not a 'private' person. I have always wanted to be able to be, openly, what I *am*. 'In *my* day', an elderly Old Etonian apparently commented sadly after reading my book – 'In *my* day, if one was – er – "like that", one kept quiet about it.' That, of course, was the trouble: one had to. The more tolerant attitude in recent years towards homosexuality, and the fact that I was eighty-two, seemed to me to justify the publication of what I had written about the early part of my life; now, at eighty-four, I risk stretching tolerance even further.

While writing my first volume I made a number of discoveries, primarily that the task presented problems wholly different from those that arise when writing the life of someone else. With the biographies of others – both the long dead such as Linnaeus or Mendelssohn, or the recently dead such as John Christie of Glyndebourne – I knew (or believed I knew) that what interested me might reasonably be expected to interest my public. Friends who read my typescripts usually thought I had got the balance about right, and if cuts were necessary there was, in general, agreement as to where they could best be made.

But with *Married to a Single Life*, though all who read the rough draft felt the book was too long, all wanted different passages sacrificed; one potential publisher even suggested that 'most of the Haileybury stuff' might advantageously be eliminated. When it became clear to me that *someone* might regret

---

6 Christopher tells me that this was the heading of a review of *My Diaries* (1919, 1920) by my kinsman Wilfrid Scawen Blunt (1840–1922).

almost any cut I made, I decided I had no objection to its being regarded as what the Swedes call a *smörgåsbord* – a sort of mixed hors-d'œuvres or cold buffet meal from which the guest selects those dishes that attract him. In the Lyttelton Hart-Davis letters (which contain much about Eton), whenever I saw that a man was about to bowl, bat or eat I turned over two pages that doubtless gave immense pleasure to many other readers. I did not ask that they should have been left out, merely that I should not be expected to read them; but I understand that quite a lot of people did. Those who are more interested in Eton than in me – which is very proper, since it is older, bigger and more important – may well prefer to skip the fifth chapter of this present book.

In *Married to a Single Life* I attempted – perhaps not always quite successfully – to tell 'the truth, the whole truth, and nothing but the truth'; in its sequel so many of the *dramatis personae* are or may still be alive that I have had to lower my target to 'the truth – disguised or curtailed in places to avoid causing embarrassment, not to myself but to others'. Of only two or three people at present living – Grizel Hartley in particular – have I written at some length.

However, if I have felt restricted I did also realise that, when I brought my first volume to a close with my departure from Haileybury in 1938, more than half of my life still lay in the future. After I had left Eton I felt that I could write more freely. As my friend and former colleague, George Lyttelton, put it when I showed him an early draft of parts of this present book, I could now 'give scope to the Rabelaisian vein' which I had had 'largely to suppress in the air of Academe which is apt to be a bit stuffy'. '*Don't* emasculate!' he wrote. 'Go on libelling right and left.' It was not quite so simple as that. While describing my life at Marlborough during the First World War and at Haileybury between the two wars, I had little competition to face. But Eton is both holy and well-trodden ground and, even if I put off my shoes, as a non-Etonian I knew I would still have to walk delicately. What I have to offer here is really little more than a handful of capriciously chosen vignettes.

I suppose it is true that until I was nearly forty I had, without realising it, been steadily indoctrinated in the belief that Etonians were 'stuck up', and that – in the words of an Old Etonian – after 'five years in a lukewarm bath of snobbery' they looked down on the alumni of nineteenth-century public (and even fifteenth-century grammar) schools. Richard Ollard, in *An English Education: A Perspective of Eton*,[7] wrote:

> My father, a country clergyman, and my mother were being entertained in the early thirties by a local landowner of long and impeccable ancestry. The hostess politely asked my mother where her children were at school. On being informed that my eldest brother was in his last year at Eton she paused in evident perplexity.
> 'Eton?' she said. 'Not . . . not *our* Eton?'

I certainly knew parents of Etonians who could have said exactly that – my Aunt Mildred Assheton for one.

One of the great merits of Ollard's book is that, though he is obviously devoted to Eton, he is far from reticent about her shortcomings. One might have imagined that, as an Old Etonian, he was at liberty to express them, just as an Englishman may criticise England but a Frenchman may not. The difference between Ollard's and my book (where Eton is concerned) lies principally in the *treatment* of the material. I had neither the desire nor the ability to write an earnest and balanced account of the school, but chose rather to record some of the stories and chit-chat that might otherwise be lost for ever. 'I care not who knows it – I write for the general amusement.'[8] I have, for example, devoted a whole chapter to Grizel Hartley; Ollard, though he dedicates his book to 'Grizel Hartley, who loved Eton and shewed so many masters and boys what there was to love in it', does not even mention her in the text, and there is only a line or two about her husband, Hubert. I would have liked Ollard to have explained how Grizel brought so many people to love *Grizel* – and this I have tried to do.

In chapter 9 of this book, a boy who was at Eton during the Second World War describes in detail how the hostility of his housemaster to music, and the general philistinism then prevailing in the school, combined to make his life there miserable. An Eton partisan suggests that some inaccuracies and even an occasional absurdity in his account make his whole story impossible to accept. I think that after a lapse of forty years they

---

[7] Collins, 1982. An admirable book, of which I have made much use.
[8] Sir Walter Scott, *The Fortunes of Nigel*, introductory epistle.

are only to be expected, and that the fact that he still so vividly harbours his grievances is evidence of the general truth of what he writes – though I do not doubt that he has overdramatised his woes. But is he to be discredited because he refers to the *Eton Chronicle* (as I might well have done) when in fact it is apparently always known either as the *Eton College Chronicle* or the *Chronicle*? Another reader – a woman who knows nothing of Eton – thought this account one of the most interesting pieces in the whole book, nor could she see any reason to doubt its basic truth.

Since it was uncertain, when *Married to a Single Life* appeared in 1983, whether any sequel would ever materialise, I included in it passages (especially about my mother and about the Haworths) which really belong to this present volume. Also, to avoid too many footnotes and repetitions, I have – perhaps over-optimistically – now in places assumed readers to be familiar with the former book. Once again, and for the same reason, I have occasionally overstepped my time-limits. I have also added a fairly substantial postscript on my brother Anthony.

The Watts Gallery,   WILFRID BLUNT
Compton, Guildford

I

Et in Etona Ego

Educ: during the holidays from Eton.

SIR OSBERT SITWELL, entry in *Who's Who*

In late April 1938, after fifteen years as art master at Haileybury, I arrived at Eton to take up my new post – that of junior drawing master at the most prestigious public school in England. I was thirty-seven, but still very immature.

After Marlborough, where I had been educated, Haileybury had not seemed so very different: it was simply that there I found myself with – mercifully – a God's-eye rather than a worm's-eye view of the scene. But Eton was a new world – and a rather alarming one. It was not merely a different species from Marlborough or Haileybury; it was a different genus. At times there could be 'snobbery with violence' on the staff (Oscar Browning had been a notable example), while J. D. Bourchier,[1] also an Eton master in Hornby's day, was reportedly so ashamed to admit to being a mere 'usher' that, when he returned home to Dublin at the end of the half (term), he would explain that he had been 'spending a few weeks in the neighbourhood of Windsor'. John Betjeman, when I asked him why, as an Old Marlburian, he had sent his son to Eton, replied, 'I think it is *so* important for a boy to go to a *really* bad school.'

At Eton, boys (and beaks on Sundays) wore 'tails' (small boys, 'bum-freezers', or short jackets – also known as 'Etons'), trousers and top hats; 'Pop' waistcoats and sponge-bag trousers – more about Pop in a moment – alone relieved the funereal black which Provost Quickswood – more about him too – hoped in vain might be replaced by blue. Thus indoors, in a poor light, one could

---

[1] Bourchier (who denied the truth of this story) was a fascinating character who abandoned an unsuccessful career as a schoolmaster for a brilliant one as a journalist. He is, so far as I am aware, the only Eton master whose portrait has figured (in 1922) on a Bulgarian postage stamp.

scarcely tell a beak from a butler, or in the street a marquess from a mortician. (In 1957, when giving a talk on Eton, illustrated with pre-war slides, to students taking the English course at Munich University, I was asked who had died, and why '*der obligatorische Zylinderhut*'.) So terrified was I of committing a social solecism that on my first Sunday afternoon I drove myself to Burnham Beeches in full regalia. Though half of one of Eton's noblest buildings was to be destroyed in the Second World War, the suspension at that time of the top hat – allegedly to save time collecting it *and* books *and* a gasmask when the sirens sounded – was for boys, who are always more conservative than beaks where traditions are concerned, a far more significant disaster. Later, top hats – and jackets also – were abolished; but I cannot conceive that anything short of the first nuclear bomb on England could seal the fate of what remains of school dress. School uniforms of any kind, though soon taken for granted and indeed cherished by the wearer, look ridiculous to the alumni of other schools; ask any Etonian what he thinks of the Harrow 'boater'. And the same applies to school slang.

But to revert to Pop (or, more correctly, the Eton Society). Founded in 1811, originally as a debating society, it consists today of some twenty members who very roughly correspond to school prefects elsewhere. It is, however, a self-electing body,[2] though with several *ex officio* members, and those who succeed in getting elected thereby attract hero-worship and acquire a peacock splendour never surpassed by prefects in other schools or, indeed, even by themselves in later life. Pop buttonholes – no other boys could wear a buttonhole except on the Fourth of June – are of almost obscene magnitude, and carefully chosen *pour épater*; Monsignor Ronald Knox, in his day a member of Pop, suggested in his poem 'The Wilderness' that School Yard might be enlivened by some vegetation, including 'Calceolarias of suitable areas / Worthy to rest on the bosoms of Pop'. Members of Pop had various other privileges and amenities, including the power to cane and a clubroom with a telephone. There were also

[2] Or rather, was. On the discovery, in the summer half of 1985, that its premises were being used as a smoking den, the wings of Pop were clipped and it is no longer fully autonomous. The matter came to light when a cleaning-lady applied, in all innocence, to the authorities for more and larger ashtrays.

Pop Room: summer 1933

certain harmless little 'perks' of the kind that schoolboys set so much store by, such as being allowed, by custom of their own creation, to carry umbrellas rolled up, to wear fancy waistcoats, and to have blobs of sealing-wax on their top hats.

Election to this august body could be achieved in various ways, athletic distinction being the most obvious but not the only one. Cold-blooded 'electioneering' by means of ingratiation – Cyril Connolly himself admitted making use of this – was another, and legend had it that an unscrupulous aspirant had once achieved his goal by procuring the services of his sister for the society's president. Good looks were not a disadvantage, especially if accompanied by good will, and even in my day it was widely asserted that a certain pretty but relatively unimportant boy had 'kissed his way into Pop'.

Housemasters at Eton were virtual rulers of their little kingdoms: more like heads of colleges at a university whose students were boys rather than young men. Thus, though the good housemasters were very good indeed, the few tyrants, fearing nobody, could almost get away with murder. I did not have to wait long to meet Eton's finest specimen of the latter class. At my first Chambers (brief daily mid-morning meetings of the

3

Head Master with his staff) I was accosted by a tall, gangling man with a weary, drooping moustache, the remainder of whose face looked as though it had been gone over two days before with a Flymo. Without any preliminaries he said, 'Name?' I replied, 'Blunt.' 'Christian names?' I gave them and he turned on his heel and passed on. This charmer, I learned, was H. K. Marsden ('Bloody Bill'), gathering data for the 'School List' which he edited.

The Head Master now mounted the rostrum, rang a tiny bell and said 'One.'

Dead silence.

'Two.'

Silence still.

'Three.'

Perhaps the staff were being taught to count.

But when we reached 'Eleven', the small voice of a disciple said, 'Four lines from the bottom, sir, Mr Douglas-Home minor should be "little a".'

Close on a hundred pens and pencils made the correction on page 11 of our little white books. And so, much mystified, did I.

These Chambers were essential in a school as decentralised as Eton. Much that was to be discussed at them remained, to the end of my time, incomprehensible; for, very fortunately, I was not involved in those tangles in the curriculum which might perhaps hang upon the employment of – say – 'θ boys in δ– hours'. Sometimes, when a highly confidential matter was about to be broached, the Head Master would ask for the doors to be closed, and the staff, assuming *News of the World* faces, would shuffle a little closer to the rostrum. Though it was widely believed by the boys that we all regaled ourselves with port and sherry during the ritual of Chambers, there was not in fact even Bovril, still less a cigarette, to comfort us while they were gorging at Jack's or Rowland's (vulg. 'tuckshops').

We filed out at last into the bright sunlight.

Eton on that early May morning: I shall never forget it! Like the trippers who were even at that moment being spewed out of the bulging coaches (Eton – Windsor Castle – Hampton Court; Round Trip, 15/-) parked by the Burning Bush, I goggled at the unfamiliar scene: dolphin Lower Boys[3] clustered and chattering

---

[3] New boys, other than King's Scholars, for their first few halves.

under the greening lime-trees; Pop aloof and splendid with their glittering waistcoats and provocative buttonholes; the black-sailed ushers, and the white-rigged chestnut by New Schools – the whole wrapped in that Etonian spring smell which is an amalgam of lilac just breaking into flower, Royal Yacht Club hair-oil, and petrol fumes from the impatient cars. With my new boss, Menzies-Jones, I strolled down Common Lane to the Drawing Schools.

I had taken rooms above an antique shop in the High Street, waiting until a vacancy occurred in one of the 'colonies' – as establishments of three or four bachelor beaks are called. And not merely a vacancy; a new beak was 'looked over', and if approved was eventually *invited* to join one of them. Thus, though another new master also lodged in the house, my first four halves were spent in an isolation wholly unfamiliar.

By day I was largely at the Drawing Schools, for a good many boys came there in their spare time. But evenings would have been depressingly boyless had it not been for the almost ceaseless round of dinner parties given by housemasters; for afterwards one was often invited to 'go round the house' – in other words, to visit in their rooms,[4] as they were going to bed, any boys whom one happened to know. Here one met them on, as it were, their own territory, surrounded by photographs of their family and dogs and horses, with the almost compulsory hunting prints on the walls and perhaps a reproduction of a Rembrandt or a Titian ('Oh, it's just one of Daddy's'). Conversation flowed effortlessly, and it seemed that nothing could puncture the famous Etonian poise.

I remember particularly an evening when I had been dining with Hubert Hartley and his wife Grizel. After dinner Grizel said, 'You *must* go and see "Gully" Mason; he's easily the naughtiest boy in the school.' I did not know him; but I knocked on his door and entered, to find an eighteen-year-old cleaning his teeth and wearing nothing but a toothbrush. I was about to retreat when he turned round and, presenting at close range what today is called a 'full frontal', said without a shade of embarrassment, 'Good

---

[4] Every boy had his own room – one of the great advantages that Eton has over most other public schools.

evening, sir; take a pew.' His clothes were on the only chair; the only 'pew' was his bed. I remained standing, and fled as soon as I decently could. I am told that today, in the permissive 1980s, boys are as coy as maidens used to be, and take refuge in the darkest corner of their rooms if surprised merely 'topless'. Often too much half-baked knowledge has led to loss of innocence and hence a reversion to prudery. But Gully was undoubtedly the kind of boy who had always known everything.

Endless stories are related of him. For example, late for school one day he apologised and said he had been to see the doctor. 'Which doctor?' asked the master, who didn't for a moment believe him. 'No, sir. Ordinary doctor.' Another story of an ingenious excuse for lateness, current soon afterwards and often to be attributed to Gully, was of a boy's claim that his watch was fast. 'Then,' said the beak triumphantly, 'you were later than you thought you were!' 'No, sir. My watch was not as fast as I thought it was.' The boy in question was in fact Lord Berners, and the event had taken place nearly fifty years earlier; but it first appeared in print in his *A Distant Prospect*, not published until 1945.

Eventually Gully was sacked. It was on the penultimate day of his last half, so it made little difference. At the same time there departed from Eton a member of the staff. No – nothing whatever to do with sex, but for foolishly getting himself entangled in one of Gully's more hilarious escapades. (Gully's most notorious achievement had been to hire an aeroplane and take off from the Playing Fields with half a dozen of his friends for a night's gambling at Le Touquet, returning at dawn with the casino entrance tickets to prove it; *and* he wasn't caught!)

Gully was one of those enormously engaging but impossible boys who make a housemaster's life hell. And he was brilliant too, having an article published in *Horizon* while still in his teens. He was killed in the war – 'accidentally', which probably meant that he was doing something heroic but totally imbecile. He was only twenty-one, and after three years in the RAF was still only a flight sergeant. Had he lived to become Lord Blackford he would undoubtedly have enlivened the Upper House.

The Drawing Schools, a substantial red-brick building designed

Visit of King George V and Queen Mary, 7 June 1925.
The Captain of the School stands extreme right, behind the low wall.

by W. A. Forsyth, had been erected in the early twenties on the site of some smelly and redundant gasworks. A photograph survives which was taken on the occasion of a visit paid by the King and Queen on 7 June 1925, cheers as Their Majesties left being led by the Captain of the School, Q. McG. Hogg, KS – better known today as Lord Hailsham. The senior drawing master at that time was the recently appointed Eric Powell – Old Etonian, winner of the Diamond Sculls at Henley, mountaineer, and a housemaster (which drawing masters normally were not, but Powell had originally come to teach modern languages). It was thanks to Dr Alington, then Head Master, that Eton acquired its large and well-equipped art school – but one which unhappily confronted the Parade Ground, an oversight that was often to lead to open warfare.

Powell was a highly competent amateur watercolour painter of the traditional English school – immeasurably better than my

7

E. W. Powell, E. V. Slater and J. D. Hills climbing in Snowdonia

episcopal grandfather but inferior to Turner, a collection of whose watercolours he rather daringly exhibited alongside a number of his own on the occasion of the opening of the building. Powell's athletic prowess and the tragedy of his death (together with that of three of his colleagues) in a climbing accident in Switzerland in 1933 had made it virtually obligatory for Eton housemasters – especially non-Etonians – to have at least a couple of Powells on their walls. You could thus proclaim to the world that you were not a philistine without risking the charge that you might be an aesthete: in fact, it almost made you an honorary OE. It was, incidentally, also safe, even commendable, and much encouraged in due course by Geoffrey Agnew, to collect early English watercolours – preferably bought at what he always referred to as his 'shop'.

Llewelyn Menzies-Jones, under whom I was about to work, was universally known as 'Mones' – not, he insisted, to be spelt 'Moans'. Powell, bicycling one day to the river, had come upon

'Mones' packing the kiln, 1956

9

Mones, also an Old Etonian, making a sketch in Keate's Lane and had invited him to lend a hand at the Drawing Schools. In 1927 Mones had been officially appointed second drawing master, and on Powell's death succeeded him. He was a tall, courtly, middle-aged, well-to-do, eccentric Welshman, a bachelor of course, gaunt as Don Quixote; and he had generously equipped at his own expense a pottery which was gradually to become his whole life. I used sometimes to tease him by asking if his 'vases' had 'cooked' well, and courteously he would each time correct me and tell me that his *pots* had *fired* successfully: in the potting world it is as solecistic to speak of a 'vase' as at Eton to speak of a 'term'. He was also a very competent watercolour painter, etcher and pastellist, more professional than his predecessor; but, like myself, he did not possess the useful knack of instantly producing those quick, witty little sketches which boys always demand. He had, however, learned how to cope with an awkward question such as, 'Sir, can you draw me a hyena?' 'Of course. But what I want is *your* idea of a hyena, not mine.'

A large part of Mones's very considerable charm stemmed from the fact that he seemed to exist in a kind of dream-world, or at all events in a different era or stratum from the rest of us. Had he said 'Prithee' one would hardly have been aware of it, and he had a handful of recurring malapropisms ('I do not wish to appear pontificial', and so on) that never ceased to delight us. He had leanings towards mysticism, and was addicted to prophecy. These 'hunches', as he called them, were often surprisingly accurate, though by 'hunching' in 1938 that there would not be a war he was later to lose the allegiance of some of his most fervent disciples.

As a Fellow of the Royal Horticultural Society I had a free ticket for the private view day of the Chelsea Flower Show, and one year, not being able to use it myself, I gave it to him. 'Were the crowds awful?' I asked. 'Indeed no. There was hardly anybody there; in fact, they didn't seem really quite ready.' It was scarcely surprising; he had gone a day too soon. If one happens to look like an old-world gardener (as he did), probably this is the best way to visit the show in comfort and at no expense. If not, then scruffy clothes, a spade and perhaps a wheelbarrow ought to serve the purpose.

The Provost-elect, Lord Hugh Cecil, later Lord Quickswood (centre), with (left) the Head Master, C. A. Elliott, and the Lower Master, A. E. Conybeare, 12 June 1936.

When Claude Elliott, a medieval historian and Fellow of Jesus College, Cambridge, was appointed Head Master of Eton in 1933, the large majority of the staff had never even heard of him, though someone who had been at Cambridge did confess that he believed there *was* a man of that name at Jesus – 'but it can't possibly be the same one'. In any case he was a layman, for which there was no precedent. However, it was soon discovered that it was the same man, and that Elliott had been an exact contemporary at Eton of Mones, who was immediately approached for further information.

'Do you remember him? What was he like?'

Mones reflected for a while, as if awaiting some prompting from on high. Then – yes – he admitted that he could recall him.

'Well – what was he like?'

'I do not recollect him with clarity.'

'Can't you tell us *anything* about him?'

Another long pause, with eyes uplifted. Then – 'Yes, I distinctly remember . . . that his second name was Aurelius.'

Indeed it was.

Elliott's most endearing qualities were his modesty and his complete absence of snobbery and pomp of office; nobody could possibly have disliked him personally. But the cloak of greatness had been thrust upon him and he wore it uneasily, never quite succeeding in looking a headmaster; indeed, he remained what he had formerly been: a very worthy but rather undistinguished don. George Lyttelton, on learning of his appointment, paid him a rather back-handed compliment when he wrote to a friend, 'They say that Elliott is a good man. His façade is not impressive, but no more is Hitler's.'[5] It was probably later on, when he became Provost, that Elliott was to make his greatest contribution to Eton by his skilful management of the College estates. And, in all fairness, I add that an Old Etonian who came to see me said, 'I imagine you will be attacking Elliott? – Well, I would like to tell you that he was the most stimulating teacher of history I ever had.' I confess that I was astonished.

It was a pity that he was a complete philistine; as George Lyttelton put it, 'Our dear headmaster & Michelangelo, I feel, would have been mere oil and vinegar.' Luckily for me, his hatred of music exceeded his fear of the visual arts, a particular brand of deafness making the former a physical torment whereas the latter merely posed a threat to morality. When joyfully informed by his wife (who *was* a snob) that they had been invited to the Castle to hear Jelly d'Aranyi play, he had replied, 'Good God! I'd rather be flung into a dungeon.' The theatre fared no better: to a young master who wanted to put on a school play he replied that he saw no objection – 'provided it's not too *good*'.

And how about natural beauty? Did it mean anything to Elliott? It might be thought that any mountaineer must have some appreciation of it; but I gather that the pleasure a climber gets is more mystical than aesthetic, perhaps at times almost military: the *conquest* of a *hostile* peak. The talk – when there is breath to talk – must surely be of couloirs, glaciers and avalanches, of ropes, crampons and climbing-irons. Did Elliott ever pause to

---

[5] Ollard, *op. cit.*, p. 169.

pluck a gentian and put it in his buttonhole? Did he recognise a gentian when he saw one? Did he even *notice* the pretty little blue flower that he trod underfoot? I very much doubt it. And did he, when he reached the summit, gasp, 'God, what a view!'? It would surprise me to learn that he did.

When speaking, he had a curious habit of seeming to be about to clear his throat, but though the larynx and Adam's apple moved to the appropriate position, nothing audible emerged. He was known to the staff as 'Mutton', and it was reported that he carried on a string round his neck a disc inscribed, 'If found, do not resuscitate'. Dead – as mutton?

Had he a sense of humour? I suspect so, though of a donnish brand, and possibly some of his more hostile remarks about the arts were, in part at least, tongue-in-cheek. During the war he made a most extraordinary temporary appointment to the Modern Languages staff: Baron George Marochetti, an Anglophile middle-aged Frenchman of Italian extraction and grandson of the famous sculptor to whom we owe the equestrian statue of Richard Coeur-de-Lion outside the Houses of Parliament. The Baron, obviously a dubious acquisition, when shown the bedroom allotted to him in a colleague's house, exclaimed, 'What? In that wardrobe there would not even be room for my *shirts!*' Orthodox members of the staff kept their distance from him; but I found him an amusing, hospitable and widely travelled snob,[6] and earned a bad mark for accepting his invitation to lunch with him at Prunier's where his old friend Mme Prunier appeared in person to discuss the choice of wines. The Baron left Eton very suddenly, in the middle of his first half. So why had Elliott appointed him? Because, he said later, he thought that the war was getting the staff down, and that this colourful addition to it would at all events create a diversion. Surely no man without *some* sense of humour would have acted thus.

In the middle of my very first half I was suddenly faced with a crisis: one morning, while 'in school' and without any warning, Mones had the first of a succession of what I am told are called 'psychotic outbursts'. In describing what occurred I do not mean

---

[6] See his autobiography, *Rich in Range*, Hutchinson, 1941.

Geoffrey Engleheart (see also pp. 187–9)

to appear heartless, for everyone loved Mones; but it cannot be denied that it was a tragicomedy. Moreover, throughout it he never seemed unhappy; it was rather as if he felt himself to be the privileged recipient of supernatural experiences not accorded to ordinary mortals. He suddenly became *exalté*, not manic-depressive – striding up and down the big gallery at the Drawing Schools, singing operatic excerpts at the top of his voice as he conducted an imaginary orchestra, ordering two boys to fetch ices for the entire division and 'charge them to Mr Blunt'. A pitched battle ensued, ices flew, desks were overturned, while I and Geoffrey Engleheart, the Drawing Schools' faithful attendant, looked on, helpless, till the attack had finally worked itself out. Suddenly Mones was perfectly calm again.

But news of this delectable free entertainment soon spread, and that afternoon half the school turned up. I stood at the entrance to the Drawing Schools and persuaded them to go away. Mones, now again *exalté*, was covering the walls with extempore verses painted with poster-colours on huge sheets of paper. One began:

14

> What ho within! What ho without!
> Beyond yon castellated moat
> There lurks the self-appointed Baron B.

To another he laid no claim to authorship:

> As my poor father used to say
> In 1863,
> Once people start on all this Art
> Good-bye, moralitee!
> And what my father used to say
> Is good enough for me.[7]

Then calm returned. At six o'clock I went home, leaving Geoffrey to complete the clearing up, and rang the Head Master. He was at Henley.

About midnight there was a frantic pealing of the bell at my lodgings. I went down to find a white and terrified Geoffrey. Mones, he said, was still at the Drawing Schools, rampaging up and down, singing fortissimo and talking of *suicide* – which seemed to me highly improbable in his present euphoric state. Having verified Geoffrey's story I went to one of the school doctors, whom I scarcely knew. I found him still up, slumped in his armchair, and told him what had happened.

'What do you want me to do?' he asked. There was a half-empty bottle of whisky beside him, and his speech was slurred.

'Mones talks of suicide. I couldn't take the responsibility of risking finding him hanged in the morning, and . . .'

He interrupted me, and I think I can remember almost his exact words: 'People who say they're going to commit suicide never do. Or if they really mean to, then they'll do it anyhow – in the end. Do you want me to have him certified? If you can get him to do something anti-social, like taking off all his clothes in the High Street, then of course I will.' It was obvious that I could get no help in this quarter, so I returned to the Drawing Schools. Mones had calmed down; the crowd of servants from nearby houses had dispersed, and Mones, Geoffrey and I passed what remained of the night peacefully but uncomfortably in the Gallery.

---

[7] A. P. Herbert, *Lines for a Worthy Person.*

There was early school at 7.30,[8] and with the arrival of the boys Mones's euphoria returned. 'You're all half asleep,' he shouted, and challenged them to a race round the Parade Ground. Though nearly fifty he could run like a hare, and was beaten only by a few yards by the fourteen-year-old Viscount Althorp, now father of the Princess of Wales. I wonder whether he too remembers it.

After breakfast I went to see Elliott. 'You know it's Henley week?' Elliott said. (I did.) 'Can't you possibly keep him in play until that's over?' Eventually Mones's sister was summoned and took him home. Later she confessed to me that she had at first thought my account exaggerated (did she imagine that I was after his job?); but she soon discovered that it was not. Apparently this had been his first attack, and by September he was considered sufficiently recovered to return for the Michaelmas half.

All went well until the summer of 1946, when the trouble returned. It was heralded by various portents, the most curious of which was the affair of the stigmata. There was a certain boy to whom Mones was deeply, but entirely innocently, devoted. One day this boy informed him that he had been beaten by the captain of his house. Mones was much distressed and brooded over it for many hours. He woke next morning to discover that his own body bore appropriately situated weals. Outside the Church of Rome, miracles are now a rarity; it was therefore perhaps understandable, though certainly rash, that he saw fit to broadcast news of this paranormal phenomenon among his colleagues. No examination is recorded and no rational explanation was ever proposed, so that the mystery remains unsolved to this day.

Mones vanished for another three or four months, and my predecessor, Robin Darwin, stood in for him. Yet once again he was allowed to come back – a remarkable example of tolerance that would have been found in few if any other schools, and even at Eton perhaps only where an Old Etonian was involved. I had been from the first in charge, *de facto*, of virtually everything at the Drawing Schools except the pottery, and soon after this I was officially appointed senior drawing master and given an assistant. Mones stayed on, unpaid, running his pottery by day and glued

---

[8] A barbaric institution, since abolished. I have taught at the Drawing Schools on an empty stomach and with the thermometer at 38°F.

Robin Darwin and Helena Lyttelton (later Lawrence)

by night to his television set (ice skating was his favourite programme) until finally he faded away to a remote village in Oxfordshire where he died in 1973.

2
Eton in Wartime

In August 1938, after the end of my first and far from unruffled half, I had an operation on both my feet, which had been giving me trouble for some time past. The surgeon at the King Edward VII Hospital in Windsor began his examination by saying, 'So you sat down on your chair rather heavily?' I rose, thinking I must have broken something; but it turned out that I had been mistaken for another patient who had thus injured his coccyx. (Such errors are far from rare, though usually discovered before the patient reaches the operating theatre. On another occasion, I had been momentarily confused with a Mrs Brunt, due for a hysterectomy. The notorious cacography of the medical profession was doubtless to blame.)

The operation was successfully carried out at the Wingfield-Morris Orthopaedic Hospital at Headington, near Oxford, by the best-known orthopaedic surgeon of his day, G. R. Girdlestone. For six weeks I was in plaster to above the knees, and the addition of 'bowler[?]'¹ irons' made me not far short of seven feet tall. At the time of Munich, I was prevented from doing much to help beyond fitting homely-faced 'boys'-maids' with gas-masks, and the following year there was no question of my 'joining up'. I confess that I felt relief rather than regret, for I am not one of nature's soldiers and had always mistrusted that 'General Switchboard', who, since he headed the War Office entry in old telephone directories, was presumably in overall charge of our distressingly inadequate forces.²

¹ Five doctors have failed to provide me with the correct spelling of 'bowler', but 'Bohle' or 'Bohler' has been suggested. At all events it seems to have nothing to do with cricket.

² This reminds me of another mythical soldier. When I was at Haileybury a card arrived in the Common Room from Bavaria addressed to 'General View, Haileybury College, Herts'. I was eventually identified as the intended recipient: I had sent a picture-postcard thus inscribed to the keeper of an inn where I had been kindly treated.

Irish Girl: *oil painting by the author*, 1939

In September 1939 I was staying with a former Haileybury pupil, Richard McClelland,[3] and his mother in westernmost Connemara, almost out of contact with civilisation, when news eventually reached us that England was on the point of war. Abandoning two portraits I was painting of the daughters of the local postmistress, I hurried back to Eton, and was at Windsor

[3] Dr Richard McClelland, now stage and film actor under the professional name of Richard Leech – still a faithful friend after nearly fifty years.

Station, helping to pack hundreds of small, bewildered children into trains, when the fateful declaration was made.

I found myself allotted to the 'Strike Force' of the Home Guard (initially called the Local Defence Volunteers) and thus came to be in very imperfect control of a 'rifle and rounds of SAA' which, fortunately, I was never to be obliged to discharge in anger – nor, so far as I can remember, in anything else. One officer alone carried a Bren gun – an obsolete Czech weapon. Four patrols operated 'at dusk and dawn' to locate the enemy, whose destruction was then 'to be achieved by the Strike Force' – in other words, by me. There followed dreadful vigils futilely guarding bridges and waterworks, often in driving rain. One foggy night I nearly shot a cow which had not responded to my challenge; but during the whole of the war there was never for me an experience half so alarming as that of being driven through peacetime central London by Rose Macaulay.

I find myself described, in an article entitled 'Eton 1940' which was published in *Etoniana*, as 'a strangely unmilitary figure' – and I cannot deny the truth of this. It was during military

The author winning the war: Eton, 1939

exercises (as awful as the Corps at Marlborough) that I was to be seen at my worst. When ordered one day to crawl 'invisibly' through an interminable bed of nettles, my behind had been so conspicuous that it had caught the eye of some passing officer, who rightly decided that I might serve my country more usefully in Air Raid Precautions. This was not really very much better, for teaching at dawn after a sleepless night on the hard floor of the ARP centre soon lost its charm. One day, when left in sole charge of the post, I received a message, 'Parachute reported descending on Windsor Castle'. The chance of its landing on the King seemed remote, so I decided to let it descend. It proved, as I had hoped, to be one of our own airmen baling out over Windsor Great Park. Had I got it wrong I would presumably have been arrested, and probably shot.

During the holidays I made a short-lived attempt to work in London in an office where a new gun – the Blacker Bombard – was being developed. When it was discovered that I did not know what a spigot was (and I still don't) my services were dispensed with. I seem to remember being 'frisked' at the door and having to sign some document pledging me to uttermost secrecy. That was unnecessary: even under severest torture I could have told the enemy nothing.

And then there were those lectures . . . Elliott had been informed that troops of various kinds encamped in the neighbourhood were so bored that they were clamouring for cultural talks on art, history, literature, science, and so on, and I was told to organise them. I was dubious from the start about this alleged enthusiasm, and not surprised to discover before long that it existed principally in the minds of the officers, who were of course too busy to attend in person. Our audiences consisted of other ranks – minor offenders, perhaps – press-ganged into a Nissen hut and potentially as mutinous as the worst schoolboys.

Every schoolmaster must at one time or another have entertained doubts as to the value and the desirability of attempting to educate the wholly uncooperative and the constitutionally incducable. I have sometimes wished that the system could have made possible an on-the-spot transference of hard cash from pupil to teacher – the connection between a parent's end-of-term bill and his son's lesson is too remote for the boy to grasp. Yet

Michael Severne: *oil painting by the author, Eton, 1939*

John Sutton: *oil painting by the author, Eton, 1939*
(Eton College Collection)

everyone really likes to see that he is getting value for money. When I was learning German at a Berlitz School in London we had to pay five shillings for an hour's lesson as we entered, and we all took good care to get our pennyworth of knowledge with every sixty seconds run.

My first, and worst, experience of lecturing to troops was at an anti-aircraft battery on Dorney Common, a couple of miles from Eton, whose commanding officer had assured me that an illustrated talk on Spanish painting would go down well; and I was so innocent as to believe it to be just possible. I bicycled to the camp in a thunderstorm, and was stopped at the entrance by a sentry who refused to let me in because I had no pass. I 'stood in' for him while he went off to inquire, and was eventually taken, soaked to the skin, to a Nissen hut, where it soon became apparent that my visit had been completely forgotten. 'Come in and get dry,' said the officer; 'I expect you'd like a cup of tea while you're waiting? Some of our chaps are being inoculated today, and things are a bit disorganised. They're off overseas soon – but keep it under your hat of course.' He could not have noticed how badly my hat had been leaking.

I waited an hour, overhearing scraps of conversation such as 'The lantern's reflector is broken, sir . . .' 'Well, borrow a shaving mirror,' and so on. Finally I was conducted to another hut and introduced. The words 'Eton' and 'art' produced groans audible even above the sound of the rain belting down on the tin roof. 'Wish I could stay,' said the officer, 'but duty calls. Good luck! By the way, some of the chaps will have to come out to be inoculated, but I know you'll understand . . .'

I called for the first slide – the El Greco alleged self-portrait in the Metropolitan Museum, New York. Two bleary eyes and a muzzy nose appeared on the wrinkled dust-sheet that did service for a screen; the rest of the picture was scattered over the walls and on the backs of the men in the front rows, and no amount of adjustment produced much improvement. I began, 'In the year 1603, the great Flemish painter, Rubens, came to Madrid . . .'

The door was abruptly flung open and a stentorian voice shouted 'A to C!' Seven or eight men sprang to their feet and vanished into the storm. And so it continued. I rejoiced when 'H to K' disposed of the ringleaders of a gang at the back who had started community singing. It was like 'Ten little n . . . . r boys' (I no longer dare to write the word in full). When 'L to P' had removed the man working the lantern I felt I could reasonably bring the lecture to a premature close. An officer *did* apologise: there was, he reminded me, 'a war on'. After other of my colleagues had reported comparable experiences, Elliott eventually agreed that the whole project should be abandoned. I only wish that I could have persuaded him to lecture on some aspect of medieval history, his subject as a don at Jesus. He would have acted sooner.

It may have been during the war, or perhaps it was soon after, that I was trapped into giving several courses of lectures to the Workers Educational Association. They had to last for an hour and a half, and included 'question time' – always an ordeal because there was usually one know-all, *agent provocateur* or genuine specialist lurking somewhere in the audience. (Even at a talk on handwriting to a Women's Institute I had been asked, 'Which of the two forms of the Visigothic lower-case "g" do you consider preferable?') A colleague, Monty Evans, an expert on Sweden who lectured on that subject to the WEA, had been momentarily nonplussed by the question, 'What is the country's annual export of pig-iron?' But he rallied: 'I believe', he said, 'it *varies*.' In such a situation I always suffer from *l'esprit de l'escalier*.

After one of the heavy raids on the City in 1940 I went up with my mother to London to see the damage. Destruction and desolation everywhere; but near St Paul's I noticed a clump of dandelions in full splendour among the rubble. When I got home I wrote a sonnet which was accepted by the *Sunday Times* but, though eventually paid for, never printed. It now seems terribly precious and dated, for, as Richard Church wrote, 'Georgian poetry was already by 1950 a movement which . . . could no longer be understood by anyone under the age of twenty-five'. But I append it all the same:

> Where scarred the face of London open lies,
>> There lodged the quickening seed that gave you root.
>> Borne on the swan's-down of its parachute
> Above her squalor and her agonies

25

It chose this resting-place, that grief-red eyes
 And hearts grown callous in the dead pursuit
Of gain might pause, resurgent, to salute
The phoenix flowers sprung from her sacrifice.

How rude and obstinate a weed! And yet
 Not Benvenuto in his vainest hour
  (Whose fretted jewels were an emperor's pride)
Dared boast the skill to gild your coronet;
 Not Jove himself in a more golden shower
  Dropped from the lip of heaven to Danaë's side.

As for the rest of the war: sirens, V1s and V2s, air-raid shelters and air-raid rehearsals, broken nights, fire practices, black-outs, gas-masks, rationing (and unattractive meals at the British Restaurant to eke out), shortage of alcohol, a ghastly patriotic allotment which grew nothing but Jerusalem artichokes, ceaseless officious officialdom . . . I will say no more. Everyone who was around at the time remembers, while those who were not will at least have seen 'Dad's Army'.

We were remarkably lucky, for Claude Elliott's firm refusal to find, at short notice, a place in the school for the son of Ribbentrop, German Ambassador to Great Britain from 1935 to 1938, might well have led to Eton – in any case a potential target

The bomb on Savile House

26

The bomb on Upper School.
It fell 4 December 1940 and exploded the following day.

because of the proximity of Windsor Castle – becoming a special one to the Germans. Except for some harmless fire bombs and two serious ones, we came through unscathed. Even the latter, though they destroyed part of Upper School and damaged Savile House (where Dr Henry Ley, the Precentor, lived), at least did us a service by shattering the Chapel's hideous Victorian glass. The art-loving beaks were quickly on the spot to collect and dispose of every discoverable fragment so as to preclude any attempt at restoration. Thus we eventually gained Evie Hone's east window and eight further windows designed by John Piper, while a brilliant piece of restoration on Upper School left it almost as good as of old.

Since I had come to Eton only a year before the war, very few of the Etonians who were killed in it were known to me personally. The friends I lost were principally boys who had been my pupils at Haileybury, and many of these I mourned – Stephen Haggard, of course, most of all. VJ Day came while I was in charge of a farming party of Eton boys on Lord St Germans's estate at Port

Eliot on the southern coast of Cornwall. I joined in the reaping; but I found it hard to keep up, and was more than once surprised snatching a catnap behind a stook. I prefer to *read* about harvesting – in the novels of Thomas Hardy or in Tolstoy's *Anna Karenina*.

3
Baldwin's Shore

The Provost and Fellows, with the strong support of Claude Elliott, had taken the brave decision that the school should not move to a safer part of the country. This boldness was justified in the event, for though those two haphazardly dropped bombs fell on us, no lives were lost and no one was seriously injured. Thus we were spared the horrors endured by schools such as Malvern, whose buildings were compulsorily taken over by the Government and their inhabitants mercilessly driven from pillar to post. When war had eventually broken out I was made air-raid warden of the house of a cousin, Richard Assheton – a nice man who hung a reproduction of Vermeer's *View of Delft* upside down in his hall to test the powers of observation, or maybe the tact, of prospective parents.

This duty meant 'living in', and since Richard's wife, Beryl, was reluctant to sacrifice (as did the wives of most housemasters) a guest-room on the private side of the house, I was allotted the room of a small boy who was absent for the half. It was tinier than many a loo; the bed, which by day was folded up against the wall, was about five feet long and uncomfortable by prison, even by Marlborough, standards. Also the door happened to be the one used as a goal for 'passage football'. It was a surrealist experience; like Mr Bultitude in *Vice Versa* I was as it were back at school again – *as a boy*! Of course I enjoyed it all much more than he did – and not least the moment when, on the first evening, a very senior boy burst in as I was dressing for dinner and asked me who the hell I was and what the hell I was doing there.

At the end of the half the policy of having a resident air-raid warden in each house was abandoned. I was not altogether sorry, for, much though I liked Richard, I did not find Beryl *simpatica*. She made me feel that I was something of a burden, and probably I was; but it was not my fault. A colleague, Francis Cruso, invented a story that was widely circulated at the time among the staff and had no foundation whatsoever; that Beryl, seeing me walking up the centre of the staircase in her house, had said, 'Walk on the boards, Mr Blunt! Walk on the boards! Carpets cost money!'

On leaving the Asshetons, I did not return to my lodgings because of a timely invitation to join the Baldwin's Shore colony.[1]

Baldwin's Shore: Eton College: Windsor

Letter heading by the author for Baldwin's Shore

This suited me perfectly, and its two other inhabitants at that time, Richard Martineau and Peter Lawrence, welcomed me kindly. Its position was perfect: it adjoined Baldwin's Bec – a boys' house of which Hubert Hartley was housemaster, and it was separated only by a strip of meadow, and a little hump-backed wooden bridge over a backwater of the Thames, from Luxmoore's Garden.

That paradise, which had previously been a Corporation rubbish-dump, was the creation of H. E. Luxmoore,[2] who had come to Eton as a master in 1864 and lived on there in retirement until his death in 1926. He was the great aesthete of his day, and a competent and meticulous watercolour painter. A generous

---

[1] 'Shore' was possibly less romantic than it sounds, being (some allege) a corruption of 'sewer' – the open drain that formerly ran past the building. During the great flood of March 1947 we had a foot of water in the ground floor of our house; Eton became an island, and on the 17th the school was sent home.
[2] Known to boys in his early days as 'Buffy' or (from his initials) 'Pandemonium'.

The Entrance to Mr Luxmoore's Garden.
Oil painting by the author, 1944.

appraisal of what Eton owed to him – which included a replica of Watts's *Sir Galahad* made at his request and presented to the school by the artist – will be found in the pages of *An English Education* by Richard Ollard, who did not know him. This judgement is confirmed by Grizel Hartley, who did, and who mentions his delightful sense of humour. A briefer and less enthusiastic portrait – 'that sanctimonious old stick' – comes

Stroud, gardener of Luxmoore's Garden

from the pen of Anthony Powell, who had a boy's-eye view which may well be equally valid in its particular context. But at all events Luxmoore left an enduring mark on Eton by making, on the banks of the Thames, a garden, available to masters and senior boys, that was an oasis of peace and beauty.

When I first came to Baldwin's Shore, Luxmoore's splendid old gardener, Stroud, was still in charge and still preserving Luxmoore's concept of the semi-wild garden advocated by William Robinson, sworn enemy of 'bedding out'. The wide and curving principal path was a glorious jungle of self-sown poppies and lupins, passable only by way of a narrow beaten track through the middle of it. In 1938, Beryl Assheton was supervisor of the garden – which chiefly meant that she felt entitled to help herself liberally to its flowers and fruit. But she also longed for everything to be made neat and tidy. Here, however, all her efforts were frustrated by Stroud, and it was only when he retired, after having tended it for forty-nine years, that she finally got her way. Paths were now ruthlessly weeded, lupins and poppies dismissed, the 'sweet disorder' banished for ever. Fortunately, the overall beauty of the garden proved indestructible, and not even the aeroplanes that today roar overhead every two or three minutes have wholly succeeded in spoiling its peaceful charm.

Stroud had many stories about Luxmoore. For example, one day he noticed on the lawn his master's penknife, and retrieved it. Soon he came upon his tobacco-pouch, his pipe, his diary and other personal possessions, which he dutifully gathered up: the old man either had holes in all his pockets or was growing senile. Luxmoore did not receive their return with the expected gratitude. They had been carefully placed by him to mark plantains – the one weed he could not abide.

TO MR LUXMOORE, ON HIS GARDEN

How well the staid, neat-fingered Dutchman drew
 The rule-straight pattern of his tulip square,
 His box-trimmed quilt of blossom! With what care
The proud Italian planned his tapering view,
His marbled grot, his shadeless avenue,
 His Triton fountain, his exact parterre!
 But you engaged that disputatious pair,
Nature and Art, and reconciled the two.

Oh, never let some slick, suburban hand
  Drill the lobelia down your tangled walks,
Or, with ill-judged devotion, neatly band
  The wayward loftiness of lupin stalks.
Long may the meadow-parsley spread at ease,
A mist of lace beneath your apple trees.

W.B., 1945

Richard Martineau

'Colonial' life was pleasant, though the inhabitants of the Shore
came and went – either moving on to become housemasters,
lapsing into matrimony, rising to greater heights in our profession or some other, or simply falling by the wayside when (or
before) their probationary two years were over. I alone went on
for ever – or at least for nearly twenty years. Among those who
spent almost the whole of their working lives at Eton was Richard
Martineau, who remained at Baldwin's Shore until he became a
housemaster in 1944.

Richard – tall, slimly built, and with the word 'scholar' written all over his kindly, bespectacled face – had been Captain of the School at Eton in 1923, the year that A. J. ('Freddie') Ayer entered College, and returned as Sixth-Form master before Ayer left Eton. Ayer describes him as 'a charming and civilised boy'[3] who ran College with a humanity that was abruptly terminated when H. K. Marsden became Master in College, also in 1923. Having private means, Richard was able to be unostentatiously beneficent, and very hospitable to old pupils and colleagues in the handsome eighteenth-century rectory he bought at Droxford in Hampshire, and to which he was to retire in 1961.

The word 'hospitable' needs some qualification here. He kept his house at Droxford full of guests largely because he hated to be alone – curious in a man of such intellectual brilliance. He was also at heart a puritan, and contrived to make the Old Rectory even colder and more uncomfortable than my mother's house at Ham. Friends, with the support of one of his sisters-in-law, eventually succeeded in getting him to buy new mattresses and to install central heating, but the latter availed little. In the winter, when the temperature had risen to around 55°F Richard would say, 'I feel very hot. Would you mind it if I took my coat off?'

'Not at all, Richard.'

Then, a little later, when the thermometer had dared to approach 60°: 'It's so dreadfully hot. I think I'll turn the heating off.'

Dinner was, as at Eton, always at eight o'clock, and around half past six guests' tongues would begin to hang out and eyes would be cast longingly at a tray on which stood a bottle of sherry and some rather small glasses. Richard made no move. Ultimately he would say, 'Oh Wilfrid, you haven't got a drink!'

'Thank you, Richard. I'd love one.'

Richard would then look at his watch; 'Oh, I see it's five to eight. We're just going in to dinner . . .'

Was this absent-mindedness? I can't believe it. Was it meanness? Hardly. Perhaps it was a kind of tease – in, I thought, very poor taste – or the puritan streak in him coming out. I could never quite decide. And even though I knew him so well, somehow or other he was not the kind of person to whom one could say, 'Richard, may I help myself to a drink?' On one occasion, several

[3] *Part of My Life*, Collins, 1977, p. 48.

35

of us who were staying with him slipped out to the pub opposite; we returned to find Richard desperate in his loneliness, a volume of Gibbon in one hand and half a glass of sherry in the other.

'I wondered where you'd all got to.'

'We just went for a stroll, Richard.'

Nor was he an easy housemate at Baldwin's Shore. There was only one bathroom for the three of us, and on a Saturday evening, when often we were all wanting a bath before dressing to go out to dinner, he would get in first, take most of the hot water, and remain immersed for an unconscionable time. This too was part selfishness, part tease; but it could be very irritating.

I often wondered why he had not become a don. He had all the qualifications: a brilliant brain, that passion for local gossip and tittle-tattle that bachelor dons revel in, and that capacity for jealousy often displayed at college high tables. (He used to be venomous about Cyril Connolly, who was his inferior as a classical scholar, but achieved a greater fame.) Perhaps he was too steeped in Eton ever to have contemplated leaving it; perhaps it was because he lacked any desire to devote years of his life to editing the works of some obscure classical author (he never wrote a book); or might it simply have been that he preferred the company of boys to that of undergraduates? He was certainly a born bachelor, and, lonely though he became in his retirement, it is impossible to conceive of him seeking a solution by marrying a middle-aged, understanding widow for companionship's sake – as sometimes happens and sometimes works out well enough.

After I was appointed Curator of the Watts Gallery at Compton in 1959, Richard came several times to stay with me. He was no easier as a guest than as a host – clamouring for draughts and what the media insist on calling 'sub-zero' temperatures, grumbling at having to dine at the non-Etonian hour of 7.30, and even asking whether he might change his seat at the dinner table so as to be spared the pain of confronting the copy I had made of El Greco's *Agony in the Garden*. Finally he developed Parkinson's Disease, and visits to him – rare, I regret to confess, though frequently requested – became increasingly a torture. His speech, always gabbled and hard to understand, became completely incomprehensible, his writing totally illegible, his gait unsteady. He had many sterling qualities, and most of the boys in his house, and his pupils, were very fond of him. But I never felt at my ease with him as I did with his particular cronies – Francis Cruso, for instance, or Kelsall Prescot. He wore his undeniable intellectual brilliance in such a way as to make lesser mortals feel their inferiority. As a boy in College he was known as 'the Hermit', and I think that, fundamentally, all his life he was a very lonely man. At Droxford, walking (so long as he was able) and books were his chief solace when deprived of the company of friends. He died in August 1984, and I believe that the excellent obituary which appeared in *The Times* (22 August) was written by his former colleague, Oliver Van Oss.

The other occupant of Baldwin's Shore at the time of my arrival there was Peter Lawrence, at whose marriage in 1940 to Helena

Peter Lawrence, Christmas 1940

37

Lyttelton (daughter of George Lyttelton and sister of Humphrey) I was – to my great surprise and Richard's equally great disappointment – best man. Peter, a mathematician, was a delightful Old Etonian, though to use the word 'old' in any association with him seems misleading: for 'Lawrence' one might well have substituted 'Pan'. He was twenty-seven when he first arrived at the Shore; but he seemed to me still a boy, with a boy's enthusiasm for scouting and for gadgets of every kind. (It was very characteristic of him that he provided me with an invaluable and meticulous three-page memorandum on the duties of a best man.) In Helena he found the perfect companion for life, had a large family, and was a very successful housemaster. Before joining the Eton staff in 1936 he had taught briefly at the Doon School in India, and apart from wartime service as a radar officer with the Royal Navy he remained at Eton for more than forty years. Since his retirement, he has become the chronicler of Eton, having compiled several invaluable volumes of photographs and reminscences of his old school which he has very generously allowed me to use.

On Peter's departure from the Shore, Richard and I were joined by poor Tom Lyon – not an Etonian but *plus royaliste que le roi* – who like Richard, but at a much younger age, became a victim of Parkinson's Disease. Because of his illness he was ultimately obliged to exchange teaching for taking charge of the College and School Libraries, a fortunate chance making both jobs vacant at exactly the right moment. To College Library, in particular, he brought new life. No longer was it usually uninhabited: he would be around, ready always to show books to any boy who was interested. No longer was its key under the doormat, thus leaving Eton's priceless Gutenberg Bible at the mercy of any thief who could break the wafer-thin glass of a small showcase. Tom died suddenly, from a stroke, in 1959, and was thus spared the long, sad decline that was to be Richard's lot.

Another inhabitant of our colony in the fifties was Raef Payne, of whom I shall have more to say later. Among Eton's birds of passage who nested more or less briefly at the Shore were Anthony Caesar, organist, who was later ordained and is now Sub-Dean of the Chapels Royal; Walter Dunlop, a charming and whimsical elderly eccentric, long since dead; the improbable

*Peter Lawrence on his wedding day, 10 August 1940
with the author as best man*

G. M. Hayward, known as 'the Wizard', who spent all night asleep in his chair allegedly writing a life of Merlin; John Bowle[4] – historian, author and Oxford don; and Kenneth Rose of the *Sunday Telegraph*, a brilliant biographer of the great and famous: a mixed bag.

There was also constant fluctuation in domestic staff in both the colonies and boys' houses, resulting at one time in such liberal importations from the Baltic shores that it was alleged that in the High Street one was as likely to encounter an Estonian as an Etonian. At the Shore, where we usually had a married couple or a cook-housekeeper and parlourmaid, we remained firmly British. Once we came to engage a couple of professional thieves. At another time, during the war, we had a highly respectable middle-aged widow and a pretty but flighty young parlourmaid named Ruby, who spent her leisure, not a few of her working hours, and no doubt many of her nights, in the arms of our gallant lads from the Windsor Barracks. (I remember the Wizard, at her first appearance, uttering a wolf-whistle.) One morning at breakfast the cook, who had unwisely attempted to 'mother' Ruby, burst into the dining-room crying, 'I won't stand it! Ruby has just called me an interfering old bitch!' She paused, then added, 'I will *not* be called *interfering*!' Exit Ruby.

There were many advantages in living in a colony – provided that one's housemates were agreeable and that one was able to get suitable domestic help. At all events it was best to live close to the school, for at Eton at that time there was no common room beyond a sort of down-at-heel dentist's waiting-room, used only by desperate non-housemaster beaks who lived at a distance and had an odd hour to fill in between two periods of teaching. Neither food nor drink was of course available, and the ashtray was emptied at the end of each half. These men were for the most part not influential enough to fight for a decent common room. They have now, I am told, at long last been provided with an adequate refuge.

[4] A Marlburian (1919–24) and in Sandford's house (see *M.S.L.*, p. 55). Sandford beat him, for an utterly trivial offence, when he was in the Sixth Form and had already won a Balliol scholarship – a monstrous act which I think scarred him for life. As William Cowper wrote in *Tirocinium: or, a Review of Schools* (1784):

> The management of tiroes of eighteen
> Is difficult, *their punishment obscene* [my italics].

At Haileybury, when I was younger, I found the gregariousness of common room life agreeable; at Eton, colonial life suited me well, and I disliked it when, as occasionally happened, I found myself dining alone. But at Compton, in old age, I never crave for company at meals. A book, the radio, my thoughts or my cat, are all that I need.

4
The Drawing Schools

You have got to be careful of artists.
You don't know where they have been.

QUEEN VICTORIA

I had not been long at Eton before I realised that the equivalent of 'Blunt's room' at Haileybury would fill a need, but also that it could be created only at the Drawing Schools. I therefore had a partition erected in one of the studios and converted half of it into a sitting-room furnished with a sofa, chairs, books, pictures, and my piano and gramophone. I also had a French window and window-seat made, leading to a derelict patch of nettles that I turned into a small garden with shrubs, flower beds, a lawn, seats, and a little pool the size of a hip-bath.

There was a lot of informal music-making. I recall one golden

The author and Jeremy Benson, making a pool: Eton, 1939

June evening when a handful of boys and myself were listening to a record of Myra Hess playing Mozart. The window was open, and through it I could see my neighbour dead-heading roses at the bottom of her garden, which adjoined mine. I thought what pleasure it must be giving her too; but suddenly she came to the boundary fence and shouted, 'Mr Blunt, Mr Blunt! Do *please* turn off that *noise*! It throbs on and on so!' I know that a good many of my former pupils remember the room with pleasure, while to some it certainly became a refuge. Only the other day I had a letter from a sixty-year-old OE saying that he wondered how he 'could have survived Eton without it and the Slough sewage farm' (his hobby was watching water-birds). I feel flattered that he put them in that order.

My successors – admirable men all – have seen to it that not a trace of my little sanctum remains beyond its French window, leading now from creative squalor to semi-jungle again. Even the twelve-foot-tall judas tree, planted as a seedling from Luxmoore's Garden, was swept away in an unnecessarily ruthless clearance when the new Farrer Theatre was erected in the sixties about thirty yards away. One ought, perhaps, never to return to places where one has been happy.

I had inherited from Robin Darwin not only a lively tradition of painting in oils but also a sumptuous marionette stage and a handful of ardent puppeteers; and though puppets were not at all in my line I felt obliged, out of loyalty, to keep them going. This was in spite of a letter I had received, at the time of my appointment to Eton, from Andrew Gow, a former Eton master who had become a don at Trinity College, Cambridge.

Gow was a devoted admirer of my brother Anthony (and of many other intelligent, attractive and – preferably – aristocratic young men). My mother viewed him with some mistrust, and took a particular dislike (as did I) to two curious outcrops of scrub (known to many colleagues in his Eton days as 'Gows') that he cultivated on his cheekbones. He belonged to the 'old brigade', was still very influential in high places at Eton, and I suspect had had a good deal to do with my getting the job there. He was a considerable authority on art but could not get beyond Degas, by whom he had some splendid drawings. He kept his praise under

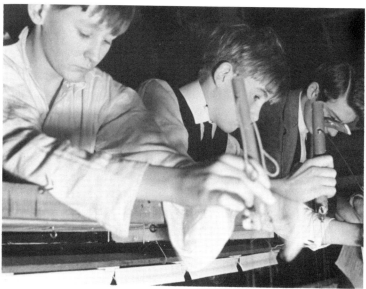

Above: the puppet theatre with the author's set for Mozart's Bastien and Bastienne. *Below: three puppeteers – from left, 'Dwin' Bramall (later Field Marshal Sir Edwin, Chief of the Defence Staff); John Sutton (see p.23); and O. C. Thomas, later drawing master at Eton.*

44

very strict control, and I remember my elation when he said of one of my paintings, 'I suppose it's not altogether *too* bad.' (I wonder what he would have thought of Eton art today.) His long friendship with Anthony, who continued to visit him fairly frequently in the hospital in Cambridge where he spent his last years, he recognised with a legacy of £100. His estate was valued at nearly three and a half million, and he was of course a bachelor.

Though his letter to me was headed PRIVATE, since he is now dead I think I may fairly quote it:

> A word in your ear. One of your functions [at Eton] will be to restore drawing and painting to a status at least the equal to that of marionettes and pots. Probably you have realised this, but in case nobody tells you so I send a line to say that the encroachments of these upon more normal school drawing have been causing some comment and anxiety both among the staff and among Old Etonians and it is hoped that you will help to restore the due perspective again. Nobody wants to abolish them so far as I know, but they obviously bulk too large at present and you needn't be afraid of criticism if you redress the balance.

As at Haileybury, so also at Eton the affairs of the old school were often discussed and mulled over at university high tables and London clubs. One day during the war a friend of mine chanced to overhear a fragment of conversation as he was leaving the Athenaeum. He identified the speaker as Lord Woolton, at that time Minister of Food; his companion he did not recognise. Woolton said, 'I suppose you go down to Eton for the Fellows' Meetings. Do you happen to know anything about a chap called Blunt? I've been told he wants watching . . .'. My informant, who missed the reply, could not suggest any reason why Woolton should be interested in me. Nor could I: I had never even (publicly) complained of the wartime fare at the Eton British Restaurant, and the mystery remains unsolved to this day.

Mercifully, the impossibility of blacking out a big room lit by skylights gave me a breathing space from puppetry during the war. But when peace returned, it was revived, and continued fitfully until my successor, more drastic and courageous than I, had the stage dismantled. One of my first and keenest puppeteers was 'Dwin' Bramall, who at the age of sixteen also had two paintings hung on the line at the summer exhibition of the Royal

Academy. He still paints and, now retired as Chief of the Defence Staff, will be able to devote more time to his hobby.

Another of my activities at the Drawing Schools was italic handwriting, and Eton became the first public school to propagate its revival. My handwriting had never been good, though not, I believe, as bad as that of either of my brothers. When my mother attempted to make a fair transcript of the manuscript of Anthony's first book, *Artistic Theory in Italy* (1940), she almost caused disaster by misreading 'obscure' as 'obscene' throughout. I tried to reform my own hand; but the result was at first, inevitably, a 'precious' script and my mother ordered me, when writing to her, to revert to my former cacography. This annoyed me: I felt like a drunkard, trying to 'dry out', who had been ordered to go back to the bottle.

At Eton itself I had the warm support of George Lyttelton, but the impetus to encourage better handwriting at the school came from Sir Sydney Cockerell, who after his retirement from the directorship of the Fitzwilliam Museum at Cambridge had for two years sought refuge from the bombing by moving from Kew, where he had bought a house, to Old Windsor. Several other members of the staff also supported me, among them Dick Routh. Cockerell (whose biography I was later to write) became a regular visitor to the Drawing Schools, where he provided the material for an exhibition of calligraphy consisting largely of letters to himself – rather too many of which seemed to have been selected primarily because they began, 'My dear Cockerell, / What a wonderful man you are . . .'.

It was Cockerell, too, who secured for us the generous patronage of the late Marquess of Cholmondeley to endow an Eton-Harrow-Winchester inter-school annual handwriting competition. Lord Cholmondeley – a delightful but simple soul – had originally proposed, in a letter to *The Times*, prizes to be competed for by *all* the Public Schools, with consolation prizes for any which entered but failed to win. However, on being told that there were now several hundred members of the Head Masters' Conference, not just six[1] as he had innocently imagined, he was obliged to write a second letter redefining the terms of

[1] The 1861 Royal Commission on the Public Schools had in fact acknowledged nine.

46

entry. Another who contributed towards the prize and was also captured by Cockerell was Gilbert Coleridge,[2] son of the Victorian Lord Chief Justice, who agreed to provide £2 a year for his lifetime; but since he was already in his nineties we were not beneficiaries for very long.

Although in my time the first prize almost invariably came to Eton, in 1952 the victor was a Harrovian Siamese prince, and this led to a television programme at Alexandra Palace. In those days the BBC did things in style, though conditions in the vast studio

Television studio, Alexandra Palace, 4 July 1952

itself were chaotic. A car collected me from Eton and stopped at Harrow to pick up the prince, and I remember the look of disappointment on the face of the driver, who had apparently understood that he had been engaged to ferry Siamese *twins* to and from the studio. A nice meal (with wine) was provided. On my last visit to Broadcasting House, to record a talk in the 'Man of Action' series, I was directed afterwards to the Cafeteria and then abandoned. I found it shut.

[2] Author of *Eton in the 'Seventies*, 1912.

The Alexandra Palace programme was followed by several interviews on calligraphy in Jeanne Heal's mixed-bag 'Leisure for Pleasure' series, at one of which Jeanne fainted as the cameras were about to open up on us – leaving me to cross-examine, impromptu, myself: 'Now I know that the question you are all wanting to ask me is, "How does a left-hander deal with the edged italic nib . . . ?" ' and so on. At another, I shared the programme with Constance Spry, with whom I was driven back to London afterwards. 'The great mercy', she said, 'is that none of one's *friends* are likely to have been watching.' I rather hoped mine *were*. Fortunately she did not ask me what I thought of her flower arrangements.

In 1954 I organised an exhibition, 'In Praise of Italic', for the National Book League, and in the fifties wrote one or two books (including *Sweet Roman Hand*). I also did a good deal of lecturing. A talk at County Hall, London, to an alarmingly vast audience of teachers, nearly landed me in serious trouble. While discussing the stupidity and impertinence of wholly illegible signatures, I showed on the screen a superb specimen given to me by a colleague who had told me nothing of its provenance. After the lecture a reporter from the *Daily Telegraph* asked whether he might reproduce it in his account of my lecture, and since not even a Champollion could have deciphered it I saw no harm in letting him have it. It appeared the following morning, accompanied by a full and accurate quotation of my comments on it.

I gave the matter no further thought; but three or four days later I found myself summoned by Elliott to his sanctum. It happened that, most unfortunately, this abstract scrawl was the widely known business signature of a millionaire and most generous benefactor of the College. I was duly carpeted, and ordered to write a grovelling letter of apology assuring the complainant that I had now retrieved and destroyed the offend-ing object. He replied in forgiving terms, graciously accepting my admission that I was a fool rather than a knave. His letter was signed – I observed with amusement – with an equally splendid specimen for my collection. I do not dare to reproduce it here.

When teaching italic to Lower Boys, I used to introduce the subject by asking any boy in the division to write, in his everyday hand, the first thing that came into his head, and I find that I have preserved a few of the texts submitted. For triteness it would be hard to beat: 'It is very cold today; perhaps it will not be so cold tomorrow', though some of Watts's table-talk, as recorded by Mrs Watts, runs it pretty close. One (from a Dutch boy) reads, 'I am a little cheese' – which I take to be the equivalent of the French 'petit chou'; another says, 'Please come to my little arbour in the South Pacific and we will rest together.' But strangest of all is the following: 'Joe Bloggs L.T.D. regretts [*sic*] that owing to the printing dispute "Bronco" Toilet Paper has been unable to stamp "BRONCO" on its last 300 sheets in each roll. Those sheets not stamped are still "Bronco".' There was seldom any difficulty in creating an interest, and the Society for Italic Handwriting – of which I find, rather to my surprise, that I am a Vice-President – still flourishes.

Sometimes colleagues sent me boys with appalling handwriting and a request that I give them remedial treatment. Illegibility can be the result of bad initial instruction, of a lack of interest or awareness, or of sheer idleness; and here I could usually help. But occasionally the cause was some physical disability, and then I could do nothing. Among those who thus came my way was a very clever Colleger, son of one of the most brilliant and famous men in England. You couldn't read a word the boy wrote. 'You see, sir,' he said, 'the trouble is that when I try to make my pen go up, it always seems to go down.' I could only suggest that he saw a doctor.

A person in charge of a LOCOMOTIVE shall not use the LOCOMOTIVE upon WINDSOR BRIDGE which is a bridge whereon the use of LOCOMOTIVES is HEREBY PROHIBITED, the COUNCIL being satisfied that such action would be attended with DANGER to the BRIDGE.

The text of the specimen of Eton italic which I here reproduce is taken from a notice, the tattered remains of which were still just legible on Windsor Bridge when I first came to Eton. Curiously enough, it was a visiting New Zealander who drew my attention to it, and I was just in time to rescue its substance from being lost for ever. Now the bridge is closed to *all* traffic, and the High Street – once so noisy, congested and dangerous – as quiet as the grave. (I was always amazed that in my time no boy was ever involved in a serious accident, though one eccentric, reading *Macbeth* as he crossed the road, was excusably knocked down by a car. He rose undamaged, murmuring 'The news of my death will kill my mother.')

In the end I grew rather bored with italic: not with the script itself, but with the preciosity of some of its exponents. The mere mention of the word 'Biro' was known to make them shudder. 'Bad writing', they were always saying, 'is bad manners'; but bad English and worse spelling did not seem to trouble them. One very supportive housemaster had a large and elegantly inscribed notice, BOY'S ENTRANCE, posted conspicuously outside his house. I felt that a hand should be *based* on italic, but that if it did not develop into something swift, spontaneous and personal it was valueless. 'A man's style in writing [wrote Samuel Butler] should be like his dress; should attract as little attention as possible.' To this day I get letters in immaculate, characterless and obviously snail-paced writing (but often beginning with an apology for the hasty scrawl) asking advice about nibs, ink and blotting-paper – and I can hardly bring myself to answer them . . . in my current cacography.

Calligraphy – like flower-arranging, playing the recorder, and craftwork of various kinds – provides harmless, therapeutic pleasure for many not over-talented adults and 'senior citizens' with time on their hands and an urge for self-expression. However, if you have not acquired an italic hand by the age of fifteen it will rarely if ever become a script suitable for everyday use. My policy was 'to catch them young', but having myself learned the script in middle age I often, when pressed for time, lapsed from a rather self-conscious italic into my pre-italic scribble, thus teaching – as is not uncommon with schoolmasters – by warning rather than by example. It gave one of my converts no small pleasure to return to me the envelope of a letter I had sent him, on which a post office clerk had written, 'Clearer writing would be appreciated.' He did not mean *better* writing – merely the old copperplate hand which he had been taught at school and with which alone he was familiar.

Teaching Lower Boys at the Drawing Schools

As for general teaching in school hours, all Lower Boys came compulsorily in groups of about thirty to the Drawing Schools for fifty minutes a week. This may sound – indeed was – absurdly little; but it did at least serve to introduce them to the place and show them what facilities were available, so that those who were interested could come in their spare time. These junior boys chiefly painted 'imaginative' subjects – *Autumn, St George and the Dragon*, and so on – in powder-colours on large sheets of grey paper, as was then fashionable. For the most part they enjoyed it, and at all events there was no danger of their work being 'torn over'.[3] In the summer we often took a division to sketch on the Playing Fields, still in those days bounded by 'immemorial' elms that, sadly, are no more. But for boys in any part of the school who were talented or keen, in out-of-school hours there were various other activities of which pottery and oil painting were probably the most popular. Over the years I organised a good many exhibitions of various kinds, and that of boys' work held on the Fourth of June was often crowded out – especially if it was raining.

[3] Unsatisfactory written work was returned with a tear at the top of the page and had to be done again.

The principal school drawing prize was for figure-drawing, a handful of the most talented boys being chosen to compete. But there were also prizes, awarded on the Fourth of June by an outside judge, which were intended to be given for the collected *oeuvre* of a boy over the whole year. Once I foolishly invited the capricious Stanley Spencer to adjudicate. As I ought to have foreseen, though I explained the 'rules' to him, he gave the first prize to a boy who had contributed a single picture – a naive affair probably done as a joke. The undeserving winner received his prize, but was never seen at the Drawing Schools again.

Another exhibition that I contemplated, but wisely abandoned, was one of 'bad taste', the staff to be invited to provide the material for it. Too many feelings would have been hurt, and, as somebody pointed out, it could have stripped the drawing-room of the Vice-Provost, Henry Marten, practically bare; indeed, he added, it might have saved trouble to have held it *in situ*. Perhaps the contents of the room were in fact the preferred choice of Miss Marten, his alarming twin sister who kept house for her bachelor brother. In 1938 the King entrusted the historical education of Princess Elizabeth to Marten, who on occasions became so absorbed in his subject that, from force of habit, he addressed her as 'Gentlemen'. I doubt whether he spoke much of matters artistic, but he did once borrow from me some fine colour reproductions of a sixteenth-century Persian manuscript to show her. Princess Margaret, to her regret, was considered too young to accompany her sister to Eton, being subjected instead to lessons from her rather formidable grandmother, Queen Mary.

I do not know who gave drawing lessons to the Princesses, unless Gerald Kelly did. The King frankly admitted to having only small knowledge of art, confessing once to my brother that when he saw a name under a portrait he was not always sure whether it was that of the artist or of the sitter. Kelly had established himself as a permanent guest at Windsor Castle, where he spent a comfortable war painting the state portraits of the King and Queen. He spun the task out, year after year, till it was finally rumoured that, like Penelope, he undid each night what he had added during the day. Even a caricature of him in a Christmas pantomime organised by the two Princesses – as 'Kerald Jelly, the immovable guest' – failed to dislodge him.

Kelly periodically visited the Drawing Schools, where, either unable or unwilling to grasp the difficulties we had to contend with, he condemned everything he saw. I was therefore very surprised when one day he rang me up and said, with unexpected humility, 'I'm stuck with the King. Come to the Castle tomorrow afternoon and tell me what's the matter with the bloody thing.' I went and, deciding not to be intimidated, pointed out that the perspective of the slabs of stone in the steps was all wrong, creating the impression that the King was about to slither down them. He seized a piece of chalk and, thrusting it into my hand said, 'Correct it!' I did – and later he made the change permanent. It was always said that the best things about Kelly were his Japanese prints and his wife's cooking. I never sampled the latter because my only invitation to see the former was cancelled at the last moment.

Dr (later Sir William) Harris, the organist of St George's Chapel at the Castle, took the Princesses' musical education in hand. Piano lessons proving unrewarding, he substituted glee-singing – in which a few officers on duty at the Castle, a lady-in-waiting, and several members of the Eton community took part. On one occasion, some last-minute military duty having prevented two of the three basses from being present, I found myself called in as a stop-gap. Miss Byron, vastest and most splendid of the Eton Dames, presided – sitting in the centre of the front row between the two Princesses – and I was just behind Princess Margaret who, as I had been told, usually managed to enliven an otherwise rather solemn affair. At the end, Dr Harris always invited Princess Elizabeth to choose a favourite song, which this time was one entitled (so far as I can remember) 'Oh! that I were but a little tiny bird'. Princess Margaret did not fail us. Turning to the officer seated on the other side of her she said in a very audible whisper, 'I think Miss Byron would have to be jet-propelled.'

Thanks to my brother and to the kindness of the Royal Librarian, Sir Owen Morshead, I had free access to the Library. This was invaluable, especially when I was working on my book, *The Art of Botanical Illustration* (1950). Owen once reprimanded me for setting foot in so sacred a place in grey flannel trousers. I was subsequently told, by the under-librarian who had overheard the rebuke, that a few days later the King himself had paid an unexpected visit to the Library similarly attired. Of course you may dress as you wish in your own Library.

The fact that practically the whole school passed, however briefly, through my hands means that over my thirty-six years of schoolmastering, I must have acquired not far short of ten thousand pupils. Most of these have some recollection, however vague, of *me*; but the reverse is, unfortunately, not true, and when I am accosted in Piccadilly by (for example) some ancient white-bearded bishop who addresses me as 'sir', I am not always able to recognise what remains of some cherub of the twenties. Occasionally, however, when the name of one of them catches the headlines, I recall an infant who more often than not showed no obvious sign of future distinction. For example, there was a bright little new boy at Eton in the fifties named Sir Ranulph Twistleton-Wykeham-Fiennes. 'I can't call you all that,' I said. 'Will "Fiennes" do?' 'Just call me Twinkletoes' came his charmingly improbable reply. I would never then have guessed that Twinkletoes might one day conquer a Pole, let alone two.

Looking back now on my twenty-one years at Eton, I am thankful that I left when I did; for the time had by then arrived when art, as I understood it, was becoming almost obsolete. By the mid-fifties boys, seeing reproductions of 'action paintings' and 'tachism' by Jackson Pollock *et al.*, had begun to tip or splash bucketfuls of paint over acres of paper and ride bicycles across them, and for all I know the resultant masterpieces are hanging on the walls of the Tate at this very moment. I would not go so far as to say 'Modern art is bunk', but I firmly believe that quite a lot of it is. If there is anything sillier than thinking that everything new is bad, then it is thinking that everything new must be good.

I read recently of a young artist who glues bits of smashed pottery to a canvas and then paints his picture on top of them. If it amuses him – well and good; if people buy his work, let him make hay while the sun shines: for fashions in nonsense are fickle. In television programmes we are shown apes and maladjusted children producing similar masterpieces; but the latter are not usually displayed in trendy London galleries, highly priced and described as the achievements of geniuses who 'stare into the eyes

The author fabric-printing at the Drawing Schools

of existential despair', and so on. Maurice Vlaminck said it all when he wrote, 'La peinture, c'est comme la cuisine: ça ne s'explique pas, ça se goûte.'

Naturally, much that shocks at first does finally come to be accepted as in the mainstream of tradition. In the First World War, when even a Gauguin was – if known at all – considered outrageous, we used at Marlborough a science textbook that contained a chapter on colour-blindness which concluded as follows (I quote from memory): 'Sometimes we see a painting in which the grass is red or a face green. This is not colour-blindness but art.'

I once asked my brother Anthony whether he shared my views

about the rubbish that was masquerading as art in the seventies, and, if he did, why he did not have the courage to declare his position openly. He replied that he *did* agree, but that certain critics whose views he greatly respected maintained that, eventually, he would be converted. In an article that he wrote entitled 'From Bloomsbury to Marxism' (*Studio International*, 1973) he confessed,

> . . . I have much lost touch with contemporary painting, and indeed cannot altogether comprehend much of what has happened in the last twenty or thirty years.
>
> This is, I think, a quite normal process connected with age and the hardening of the arteries. But I know my place in history. It was once defined for me with absolute precision by my friend Ernest Gimpel. I went to see one of the exhibitions of more or less abstract art and I could not make head or tail of it; and on the way out I said to Ernest, 'I'm very sorry, I just can't get it,' and Ernest looked at me very sadly and said, 'Pity, because you got as far as Picasso.'

Cumulative evidence appears to suggest that Anthony's views on ageing and hardening arteries may very well be right, and that the main trouble at Eton was that, by the fifties, I was becoming an anachronism. On visiting the Drawing Schools in the summer of 1982 I found both the staff and the buildings almost doubled in size, money apparently there for the asking, a new library and lecture room, and signs of much activity. Pottery still continued to flourish under the able direction of Mones's successor, Gordon Baldwin, though Mones's chaste 'Chinese' bowls – he was an ardent admirer of Bernard Leach – had been superseded by more adventurous polychrome objects and gigantic white elephants. The wife of a retired housemaster wrote to me recently: 'The other day I sent to a local charity auction sale a pottery dish made in the Drawing Schools and given to us by a leaving boy. It was entered in the catalogue as "large oval dish, probably East African"!'

Elsewhere there was a lot of tortured metal around, and virtually everything, both two- and three-dimensional, was abstract; but in a corridor I noticed one small representational watercolour of the Playing Fields that might have been painted in my day (indeed, just possibly it was). Its scarlet bridge, clearly identifiable as a bridge, seemed to blush for shame. I thought that this was the only single object surviving that showed at least the influence of my twenty-one years as drawing master. On a further visit a few months later I found that it had disappeared. I did discover, however, in the lavatory, a cheap reproduction of a Japanese print that I had framed and hung there, and which none of my successors had as yet had found time to burn.

Then, in December 1983, I paid what may well prove to be my final visit to the Drawing Schools. And I am very glad that I did, for in addition to the abstract work, there were a number of representational drawings and paintings of an exceedingly high quality, and the senior drawing master, John Booth, was obviously generating a lot of interest and enthusiasm. Perhaps the pendulum was at last beginning to swing back again.

5
Morocco: A Necessary Interlude

Compound for sins they are inclin'd to
By damning those they have no mind to.

SAMUEL BUTLER, *Hudibras*

I revert for a moment to the spring of 1928, when I went with my Haileybury colleague Edgar Matthews to Algeria and Tunisia.

I was at that time still very innocent, and though far from impervious to the charm of those smiling Arab and Berber boys who followed us everywhere, was not fully aware of what they expected us to demand of them. My copy of André Gide's *Si le grain ne meurt* was, I see, bought two years later, and after reading his courageous, uninhibited account of his visit with Oscar Wilde to a boys' brothel in Algiers my eyes must certainly have been wide open. Yet when, in 1939, I decided to spend my Easter holiday in Morocco, it happened suddenly and fortuitously. I had had no thought whatever of following in Gide's footsteps.

With the threat of war hanging over us I had not, as I generally did, planned anything ahead; so I went to my usual travel agent, who said, 'Why not Morocco?' And old Omar Khayyám whispered in my ear, 'Why not?' I went alone by sea to Tangier (£11 return), and on the boat made friends with two young English botanists who were then unknown but who have since become famous in their chosen fields: Oleg Polunin[1] and Peter Davis, authors respectively of floras of Europe and Turkey, who were making a sponsored journey in the capacity of plant-collectors. With them I visited Tetuan and Chechaouane (Xauen)[2] in Spanish Morocco. At the former, while they climbed a mountain I didn't like the look of to collect a remarkable

[1] Died July 1985.
[2] I have neither the time, the energy, nor the desire, to fuss over the various ways of spelling these place-names.

58

The hall porter at Xauen

cabbage that apparently grows nowhere else, I remained behind and sketched the dazzlingly white town, and on their return tried to show appropriate enthusiasm for a vegetable that to me seemed almost indistinguishable from every cabbage I had ever eaten.[3] From Xauen, a delightful little hillside townlet on the lower slopes of the Rif mountains with streams everywhere and a Spanish-style *posada* as its only European building, we passed on to Azrou, in the Middle Atlas, where peonies flowered in profusion under the shade of a grove of Atlantic cedars. At this point I left the botanists to continue on their way southwards across the Atlas, while I went on alone to Meknès, Fez, and finally to the great palm-girt oasis of Marrakech.

In those days Marrakech had not yet been discovered by Winston Churchill or opened up to conducted tours. The muezzins still called the faithful four times a day to prayer from the summits of the minarets, innocent as yet of the unromantic convenience of canned music. It had, however, like all the *Moghreb* (Islamic north-west Africa), long been the most easily accessible hunting-ground for European male homosexuals. Homosexuality – paedophilia in particular – was accepted there, and indeed throughout the whole of the so-called 'Sotadic zone', as naturally as it had been in ancient Greece, the Koran being interpreted very liberally in the extreme western outposts of Islam, especially by the Shluhs (Moroccan Berbers) who were the original inhabitants of the country before the Arab invasion in the eighth century. For the boys, who were trained in the duties expected of them, paederasty was little more than a game to which, since it was socially acceptable, no stigma was attached and no emotional 'hang-ups' were involved. Many of them came in from the country, earned some money, and then returned unharmed to their mountain homes to marry and – one hopes – live happily ever after. The Shluhs are no darker-skinned than southern Europeans, and often astonishingly beautiful. But so, in their own way, are the Arabs.

On my third and last night at Marrakech (for I had to hurry

---

[3] Professor Peter Davis informs me that this very ancient and curious plant, *Hemicrambe fruticulosa*, was long believed to be the only species of its genus, but recently a second species has been discovered on a cliff in Socotra. It is apparently far less like the common cabbage than I had remembered.

Street scene, Marrakech, in the thirties

back to England to sing the baritone solo part in Dyson's *The Canterbury Pilgrims* at the Devizes Festival before the half started) I wandered into the native town, where I was soon accosted by a 'guide' – i.e., a pimp. 'Vous désirez un beau garçon, monsieur?' I knew, of course, that I did; that it was something I had to experience *once*, but under conditions where it was a part of the traditional way of life. However, I rejected his offer and continued on my way till I reached the Koutoubia, the great twelfth-century mosque whose immense ithyphallic minaret towered above me into the moonlight. The air was spice-laden. Veiled women flitted from shadow to shadow.

Another pimp: 'Vous cherchez quelque chose, monsieur?'

This time I hesitated. 'Ça se peut.'

'Un joli garçon, peut-être?'

One's pupils – boys in the school – were, of course, 'out of bounds', sacrosanct – and were to remain so to the end. In all my thirty-six years as a schoolmaster I never so much as kissed one. But here, surely, it was different. In Rome, might not one do as the Romans? – or, as Samuel Butler put it, 'Cannibalism is moral in a cannibal country.'

I said, 'Je veux bien.'

Following him down a labyrinth of dark and sinister alleys, I came at last to a nail-studded door on which the pimp knocked five times. It opened immediately, and, crossing a small courtyard with lilacs in full flower, we entered the brothel. It was a large room. Several ancient men were smoking hookahs, two more played fitfully on one-stringed musical instruments, while seven or eight boys, dressed in spotless white burnouses, sat apart in a group on the floor, chattering away happily together like choristers waiting for a choir practice to begin. As we entered they were instantly silent; clearly discipline was strict. I appeared to be the only client.

'This is a good place, a safe place,' said the pimp. 'Why, even the manager of your hotel comes here regularly.'

'How do you know which my hotel is?'

'I am Achmad. Achmad knows everything. Look at that boy there; does he not have beautiful eyes? He is a Shluh.' He had indeed: eyes like sucked toffee, and glittering white teeth. I had noticed him at once.

A price was agreed with the manager, but when I indicated my choice he said, 'Ah, monsieur, Muhammad is special. For him there will be a *petit supplément* . . .' Probably whatever my choice it would have been the same story.

At a nod from the manager the boy rose and came towards me.

I guessed him to be about fourteen or fifteen – at all events a teenager, not a child; most of the others were younger.

'Muhammad speaks no French, but that need not trouble you. He will do whatever you wish.'

The boy took me by the hand and led me silently to a divan in a far corner of the room, still in view of the other boys and the musicians; but for them, what was to follow was too routine to arouse their interest. Muhammad stood before me. Then, with a sudden shrug of his slender shoulders, his burnous fell to the ground, leaving him stark naked. So, with the pull of a cord, might a newly acquired bronze statue of Ganymede have been unveiled by a visiting dignitary to a European museum . . .

Next morning I left for England.

In the months that followed, I reflected long and often upon that unforgettable evening. The sex-play had been of the most elementary kind (and with adult partners later was to remain so): simply that indulged in by hundreds of boys at most unisexual public boarding schools and which, unless discovered and punished by expulsion, provides – in moderation – harmless pleasure to both parties. It was an experience that, thanks to my retarded sexual development, I had left twenty years too late. It had indeed proved enjoyable; but what most surprised me was the discovery that satisfaction had been derived principally from the exquisite joy of holding in my arms, embracing and caressing this perfect young lithe body. Sexually it had not been really fulfilling, and the experiment was never repeated. Muhammed was to remain the only *boy* I ever 'slept with'.

This brief encounter, though at first I hardly realised it, was gradually to change my life. It had shown me that I was not, basically, a repressed boy-lover: that for sex I needed an *adult* homosexual partner. I am by nature monogamous. I now knew that what I wanted was to love another young *man* as I had loved Stephen, but to be loved in return – and for ever. Most homosexuals become promiscuous chiefly because society still makes even a discreet stable relationship very difficult. For many long years I remained chaste. The company of attractive – and not only *physically* attractive – boys continued to be for me as enjoyable as ever, but the adult sexual partner still eluded me.

Further, until 1968 the sexual act, even with a consenting adult in private, was a criminal offence.[4]

To conclude the story of my active sex-life I will add only this, for I am still unwilling to write more freely. Eventually I fell in love with a man little more than half my age, whom I discovered to be a practising homosexual; and because my natural instinct had been for so long repressed, when once set free it was all the more violent. Rendezvous were hard to arrange; but though I soon realised that it could not become a permanent relationship – for I proved to be an incompetent, impatient, possessive and over-demanding lover, and the disparity of our ages was too great – I experienced for some months the ecstasy of physical love. I understood, for the first time, how a heterosexual could sacrifice everything for the love of a woman. But 'Dans l'amour il y a toujours un qui aime et un qui se laisse aimer'. Inevitably his ardour began to cool while mine remained unabated, yet foolishly I refused to accept this until the matter was taken out of my hands by his firm transferring him to a job in the north of England. No doubt it was all for the best. Had he not then made his position clear, I might well have sacrificed my career in order to join him.

Not long afterwards I fell in love again, but this time with a man who was basically a lover of boys and I no more than a *faute de mieux*. My feelings were even more passionate; but once again I was soon forced to admit that what I felt for him could never be fully reciprocated. The first of these two men died before he was

[4] Until 1861, sodomy had incurred the death penalty, though in the nineteenth century it was rarely carried out. It was then changed to 'penal servitude for life, or for not less than ten years', and remained so, theoretically, until 1968, when sex in private between two (not more) consenting males over the age of twenty-one was legalised in England and Wales. Scotland followed later, and Northern Ireland in 1982. In the Isle of Man and the Channel Islands, as well as in the Armed Forces and the Merchant Navy, the act still remains criminal. Lesbians (except those in the Forces) have not suffered similar persecution – surely a case of sexual discrimination? Where a male under the age of twenty-one is involved, the charge is one of criminal *assault*, however willing, or even provocative, the younger partner may be – and indeed often is. There has recently been a good deal of campaigning to reduce the age of consent for homosexuals to sixteen to bring it into line with heterosexuals, but so far without success. The main physical consequence of teenage sex, in the form of unwanted pregnancies, should logically require a *higher* age of consent for the heterosexuals, rather than a lower one. It may also be noted, for what it is worth, that psychologists are increasingly convinced that homosexuals are not made so by homosexual experience.

forty. With the second, who now lives in South America where he made a marriage he soon came to regret, I correspond regularly, and I always see him when he comes to England. He is completely hag-ridden by his Argentine wife, who has even forced him to grow a beard.

As I look back I am ashamed, not for what I then did but that I did not sooner and more readily accept, when it had been made abundantly clear, the fact that I had ceased to be desirable. My failure was in part due to the age disparity, but also to my utter ignorance of how to behave in bed, and especially of 'foreplay' for which I – impetuous always – felt no need. There is, I presume, every kind of guidebook to *heterosexual* love-making; and for homosexuals even the television now produces programmes that practically serve the purpose. I was nearly eighty when, by mere chance, I found myself seeing my first (and only) homosexual blue film. If only such a film could have been made, and come my way, sixty years earlier!

Apart from several very brief, casual and purely lustful adventures – all so long ago now! – and one or two rejected 'passes' where I did no more than play the humiliating role of an unrewarded sugar-daddy, I have nothing more to confess. I had left it too late. I knew that the permanent, reciprocated partnership for which I had yearned was now unattainable. I had innumerable friends but, like King Ludwig II of Bavaria, I had failed to find the Friend.

Had I been heterosexual, or had I married an understanding woman for companionship, would I have led a happier and a more fulfilled life? And how would *she* have fared? I discussed these matters on the closing page of *Married to a Single Life*, and concluded that, if there had been children, my life would certainly have been less productive in other fields. As Bacon wrote in his essay, 'Of Marriage and Single Life':

> He that hath wife and children hath given hostages to fortune; for they are impediments to great enterprises, either of virtue or mischief. Certainly the best works, and of the greatest merit for the public, have proceeded from the unmarried or childless men, which, both in affection and means, have married and endowed the public.

His advice on the subject of marriage was, to a young man, 'Not yet', and to an older man, 'Not at all.' The former has been neatly updated by Cyril Connolly in *Enemies of Promise*. 'There is no more sombre enemy of good art than the pram in the hall.' Ouida's letter to Sydney Cockerell to 'congratulate' him on his engagement to Kate Kingsford in 1907 has often been quoted:

> I am very sorry to hear the news you give me. Your golden hair will soon grow grey. You have such a charming life, and are so welcome everywhere, that it is really suicide. No woman, were she the loveliest of living creatures, is worth the sacrifice of a man's life . . . With sincere regret for the irreparable error I am
> ever your friend
OUIDA

However, I continue to be amazed that so many married, quiverful men *do* contrive to find time to lead creative lives. Usually in such cases either the wife is superbly understanding, or has interests of her own, or the husband is selfishly neglectful. I was much surprised to learn, only quite recently, that my brother Anthony had in the early thirties kept a mistress – a liaison hastily terminated when her husband threatened to cite him as co-respondent. I was further told that he had actually proposed, unsuccessfully, to another woman. For me, marriage on any terms would have proved a disaster. 'Marriages', said Anthony Hope, 'are made in Heaven . . . I thought of waiting till I got there.'

Connolly, who was three times married, wrote to his great friend Noel Blakiston in November 1929, shortly before his first marriage (to an American):

> Of course the trouble is that I'm emotionally homosexual still – I see red at the idea of an infringement of my liberty by *la femme*, of any theories of gallantry that I will have to apply . . . Every Englishman, don't you think, is really contemptuous of women – the sanctity of the smoking room is always at the back of his mind . . . I think we have the fear of being run by them, as well as the feeling that they are obviously inferior . . . In America the women rule the roost. The men fool them, of course, but they boss the men.[5]

[5] *A Romantic Friendship: The Letters of Cyril Connolly to Noel Blakiston*, Constable, 1975, pp. 327–8. Connolly was born in 1903 and died in 1974. Blakiston, two years his junior, married in 1929 and died in 1984; his widow survives him.

Antinoüs (Museo Nazionale, Naples)

Only a very brave man would dare to write like that of women today.

The psychiatrist whom I had shyly visited in London in 1929, when I first realised that I was a homosexual, had told me that I would have to learn to live with my 'disability', as do people born autistic or incurably deaf. The burden of innate homosexuality *can* be relieved, and perhaps eventually almost eliminated – but only when heterosexuals learn to recognise and accept that, whether they like it or not, such mutations *do* exist,[6] and in far greater numbers than they imagine. Writing of Hadrian and Antinoüs, Gibbon commented, 'We may remark that, of the first

[6] Bernard Shaw, on receiving in 1939 from Lord Alfred Douglas the manuscript of a priggish biography of Oscar Wilde, replied: 'It is now known that a reversal of the sex instinct occurs naturally, and that the victim of it is greatly to be pitied and may be a person of the noblest character... You must clear your mind of Sodom and Gomorrah ... It is not necessary to pester the reader with assurances that you are bound as a Catholic to proclaim Pickwickian opinions and values that are now obsolete, irrelevant, and ridiculous.' (H. Montgomery Hyde, *Lord Alfred Douglas*, Methuen, 1984.)

fifteen emperors, Claudius was the only one whose taste in love was entirely *correct*.' In modern times, until very recently, 'l'amour qui n'ose pas dire son nom' had revealed no more of itself than the tip of the iceberg. Perhaps the day will come when two men living openly together and leading full sexual lives will be as generally acceptable as is the conventionally married couple: for the sake of an over-populated world, it is to be hoped so.

Even certain sects of the Christian Church – the Roman Catholics, of course, not among them – are now beginning to show a more tolerant attitude towards homosexuality, agreeing with the new law of 1968 that (in certain circumstances) it should no longer remain a criminal offence even if it remains a sin. The Archbishop of Canterbury, Dr Runcie, balances cleverly on the archiepiscopal fence, accepting the 'admitted' but not the 'practising' homosexual. This, wrote John Mortimer, is like saying that some people should be given driving licences but denied the use of a car.[7]

After I had finished this Moroccan section I showed it to several friends whom I knew I could trust to give me their frank opinions. One was a bachelor in his fifties who understands my problems, another a charming and intelligent married woman who has led a very sheltered life.

The former praised my handling of a delicate matter even more generously than I had dared to hope. From the latter, though she had eventually brought herself to accept my falling in love with a young man who had previously been my pupil at Haileybury, I had naturally awaited a more qualified response. Not for a moment, however, had I expected that she would react as strongly as she did.

She talked of the involvement of a *child*, as if I had corrupted an innocent eight-year-old. Muhammad was a teenager, past the age of puberty – a professional catamite fully aware of what he was doing. This was not a question of what the French call 'détournement de mineurs'. Yet – strangely, it seemed to me – it was *not* the details themselves, but my wish to publish them, that she found

[7] *Sunday Times*, 13 November 1983.

'so distasteful and upsetting'. In my first volume, she said, I 'had elicited much compassion' from my readers, 'and even perhaps some understanding from many people who are otherwise antagonistic. It showed, compared to this Eton part, so much more restraint, and *dignity*.' It was 'much more effective in putting forward your case'. Even were the book to be published posthumously (which I had originally intended, and may of course still happen), it would be 'a source of great regret, distress and unhappiness to your many friends and admirers', who would thus 'have their happy memories tarnished'.

I was amazed – and saddened, since she is a woman for whom I have the highest regard. I had, I thought, made it absolutely clear in my first volume that I accepted André Gide's dictum that 'it is better to be hated for what one is, than loved for what one is not'. I am trying to write an honest autobiography, not a dishonest autohagiography; and if, as Harold Nicolson observed in *Some People*, an author always paused to consider what Aunt Julia at Bath or Uncle Roderick in Littlehampton might say of his book, little worthwhile would ever get written.

As for 'putting forward [my] case' – well, I was thinking at least as much in terms of purgation as of propaganda. Here is where Christians are so lucky: they can confess to their God – who does not blab. They can have the best of both worlds: clear themselves at top level, yet leave their public image untarnished; and apparently they see nothing shabby in this. Those who are famous will almost certainly risk posthumous exposure. Those who, like myself, are not, can – if they so choose – carry many of their secrets with them to the grave, and beyond it. I could have omitted a part of this chapter, and nobody would ever have known what took place that night, now nearly fifty years ago, in Marrakech. I do not so choose.

Total repression in a highly sexed man who is very susceptible to male beauty often leads to a breakdown in middle age. A. C. Benson [8] – one of the three brilliant sons of an Archbishop of Canterbury, an Eton housemaster, and finally Master of Magdalene College, Cambridge – worshipped boys and young men, but apparently never entered that paradise on whose brink he

---

[8] 1862–1925. See David Newsome, *On the Edge of Paradise: A. C. Benson, the Diarist*, John Murray, 1980.

perpetually teetered. It was surely this that was responsible for the breakdowns from which he suffered in 1907–8 and 1917–22. Indeed, towards the end of his life we find him seemingly in agreement with a septuagenarian general who said to him that 'the one regret he felt in his old age was that he had not *sinned* more as a young man . . . As [A.C.B.] grew older, he envied those who were prepared to take risks, especially for love. He had no sexual life; all his sexual instinct had been sublimated, mainly – he thought – through his timidity, which itself sprang from his upbringing.' He told his friend Geoffrey Madan, 'I think . . . I have suffered by being brought up to regard all sexual relations as being rather detestable in their very nature: a thing to be ashamed of.'[9] What he saw as his failure to achieve his full potential, and attributed in part to his lack of moral courage, might perhaps have been more accurately ascribed to a lack of *im*moral courage.

The writing of these two autobiographical volumes has given me plenty of occasion to reflect on a long and, sexually speaking, not always easy life. I will try to sum up my conclusions. It must be self-evident that those whose professions bring them into close contact with boys must *never* interfere with any who are *in statu pupillari*. This said, I consider that two persons, whether of the same or of different sexes, if they both believe themselves to be free agents of a responsible age, are morally entitled to find whatever pleasure they both wish in whatever kind of sex-play they like – provided that in so doing they are not damaging other lives. (And, incidentally, how many *divorces* do just this!) I throw no first stone at any whose code of conduct is at variance with my own, being unwilling to compound for sins I am inclined to by damning those I have no mind to.[10]

---

[9] Newsome, *op. cit.*, pp. 382, 368.
[10] T. C. Worsley's *Flannelled Fool* (Alan Ross, 1967) describes how another schoolmaster dealt with the same predicament as mine.

6

Beauty and the Beast

Most good schoolmasters are homosexual by nature –
how else could they endure their work . . .?

EVELYN WAUGH

Rich[1] or aristocratic young men, however plain or stupid, have always tended to find at their disposal a wider choice of wives than the rest of the population. If the criterion that governs their choice is (as often happens) beauty, then those of their offspring who take after their mothers are above averagely good-looking; thus Eton has always had more than its fair share of handsome boys. In the eighteenth century a fortunate chance led to the recording and preservation for posterity of a cross-section of the school's *jeunesse dorée* over a period of about a hundred years.

By the end of the seventeenth century it had become virtually obligatory for a boy, when at the end of his last half he came to take leave of the Head Master, unostentatiously to deposit a sum of money on his writing table as he received his 'leaving book'. From a commoner £10 was considered the decent minimum, but of a nobleman at least double that sum was expected. It was said that Dr Hawtrey, Head Master from 1834 to 1852, used tactfully to rise and open (or shut) the window to make the transfer less embarrassing. This practice of 'tipping' the Head Master – for let us call a spade a spade – continued until it was abolished by Edward Balston in 1868; but in the middle of the eighteenth century some of the scions of wealthy and ancient families began to be invited to present, in lieu of money, their portraits painted by a leading or up-and-coming artist of the day. These remained in the College, which thus acquired a unique youthful male

---

[1] It must be remembered that not all Etonians – and especially Collegers – are rich, though many are better off than they realise. I like the essay by an Eton boy, on 'My Home', which began, 'Our family is very poor, and even our butler is poor.'

Schönheitsgalerie[2] of works by artists such as Reynolds, Gainsborough, Romney, Hoppner, Beechey, Lawrence, and finally the little-known though far from negligible Margaret Carpenter (1793–1872). An attempt was made in the 1920s to have further portraits painted, but it failed. However, the present Provost, Lord Charteris – himself a sculptor – is now trying again.

Today we have the more modest but more widely disseminated 'leaving photograph', given by boys to friends in the school and to the masters who have taught them. (These in fact largely replace the exchange of expensive books, though gifts continue to pass between beaks and boys who had a close relationship.) Over the years most beaks acquire boxfuls of photographs that are sometimes used by the more frivolous among them for a kind of card game, the trumping card being the more handsome, ugly or aristocratic, as agreed in advance. In my time these photographs were usually formal, inscribed on the folder, 'W. J. W. Blunt, Esq.' and signed 'John, 1949' or whatever, though a few of the more aesthetic or unconventional boys had already begun to break away from the standard school-dress, head-and-shoulders format. Now, I observe, total informality is *de rigueur*, and effusive tributes of gratitude and affection, signed 'With much love from' are the rule rather than the exception.

Eton's plethora of beauty was not without its dangers. We have to go back to the reign of Henry VIII to find an Eton Head Master – Nicholas Udall – imprisoned for seducing a pupil. (His case was truly extraordinary, for he was also involved with this boy in the theft of some of the College silver; yet after his release from the Marshalsea Gaol he was repaid the arrears of his salary, and subsequently appointed Head Master of Westminster.) But in 1872 William Johnson (Cory), probably the most inspiring teacher ever to grace the Eton staff, was summarily dismissed by Dr Hornby in circumstances that have never been completely clarified.

Much has been written about Cory (the name Johnson adopted after his dismissal). He is best remembered by Etonians as the author of the words of 'The Boating Song' and by a wider

---

[2] King Ludwig I of Bavaria created a famous 'Gallery of Beauty', comprising portraits, painted to order, of the women he admired.

William Young
by Benjamin West, c. 1770

Hon. Henry Howard
by Allan Ramsay, c. 1757

Frederick Howard,
5th Earl of Carlisle,
by Sir Joshua Reynolds, c. 1764

John Dawnay,
5th Viscount Downe,
by Thomas Gainsborough, c. 1781

Leaving portraits

73

1957

1942

1959

1952

Four leaving photographs: an ambassador,
a peer, a publisher and a field marshal.
I leave the reader to decide which is which.
(Answers at end of index.)

audience for his 'Heraclitus'. That he loved youth was undeniable. He had surely already foreseen the risks he ran on accepting, at the age of twenty-two, an invitation to join the Eton staff – hesitating because 'I distrust the purity of the motives which have this long time past swayed me towards a wish to be an Eton master'.[3]

Three years after Cory's dismissal, Oscar Browning, another man with remarkable gifts for inspiring youth, suffered the same fate. Browning was sacked ostensibly for a technical irregularity: he had, without permission, taken more pupils than was permitted. However, in his biography of Browning,[4] Ian Anstruther makes no attempt to conceal the fact, revealed in every detail in recently discovered correspondence, that what Hornby really feared was at the very least founded upon reasonable suspicion. Two of Browning's especial interests – his attraction to his own sex, and his snobbery – revealed themselves at an early age. While still a boy at Eton he wrote in his diary: 'A half or two ago, I saw a boy named Dunmore. I was struck by his eyes. I have been more so by his manner and everything about him. My wishes, my hopes and fears begin and terminate in him. I have found that he is a lord, but I loved him before.'[5]

When I first arrived at Eton I found that it was common though discreetly whispered knowledge that there had been several 'bad' houses and several unorthodox housemasters at Eton in recent times. Indeed, they were not extinct. Only the other day I received a letter from a former pupil of the early fifties, whose house seemed almost to have been 'jinxed'. He wrote: 'There were about half a dozen other new boys when I went there. Four of these are now dead, and a fifth has turned into a woman, so I sometimes feel that there must have been some baleful influence at work.'

Occasionally, as can now be told, a bachelor housemaster's unorthodoxy went dangerously far. Ollard writes:

Ian Fleming's housemaster[6] used to insist on inspecting the whole

[3] Ollard, *op. cit.*, pp. 62–3. Ollard feels that this statement is open to other interpretation.
[4] *Oscar Browning: A Biography*, John Murray, 1983.
[5] Christopher Hollis, *Eton*, Hollis and Carter, 1960, pp. 282–3.
[6] E. V. Slater – a housemaster from 1920 to 1933.

house in a state of nakedness at regular intervals. The alleged purpose was to make sure that they had not contracted venereal disease. Other motives naturally suggested themselves. The creator of James Bond perhaps owed something to this early introduction to sexual fantasy.[7]

Hallam Tennyson, a great-grandson of the poet, still a boy at Eton when I arrived there (though our paths never crossed), describes his bisexuality in every detail in his astonishingly frank autobiography.[8] Eton in his day, he writes, was 'humming with sexual activity', and confessions of mutual masturbation, extracted over the Confirmation season by the Conduct (Chaplain), led to the exposure of 'well over two hundred' offenders before a halt was called to avoid scandals reaching the press. 'One boy, a peer, was sacked for sodomy.' The Conduct (the Revd Robin Hudson), described by Tennyson as 'an odious hypocrite' and 'a round cock-robin', comes in for some pretty savage attack for the dubious methods he employed to collect incriminating material.

Tennyson's housemaster, Richard Young, seems to have been amiably unaware of what went on in his house:

> During my brief sojourn in 'the library' (the senior house common room) my colleagues kept a public score sheet on which they numbered the progress of their *affaires du coeur*. '1' meant a glance returned, '2' a word exchanged, while the meaning of '3' was left to the imagination. When our housemaster peered at it myopically one day he was told it was our 'ping-pong' rota. 'Why aren't you on the list, Tennyson?' he asked mildly. 'I thought you were keen on table-tennis.'

Tennyson preferred male sex partners maturer than himself, and was thus to be saved in later life from dangerous involvement in acts 'execrated by both society and the law'. Yet even here he shows himself remarkably – some may feel excessively – tolerant:

> Not that I myself think 'paedophilia' intrinsically monstrous. In fact, if boys or girls consent to sexual advances from adults I am sure they suffer a great deal less harm than most of us seem to want to believe. I stress the word 'consent' of course. To my mind the Dutch have got it about right. In Holland sex between adults and children over twelve is not in itself criminal. Violence or undue influence has to be proved.

[7] *op. cit.*, p. 123.
[8] *The Haunted Mind*, André Deutsch, 1984.

76

In fact the Dutch have not as yet implemented this proposed change.

It was Rupert Hart-Davis who first dared to disclose in print the unconventional behaviour of a former master, Tom Cattley, who after his stint as a housemaster (1914–30) was still teaching when I joined the staff in 1938. On Cattley's death in 1958 Hart-Davis had written to his old friend and mentor at Eton,

Tom Cattley

Richard Young

George Lyttelton, 'I never knew him to speak to, but didn't much like what I heard about him . . . I'm sure he was a suppressed paederast.' Lyttelton agreed: 'Like many bachelor beaks . . . many of them excellent beaks . . . he was a sublimated homosexual, the adjective, or rather participle, being just as certain as the noun. He was perhaps a little too frank in his preference for bright boys of fourteen to all boys, bright or not, of eighteen.'[9]

[9] op. cit., p. 123.

It was, however, whispered over the port at Eton dinner tables that Cattley had allegedly interpreted his *in loco parentis* status as entitling him to kiss *all* his boys goodnight, whether they were fourteen or eighteen, when he made his evening round of the house; possibly he felt that there was 'safety in numbers'. But I never heard any suggestion that his display of affection went further, and one former member of Cattley's house told Ollard that in his day there was no greater danger than that of 'the encircling arm'. It was, of course, reckless of Cattley to have kissed (if he did) the boys in his house, and he was fortunate to have 'got away with it'. Kissing is a positive and, even if not a criminal, certainly a perilous act, whereas a casually encircling arm is surely too imprecise a one to constitute a hazard. At all events, Tom survived his full time as a housemaster, and was on the staff continuously from 1899 until his death, at the age of eighty-four, in 1958.

It sometimes happens with suppressed paederasts that over the years the age group that attracts them shifts upwards. Only thus can I now understand how, soon after my arrival at Eton, I came to be the surprised, undeserved, unembraced and even un-arm-encircled recipient from Tom of a handsome Japanese painting and other gifts – for really I knew him only very slightly. Or am I letting my imagination run riot?

If the appointment to the staff of a suppressed homosexual involves an element of risk, as a rule it proves to be one worth taking; the appointment of an unsuppressed sadist, on the other hand, must surely always be folly. In all my years as a schoolmaster I was aware only of one: H. K. Marsden. A mathematical Colleger who had left Eton in 1906, Marsden had passed on to Merton College, Oxford, and after a brief spell of teaching at Osborne had joined the Eton staff in 1912. (On being asked, many years later, whether he had ever been a dancing man he had replied that his last dancing partner had been the Prince of Wales, the future King Edward VIII – his pupil at Osborne.) In his summer holidays during the First World War he had regulated railway timetables involving troop movements – a task which many users of British Rail today will surely agree gave ample scope for his sadistic talents and which he carried out with

Watkin Williams, H. K. Marsden and the Revd Bernard Harvey:
caricature by Robin McEwen, c.1942, rescued by the author
from the floor of the Drawing Schools.

remarkable speed and efficiency. The *five* men originally allocated to the task were sent on leave. In 1923 he became Master in College, and was subsequently a housemaster from 1930 to 1946.

Freddie Ayer, doomed to spend his Eton career in College under Marsden, said that Marsden 'was exceptional in that his whole mental outlook was bounded by Eton'. Though a kindly man, Ayer dipped his pen in vitriol to describe his tormentor. Marsden's close contact with Eton, he wrote,

> at least led him to take an interest in boys, which might have borne better fruit had he not been a sadist and a repressed homosexual. He used to prowl about the passages at night and I could not go to the lavatory after lights out without his coming to my room and asking me where I had been. Being an innocent boy, I did not realise until long afterwards that he was suspecting me of homosexuality. He was not allowed to beat the boys himself, but he contrived to have them beaten by his sixth-formers, and later when he had an Oppidan house he blackmailed at least one boy, to my knowledge, into letting him [Marsden] beat him. He was much concerned about our masturbation and used on his nightly rounds to question us about our apparent loss of vitality . . . I hated him at school and for some time after, until I saw him drunk at a Christ Church dinner and thought him more pathetic than odious. He was reported to have run his Oppidan house very efficiently and many of his boys were devoted to him, so that I suppose he must have had some better qualities . . . Nevertheless I was angered by the fulsomeness of some of the tributes which were paid to him in *The Times* when he died some years ago [15 January 1967].[10]

Richard Ollard, who was in College at Eton from 1937 to 1942, refers to 'an older master of notably tyrannical habits' (whom the index betrays as being Marsden), and also to Ayer's indictment. He adds later, now mentioning Marsden by name:[11]

> Regulations, and the penalties attendant on their infringement, were his ruling passion. It is ironic indeed that a spirit so essentially hostile to everything that Eton stood for should have cast himself for the role of guardian of its traditions. His siege mentality evoked loyalty and *esprit de corps* from the boys in his house, whom he defended, like some clan chieftain, from the official punishments he was zealous in

[10] *Part of My Life*, pp. 48–9.
[11] *op. cit.*, pp. 106, 192–3.

securing for everyone else. If his boys were to be chastised he desired to be the sole arbiter and, it was said, executor of the matter. Deplorable as all this might be it seems to have worked. His house was a good one by the only known tests, namely that his boys seemed generally happy and successful and their subsequent contribution to the life of the nation has not been negligible.

Endless stories are told about Bloody Bill. It was alleged that he never slept, though Walter Hamilton – a colleague with a pleasantly dry, donnish wit who later became Headmaster of Rugby and then Master of Magdalene College, Cambridge – when asked whether this was true, opined, 'Oh, I don't know . . . I dare say he takes an *angry snatch* from time to time.' Another story is of a boy in his house who returned late from dining at Windsor Castle and asked his host whether he would be kind enough to give him a line of excuse to his housemaster. The King (George VI) graciously wrote a brief word of apology. Marsden read it, observed that the chap hadn't even bothered to date it, crumpled it up and threw it into the waste-paper basket.

By sheer good fortune I happen to have a caricature of Marsden with two of his colleagues, dashed off by a boy (Robin McEwen) about 1942 and rescued by me from the floor of the Drawing Schools. I say, 'by good fortune', for Eton – in Elliott's day, at all events – frowned upon even relatively innocuous essays in this art-form. Julian Slade (of *Salad Days* fame), another very talented caricaturist, was savagely carpeted by the Head Master for including in a brilliant cartoon, published in the *Eton College Chronicle* (5 June 1948), a tiny figure unmistakably portraying

From Julian Slade's offending cartoon

81

the very corpulent wife of an Eton master. The attitude at Haileybury, in my early days there, was very different, and the staff almost queued up to be caricatured by an exceptionally talented boy, Richard Payton.

Both Ayer and Ollard state that Marsden, after his dubious reign as Master in College, came to have a reasonably good boys' house. Any housemaster who takes the side of his boys against all complaining colleagues, however just their complaint, must win a certain following; and undoubtedly some of his products were also successful in later life. But not all enjoyed being in his charge, and a kinsman of mine, who was in his house before I came to Eton, hated every moment of it. Certainly he was the most unattractive species of the genus schoolmaster that I encountered in the course of thirty-six years of teaching. It is not difficult to understand how a housemaster's wife came to say, at a luncheon party a few days after Bloody Bill's death, 'I've been going to funerals all this week, and Billy Marsden's was *much* the nicest because no one could possibly mind.'

It needs only one rotten apple to infect a whole barrel, and several Old Etonians, the products of houses run impeccably by conscientious men, ended up in gaol. The press were never slow to spot and headline their fall. So far as I am aware, no statistics are available; but a remark allegedly once made by a Governor of Maidstone Gaol about an Old Etonian in his charge is not without interest: 'There *must* be something wrong with him, because none of the other OEs here like him.'

An odd story of what may have been the gaucheness rather than the malice of the provincial press is perhaps worth recording. William Hope-Jones ('Ho-Jo'), an eccentric but wholly respectable housemaster of my day, had once been run in by the police for nude bathing 'with a boy' near St Davids. A local newspaper, when reporting the case, described the accused as 'The man Jones, alleged to be an Eton master', but omitted the important fact that the boy was his son. It must be admitted that Ho-Jo's unconventional behaviour tended to be provocative: I was told that one Fourth of June he was seen in tattered gardening clothes, wheeling a barrowload of manure through the heart of Eton just as immaculately dressed parents were arriving.

William Hope-Jones ('Ho-Jo')

Reporters were a perpetual menace at Eton, and neither Elliott nor his successor, Robert Birley, would ever do anything to placate them – which merely made them even more savage. '*Do* be careful about these people,' Birley wrote to a housemaster. 'The *only* thing to do is not to trust them an inch!' Sometimes, however, they were not so smart. I recall the young Duke of Kent leaning, languidly and decoratively, against a pillar at the entrance of the Drawing Schools one Fourth of June when a press photographer appeared from nowhere and snapped him. I thought, 'Poor boy . . . !' The photographer then approached his victim and said, 'Excuse me, sir, might I have your name?'

Not long ago I heard an old man, clearly of humble origin, being interviewed on the radio on the subject of corporal punishment.[12]

---

[12] For corporal punishment at Eton, see Henry S. Salt's *Memories of Bygone Eton*, p. 59ff. Salt, though an Old Etonian, a housemaster (from 1875 to 1884), the husband of the daughter of a Lower Master, and – incidentally – the tutor of Edward Lyttelton (Head Master from 1905 to 1916), was a crank whom most writers on Eton prefer to forget or to dismiss briefly. His *Memories*, however, forms perhaps the most witty, if also one of the more irreverent, books ever written about the famous school, and Eton ought surely to be able to take it in her stride.

He had, he said, been subjected to it time and again in his youth – sometimes, indeed, twice on the same day – and it had done him nothing but good. It had made him the man he was and though we could not see him, we were left in no doubt that he considered that he had survived it psychologically undaunted and physically undented. That was what he had *meant* to say; but unhappily he had each time referred to *capital* punishment, and his tactful interviewer had not corrected him.

I will not plead either for the retention or for the total abolition of corporal punishment. (It is, however, worth bearing in mind that though their origin is Biblical the actual words 'Spare the rod and spoil the child' are to be found in Samuel Butler's *Hudibras*,

*A master at Sherborne School birching a pupil;
from a choir-stall in Sherborne Abbey*

where the child in question is Cupid and the adviser a woman urging a man to allow himself to be flogged to stimulate sexual arousal.) When I first arrived at Eton, birching (on the bare buttocks) by the Head Master of Upper Boys and by the Lower Master of Lower Boys was not yet extinct, though I believe that the former never indulged in it and the latter only rarely. Now – and very properly – it is a thing of the past. Ordinary beating has also steadily become less frequent. How much of it there was in my time it is hard to say; but I recall one afternoon during the war, as I was walking in Richard Assheton's garden with his wife, Beryl, there came from the House Library the sound of at least a dozen boys being caned in swift succession. Beryl became

84

embarrassed, and breathlessly embarked upon a monologue on the care of delphiniums.

As at all schools there was the very occasional suicide. After one such, the house was assembled and the boys asked if anyone could suggest a possible reason. The late Lord Harlech, then David Ormsby-Gore – and a new boy – is credited with the inquiry 'Do you think, sir, it could have had anything to do with the food?'

Though there were at Eton, as there had been at Haileybury, innumerable boys to whom I felt attracted, in all my twenty-one years there was only one with whom I came very near to falling in love. Those of whom I was merely fond were of exactly the same kind as those who had attracted me at Haileybury, though now sometimes in an older age-group: bright, eager, vivacious, naive, slightly pert, and usually (but by no means always) reasonably good-looking. They were aware that I liked them, and I think that most of them liked me; but they also knew that this was the beginning and the end of our relationship. Their company gave me pleasure; their absence caused me no pain. But when the feeling is deeper, everything is different – as I described in *Married to a Single Life* when writing about Stephen Haggard.

Stephen, though I never thought him particularly handsome, possessed every other quality, and his charm – or, as they say today, 'charisma' – was irresistible. But Colin (as I will call him) was about fourteen and, with the exception of dazzlingly white teeth and the roguish smile of Frans Hals's *Boy with a Flute* to display them, had little to commend him physically: his complexion was sallow, his unruly hair mousy. He appeared to have no aesthetic or intellectual interests of any kind; he would certainly have been useless as a flautist. Nor was he particularly intelligent, and his conversation was boring. It might almost be said that I fell in love with two rows of teeth and a *gamin* smile. But I brought myself to worship him with such discretion that I believe he remained totally unaware of my feelings for him throughout the brief weeks my infatuation lasted. I do not think that Colin actively disliked me, but I would not put it much higher than that; indeed, I believe he was hardly conscious of my existence.

Of how many married couples does one not say, 'How on

Frans Hals's Boy with a Flute

earth could he have fallen in love with *her*?' or 'How could she have married *him*?' – and how many are forced, when it is too late, to ask themselves the same question? I like the definition of the word 'honeymoon' given by Thomas Blount (or Blunt – obviously a kinsman) in his *Glossographia* (1656): 'H*ony-moon*: applied to those married persons that love well at first and decline in affection afterwards: it is hony now, but it will change as the moon.' As Thoreau wrote, 'the mass of men lead lives of quiet desperation'.

It happened in my early years at Eton, before I had fully realised that young men attracted me, physically, more than did boys. Certain wartime duties had chanced to bring us for several weeks into dangerously close daily contact, and this indubitably played an important part in it; I suppose it could be compared to a 'shipboard romance'. Then circumstances altered and sent us on our separate ways. But for the next month or two my whole life continued to revolve round him. I knew his timetable by heart and would contrive to be passing as he came out of school, just for the joy of catching a momentary glimpse of him. One day, in a flash as it were, my eyes were opened. It had been a mirage. Except for those dazzling teeth and that smile there was – nothing! I have no idea what became of him, even whether he is alive or dead. My Old Etonian Association's list of members includes his name but gives no address, and I shall not bother to inquire further.

7
'Male and Female Created He Them'?

WOMAN, *n.* An animal usually living in the vicinity of Man,
and having a rudimentary susceptibility to domestication . . .
AMBROSE BIERCE, *The Devil's Dictionary*

The fact that a man does not respond to amorous advances from women often seems to arouse their curiosity rather than their suspicion: to pose a challenge. At all events this was so until the publication of the Wolfenden Report had led to changes in the law and widespread and persisting publicity in the media. Previously many women were so ignorant of the very existence of homosexuality that they could not conceive that apparently 'nice' men might be more attracted to the male than to what the French (I think mistakenly) call '*le beau sexe*'. Those who did realise that there were indeed such 'perverts' – men like Oscar Wilde – no doubt classed them with lepers. Some still do. And not only women led such sheltered lives, for we find the sixty-two-year-old Lord Stonham writing in 1965, 'During a fairly active life, including twenty-two years playing games, I have never encountered homosexuality.'

'I have reason to believe that women of our generation and upbringing are wishing that you hadn't included the very distressing course of events described in chapter 7 [of *Married to a Single Life*],' wrote a frustrated and clinging elderly widow, referring to my account of my abortive love affair with Stephen Haggard. I am sure she is right: but my book was not intended for old trout with set views and antiquated standards who prefer to shut their eyes to all that is not rosy in the ornamental fish-pond.

'Male and female created He them', we are told in Genesis i, 27. How nice it would be for many of us if it were so simple as that! It has been calculated that perhaps some ten or fifteen per cent of the inhabitants of this country are basically more homosexual than heterosexual, and since the majority of these do not produce children, thus passing on the inconvenient gene (if that is the cause) to a future generation, the 'abnormality' must be deeply ingrained. Alfred C. Kinsey[1] went so far as to claim that at some time in their lives one third of all (American) males have a homosexual experience to the point of orgasm.

To take my own family – my parents were unlucky: two homosexuals out of three children. My maternal grandparents had twelve grandchildren, three of whom were homosexuals. Of my paternal grandparents, certainly two, and possibly three, of their four spinster daughters were 'not the marrying kind', and indubitably they all died virgins. Aunt Edith was 'masculine'; Aunt Hilda was 'feminine', and had once had a very dear female 'friend' who had died and whose name was always mentioned in hushed tones. Aunt Win was almost certainly heterosexual and – so I was given to understand – prevented from making a very suitable marriage with a curate only by the selfishness of her father, the Bishop of Hull. Aunt Mabel, the intellectual, is hard to place: her father needed her services as a secretary, and she would in any case have put his convenience first.

Anthony and I were very much Blunts, whereas my brother Christopher was much more a Master (my mother's family). His three children are all heterosexual. All are married, and have children who, to the best of my knowledge, show no signs of homosexuality. At all events it would appear that the homosexual tendency comes principally from my father's side of the family. (Curiously enough, cancer, from which my father and two of his sisters died and which was passed down to Anthony and myself, has also left Christopher and his descendants so far untouched.)

To speak of bachelors in general, I would guess that possibly more than half of those over the age of forty are to some extent homosexual, whether actively or not, while not a few married men are bisexual ('playing for Middlesex', I believe it is called) and have taken wives, and indeed often produced families, in an attempt either to disguise or to overcome their ambivalence. Totally heterosexual and totally homosexual males (and indeed

[1] *Sexual Behaviour in the Human Male*, W. B. Saunders Co., 1948.

89

females) are presumably the exception rather than the rule, even though some have so small an element of the homosexual in their make-up that they do not recognise its existence.

There are also bachelors and spinsters apparently devoid of sexual drive of any kind – or are some, perhaps, merely deprived of arousal by Nature's almighty blunder in locating the organs of sex and excretion in such distasteful proximity? One of my middle-aged colleagues at Eton was reported to have remarked, 'Sex? I simply can't understand what all the *fuss* is about.' Another, however, found sex everywhere, and even attempted to get a reproduction of Botticelli's *Birth of Venus* removed from the

The Birth of Venus *by Botticelli,*
considered pornographic by a housemaster

walls of the School Library, and one of Poussin's *Kingdom of Flora* from the Modern Language Reading Room because he believed he had spotted a hermaphrodite lurking in the middle distance. 'Honi soit qui mal y pense!'

In many biographies, and indeed autobiographies, it is easy for the initiated to read between the lines and understand what is intentionally not stated explicitly in the text. Rupert Hart-Davis, for example, though writing of Hugh Walpole a decade after his death in 1941, prided himself on having produced 180,000 words on his subject without overtly mentioning his homosexuality. He was, of course, thinking of Walpole's brother and sister, who were still alive and would have been horrified by the undisguised revelation of something that they did not know about and could not have understood. There was Walpole's public too, and the climate was still hostile. It was a *tour de force* to have achieved so discreet and yet so brilliant a biography, but I myself could never have agreed to undertake such a task. I know only too well how deeply the burden of sex affects every aspect of the life and the creative work of a homosexual.

What, however, seems to me almost more strange is that Rupert, when I asked him whether he would have treated Walpole's homosexuality more openly had he been writing the biography today, replied: 'I should certainly do exactly what I did then. This country has for centuries produced magnificent literature without the use of four-letter words and blow-by-blow bedroom scenes. Their advent with "the permissive society" seems to me to have weakened rather than strengthened novels and biographies.' I was certainly *not* advocating the use of 'four-letter words' or 'blow-by-blow bedroom scenes'. But surely it is possible to twitch the fig-leaf off without titillating the readers or inviting a snigger? That has been my aim throughout this book.

Siegfried Sassoon, who died in 1967, requested that his homosexuality *should* be disclosed after his death; yet Hart-Davis's obituary of him in the *DNB* skates over the issue by merely referring to an unhappy marriage and Sassoon's enjoyment of 'the company of chosen friends, many of them greatly his juniors'. Even their sex is not specified. Possibly the *DNB* still demands this discretion. Evelyn Waugh once suggested that there should be a set piece attached to all entries: 'The above was sober, honest, chaste, maritally faithful, sexually normal, courageous, sweet-smelling, etc.', the omission of any quality being 'recognised as significant by regular readers'. References for servants – in the days when there were any – were treated similarly, to avoid risk of a libel action.

However, Hart-Davis, as Sassoon's literary executor, has recently edited three volumes of his Diaries (1915–1918, 1920–1922 and 1923–1925, all published by Faber and Faber), in the second of which the torment that Sassoon suffered from his homosexuality, which plagued him incessantly, is fully though discreetly revealed. Hart-Davis was sure that Sassoon wanted the text to be published without excisions. Yet it was Sassoon himself who removed all 'affairs of the heart' from the manuscript of the third volume.

Where 'the monstrous regiment of women' is concerned, I found to my astonishment that, though I have never been listed for conservation as 'an object of outstanding natural beauty', both while I was at Eton, and even more so subsequently at Compton, I continued to be in demand; for there appears to be no limit to the number of lonely elderly widows and spinsters pining to take over a *man* – almost *any* man. I was already into my eighties when a middle-aged widow suggested to me that it might be 'rather fun' for us to be photographed together – in the nude. It is, of course, even worse for the famous, and we find poor Arthur Benson, pursued by lion-huntresses, complaining of being 'persecuted by these d – – – – d women . . . The typical woman is horrible.'

But there are many who are *not* 'typical': I know plenty who are warm-hearted, and overflowing with a genuine desire to comfort and sustain a male who is often older and more enfeebled than themselves. Others need a masochist on whom to exercise their domineering instincts, and I can sympathise with Julia Brewster when she observed to Dame Ethel Smyth, 'One has to be very well, Ethel, to enjoy your company.' One of their deadliest weapons is the telephone.

I feel especially sorry for those nice but rather dim elderly widows who had shone only with the light emitted by their more luminous husbands. Following upon the death of the latter, an afterglow of pity lingers for a while in some rather guilty consciences; then, gradually, those 'friends' for whom so much hospitality had been provided begin to fade away. It was, the widows now realise, only their beloved Johns or Davids or Henrys who had been the magnets that drew people to the house. Some of them contrive to build new lives for themselves and are soon welcome everywhere; some wallow in self-pity and become bores, but a few become positive pests.

'Women do not find it difficult nowadays to behave like

men,' wrote Compton Mackenzie in 1962, 'but they often find it extremely difficult to behave like gentlemen.' In a world increasingly subjected to women's campaigns for sexual equality (at all events where it works to their advantage), though the attempted rape of a woman by a man remains a criminal offence, the reverse still seems to be considered no more than a flattering gesture for which the man should feel honoured, or at all events be easily capable of repelling. Only once in my life have I had actively to deal with such a situation. It happened in August 1950, while I was spending a holiday in Bavaria researching for a book on King Ludwig II that I did not in fact write until nearly twenty years later.[2]

I was staying near Lake Starnberg with a friend whom I had known when I was studying singing in Munich in the thirties – an Englishwoman who had married (and soon been obliged to shed) a German. Her little daughter, at that time about six or seven years old, had in the meanwhile developed into a very pretty, flaxen-haired, stage-struck young nymphomaniac, still less than half my age, who immediately decided to attempt to seduce me. (Why *me*, when she could presumably have taken her pick of dozens of good-looking young Germans? I suppose – as mountaineers say – 'because I was there', and almost any male under the age of seventy could have been expected to satisfy her immediate requirements. I do not really know my stuff about nymphomania.)

On the second night, soon after I was in bed, a long letter (in English) was slipped under the door of my bedroom, which adjoined hers. My heart, she assured me, was beating – less than a metre or two from hers:

> Yes, there you are, breathing and alive, almost within reach, and time passes, the hand runs round the clock, and there is a wall I cannot get through. O God, I would! . . . The terrible, commanding flame which was my body tells me to wait till midnight, and then, when all the house is asleep, find my way to the heart of my love . . .

And so on. But how? Not through the wall, *à la* Pyramus and Thisbe, and   suspecting trouble ahead – I had taken the precaution of locking my door. I am sure she *could* have burst in,

[2] *The Dream King*, Hamish Hamilton, 1970.

King Ludwig II of Bavaria, aged eighteen

for she was something of an Amazon; but the noise would have woken her mother.

Next morning I was going to Schloss Berg, on Lake Starnberg, where the unhappy Ludwig had drowned in 1886, and she insisted upon accompanying me. In the Starnberg station underpass – a little used and at the best of times unromantic spot – I suddenly found myself caught off my balance and pinned against the wall. Ominous gropings began; but I was saved from what was intended to terminate in a 'fate worse than death' by the timely though unexpected arrival of two other passengers. (Yet *why* choose a sordid station subway on a summer's day with glorious woodlands all around?)

I left for Munich sooner than originally planned – in fact, of course, the very next morning and on the flimsiest of excuses. The mother's changed attitude to me that evening had made it plain that she considered me a vile seducer, and I did not trouble to disillusion her; the girl had no doubt persuaded her that she was the constant victim of lecherous, middle-aged males. All I wanted to do was to *escape* – anyhow, anywhere.

More passionate letters followed when I got back to England; and sonnets galore – one comparing me to a summer's day but finding me more lovely and more temperate – till finally I began seriously to wonder whether I would suddenly discover her on my Eton doorstep, or even installed in my bed. Then, at last, came the welcome news that she had set up house with 'Heinrich'. In her next letter she was, predictably, already 'in trouble with Heinrich right now and rather out of my nerves'. Soon Heinrich (sensible chap) had bolted to America – 'It was the best thing he could do' – and she had become engaged 'after only ten days of acquaintance' to a young German paediatrician; she should have chosen a psychiatrist. They married and – thereafter, blessed silence. Poor creatures! I wonder what has happened to them both. I still have her letters, and a photograph (with Shakespeare sonnet on back) that confirm that she really was extremely pretty. I wish I could reproduce it, but I cannot take the risk.

There were other women who, though they did not carry things to such extremes, sometimes presented problems. One – an elderly widow without children – made a will leaving me a substantial house not far from Compton, but her relentless importunity and incessant jealousies became in the end so intolerable that I was forced to break with her. Not surprisingly, she changed her will. Another – a charming widow also several years older than I – did in fact leave me a tiny house in St Ives, and its contents. She was rich, enormously kind and hospitable, not unduly demanding – and the only person I have ever known who remembers having been tickled in her pram on Putney Heath by

Swinburne. But she suffered from angina, and on 1 December 1969 dropped dead in my arms in the foyer at Covent Garden, just as we were going in to hear *Pelléas et Mélisande*.

I tried to refuse the house and wrote to her solicitor about it, but he begged me not to; she had, he said, left her two daughters more than adequately provided for, and whatever I did would only lead to further family bickerings (he had clearly suffered from that already). One of the daughters did indeed write to me saying that she *knew* her mother had always meant her to have the house, but I took the solicitor's advice. The house was useless to me: much too far away, much too small ever to live in – and I hated what I saw of St Ives. So I sold everything except a clock which she had specifically mentioned that she wanted me to have, and a very pretty little table, by which to remember her and her many kindnesses. I have them to this day.

Christopher Hassall said of Stephen Haggard that he found it as easy to *give* affection as he found it hard to *accept* it and I think that this also applies to me where women are concerned. I cannot bear being 'pursued', as all my dearest friends soon came to understand; those women too insensitive to grasp this had ultimately to be shed – sometimes, I fear, rather brutally, because the pachydermatous do not respond to gentler treatment. I think of one in particular – a keen musician and genealogist who helped me in many ways, but who could not be brought to accept that I was unable to become involved in an emotional relationship.

Peter Ustinov claimed possessiveness to be 'the most dangerous and underrated of all human vices', and I agree; however, I admit with shame that I have been not only the victim but also the perpetrator of this particular viciousness. There are times when *things* – books, pictures, flowers, television, and, as I was later to discover, cats – afford more reliable comfort and support than *people*; and a 'voyage autour de ma chambre' provides, when needed, a hundred happy memories.

One of the problems that face the autobiographer is that certain people whom he wishes to include simply refuse to find a comfortable seat in the text. In this book, one such is my brother Christopher; and though others may finally have to be excluded, he most certainly must not.

First, Christopher is a man of total respectability and integrity: what can he have done to deserve such brothers as Anthony and myself? By profession a merchant banker of repute, happily married for nearly half a century but now a widower, at the age of eighty he lives in retirement in a beautiful Queen Anne house in Wiltshire, constantly entertaining his innumerable friends, never for long without a visit from some member or other of his family, never for a moment idle or bored.

Christopher, like Anthony, is a scholar. It must be from the Blunt side of the family that he has inherited his multifarious artistic interests, though in his case they are largely directed towards archaeology and, in particular, numismatics. He is the leading authority on Anglo-Saxon coinage – to my mind, I regret to say, the most boring artifacts (flint arrowheads excepted) that have come down to us from the past. His friends in the numismatic world clubbed together to have a silver medal, bearing his portrait, struck in his honour; it was presented to him

Christopher's medal

on his eightieth birthday in July 1984 and gave him enormous pleasure. I have seen it and have only one criticism: though the likeness is excellent, there is something about the nostrils that suggests trouble with the drains.

It would be true to say that, when we were young, both Christopher and I were closer to Anthony than we were to one another. Not that there was ever open animosity: it was chiefly that Anthony was so obviously brilliant and successful and attractive. I found the young Christopher somehow 'different', though of course I did not then realise what that basic difference was. And – dare I say it? – I think both Anthony and I thought him a shade pompous; we had our own little private jokes about him, just as, no doubt, he and Anthony had about me. It was undoubtedly Christopher's experience in Military Intelligence during the war that 'loosened him up'; Cambridge would probably have done it, and my father, though it would have been a financial strain, was prepared to send him there; but he had been so unhappy at Marlborough that he had preferred to get away from organised education and chose instead to study modern languages (especially Spanish) abroad. Anthony won so many scholarships that Trinity literally paid to have him. Now, like a good wine, Christopher becomes more splendid with every passing year. He is by far the best of the Blunts.

8

Grizel

On firmer ties his joys depend
Who has a polish'd female friend.

CORNELIUS WHUR, 1845

To list the names of all those 'polished female friends' with whom, over the years, I have had long, close and deeply valued platonic relationships would be almost impossible, and I do not intend to try; it would in any case make for tedious reading. A dozen immediately spring to mind; but I must be firm, and I trust that none of those whom I have omitted will think me ungrateful. However, to write about Eton in my time without mentioning Grizel Hartley would be like writing about life at Windsor Castle today without mentioning the Queen, though Ollard manages to do so.

Grizel, daughter of Sir George (Seaton) Buchanan, is the same age as myself – actually three weeks older, which she never allows me to forget. When I first met her she was in her late thirties: tall, splendid, with wild auburn hair that invited every wind to tousle it, high cheekbones and a complexion that confirmed her love of the open-air life; I thought of Charles Furse's once popular *Diana of the Uplands*. She was in fact a fearless rider, and when sailing also braved storms such as most of us prefer to see on television from the comfort of our armchairs; for few things are more enjoyable than watching the deliberately self-inflicted miseries of others.

Yet she was also an intellectual, and though she took her degree at Cambridge in Natural Sciences (she wanted at first to become a vet) she had a wide knowledge of English literature and more than a nodding acquaintance with mathematics and the classics. She had a man's mind in a woman's body; yet she had no lack of feminine foibles, together with a certain naivety that often led her

99

Grizel, 1929

to think the best of everybody and to believe the world a far better place than it really is. (For example, she has always understood that 'nothing actually *happened*' at those Edwardian house-parties where in fact adultery and fornication were virtually obligatory, and was later to be genuinely shocked when various explicit biographies revealed that it did.)

And then there is the beauty of her voice. I think I am attracted (or repelled) by a voice even more immediately and more strongly than by physical appearance. I find listening to most female radio and television 'personalities', Members of Parliament, and others who have screamed their way to the top in public life almost unbearable. I do not care for bright, schoolmistressy voices, nor for those of upper-class women who speak as if they were sacking housemaids; yet, equally, I am fairly impervious to Viennese charm and dulcet cooing. In short, I am totally prejudiced and unreasonable where women and dogs are concerned, having in my time been bitten by both. But Grizel's unique soft staccato is irresistible. She is the only woman I know who can call me (as indeed everyone) 'darling' without my wanting to bolt for cover. She is the wittiest, pluckiest, and most enchanting woman I have ever been privileged to count as a friend. Her letters, too, are wonderful.

I can even, almost, condone her passion not only for dogs, but also for horses and her native Scotland. I find Scotland (visited once only) draughty, while horses certainly live up to their reputation of being 'dangerous at both ends and boring in the middle'. But Grizel, though she worships horses, is not 'horsy'. As Saki said, 'there is as much difference between a horseman and a horsey [sic] man as there is between a well-dressed man and a dressy one', and of course the same applies to women.

I once offered to lend Grizel some book or other – I forget what.

'Are any horses killed in it?'

I tried to remember. 'I don't think so; but there are quite a lot of murders.'

She immediately accepted it, read it and enjoyed it. One of her favourite quotations was Mrs Patrick Campbell's famous *mot*, 'It doesn't matter what you do in the bedroom as long as you don't do it in the street and frighten the horses.' I think that her chief difficulty in believing in an afterlife was that most Christian theologians (John Wesley was an exception) maintained that animals had no souls. The prospect of a heaven without dogs and horses was hell to her, and doubtless contributed to her loss in later life of at all events a degree of faith in what she once described to me as 'that second-grade social worker called God'.

Incidentally, had she been an opera singer (and in middle age she acquired the figure of a prima donna), what a magnificent Marschallin she would have made in *Der Rosenkavalier*! I made undisguised use of Grizel, fictionally in *Of Flowers and a Village*,

Hubert Hartley
Silhouette by Robert Austin, 1935

and I have never been able to understand why, although she 'passed' the book for publication, she always disliked it; and many of her friends have told me that they are equally perplexed.

Grizel's husband, Hubert, was an Old Etonian: a man her equal in courage, charm, kindness and unpredictability. They had met at Cambridge, where Grizel was the Zuleika Dobson and Hubert the great oarsman of the day, and married soon after. At Eton, Hubert, with Grizel at his side, had what was generally agreed to be one of the best houses of its time; the devotion of their Old Boys speaks for itself.

Though Hubert knew that I was a Marlburian, it was not until very recently that I learned by mere chance that his father, Sir Percival Hartley, was also. I wrote to Grizel asking her to tell me more, and she replied (28 March 1984):

Sir Percival and Marlborough. Yes, indeed, and his two brothers, Lionel & Raymond. He was a MARTINET. He was very much the King of Bart's – a tuberculosis specialist – and I have met Bart's men who have told me so much, e.g. that he would only use a quill pen for his prescriptions – and that in a long ward of patients, nurses would bring him a clean towel and a NEW piece of soap to wash his own hands before every patient. Meticulous to the nth but awfully good at his job.

I am afraid that his first blow was that Hubert, nourished and brought up for the Diplomatic Service, chose to be a mere schoolmaster. The second was – the awful disappointment of his marriage. NO MONEY! & he refused to give Hubert a penny if he married me. I had £150 a year from my father, & you may imagine . . . But four years later an Old Harrovian cousin of Hubert's left Hubert a lot of money. I am sorry to say that we spent it all, & yet I am not *really* sorry – you will understand. And I have got everything I want – twenty stylosas today! and a lot of W. P. Milner daffodils – my favourite.

Needless to add, she did not mention the whole catalogue of physical disabilities from which she was by this time suffering.

Hubert fought in both World Wars. In the first, the horrors that he experienced as a young man of barely twenty left him for many years afterwards the victim of recurrent nightmares, while the second resulted in his being absent from Eton for five years. His house was temporarily run by Francis Cruso, and there was some uncertainty as to whether he really intended to return to Eton. In September 1939 his faithful manservant and butler, Heath,

Grizel and Francis Cruso.

resurrected his master's First World War uniform and, noticing a small moth-hole in it, observed, 'But I don't think it will show in action, sir.'

It was very inappropriate that Hubert, most ardent of patriots, should have had the brachycephalous head, closely cropped hair and steel-framed glasses of a benign German professor. He was never – except in his rare and usually quite unexpected moments of anger – less than smiling, and when laughter came it was in great gales that shook the room. I think I admired above all in him, even above his total integrity, his intrepidity. He saw all danger as a challenge to be accepted, whereas I saw it as something to be avoided if humanly possible. 'Had a good holiday?' I remember asking him on one occasion. 'No, not really; I was never frightened once.'

Hubert's reckless (if petty) extravagances, and his vagueness as a teacher, must not be allowed to pass unrecorded. Grizel told me that after playing fives he quite often left his gloves behind in the court, then simply bought a new pair when he played again. In school he taught with enthusiasm, but not infrequently using the wrong book; thus sometimes a special Trials paper had to be set 'for Mr Hartley's Division'. Grizel always spoke with admiration of Hubert's talents as a linguist, but I was never quite so sure.

He died in January 1977, at the age of eighty, having always been determined to reach that watershed in order to demonstrate that rowing does not damage the health. Grizel and I, now both octogenarians, can at least testify that *not* rowing does not either.

Grizel is – or at all events was – an indefatigable matchmaker, who scored one or two notable successes. Over the years she found at least half a dozen potential wives for me. Her first (and I don't think very serious) candidate was the attractive but far too young daughter of a housemaster. Grizel's technique was a shade naive: I was informed that the girl in question was longing for me to paint her portrait, but was too shy to suggest it; she in her turn was no doubt told that I was equally eager and equally shy. Mrs Prinsep and Tom Taylor had adopted much the same plan of action when trying to 'marry off' George Frederic Watts – with disastrous results.[1] I was more fortunate: though I did in fact

[1] See my *England's Michelangelo*, p. 104.

paint the portrait, neither the sitter nor I ever had the faintest intention of pursuing the matter further. She remained unmarried for seventeen years, and is now a viscountess.

There was another, of more suitable age: 'Darling, Patricia's *terribly* rich, and she's mad about hunting . . . But that wouldn't really matter a bit, and you'd soon get to love horses.' This, of course, did not even get off the ground, nor did any of the others; yet apparently Grizel never guessed the perfectly simple and obvious explanation. I might, just conceivably, have got to love horses. But Patricia? – never.

The hospitality of Baldwin's Bec – the Hartleys' house – was legendary. These were the days when cooks still cooked and took pride in their cooking. Even in wartime not everything came out of tins, and Grizel's dinner parties, like Grizel herself, were unique. You never knew what hidden 'party' talent she might suddenly reveal, such as blowing one smoke ring through another. You never knew who might be there: for example, one evening a lady fencing champion from Tasmania called (one could hardly forget) Mrs Bracegirdle, who did not quite get the Eton wavelength and said when I left, 'Off to correct your nudes, I suppose?'[2]

There would probably be music. Since Grizel has now given me *carte blanche* to write what I like about her, I think it may be admitted openly that she is not really musical; I suspect that she prefers Offenbach to Bach, and bagpipes to either. But she loved to have music going on – 'wallpaper music' – and it often went on so far into an open-windowed summer night that Hubert, who had slipped away to work in his study next door, would storm in and put a stop to it. After all, the boys did have to get *some* sleep.

Grizel's piano was always much cluttered, and a professional pianist who sometimes played at her salons used – and very properly – to insist on having the decks cleared, the lid opened, and a respectful silence established before she would begin. One night, as she was poised to start and the conversation showed no

[2] Even a long-standing member of the staff was alleged to have got the wavelength surprisingly wrong. Sir Edward Marsh, in his *Ambrosia and Small Beer*, mentions 'a French master at Eton who, after teaching there for thirty years, brought out a little book of instructional dialogues, the first of which began: "One of the boys in our house has three balls." "Has he? Hurrah!" The book had to be recalled and another first page substituted.'

Grizel riding on the Brocas

signs of abating, she struck a thunderous chord: then Robin Darwin, who was among the guests, said, fortissimo, 'Christ!' The lady rose in her wrath: 'Who said "Christ"?' Ghastly silence. Then Robin, quite unabashed: 'I think it must have been one of the dogs.'

(It is, perhaps, worth recalling that professional musicians had once been treated like servants, kept apart from the guests and required only to provide background music to accompany conversation. Musicians remember with gratitude the famous snub delivered by Liszt to Tsar Nicholas I, who began to talk while the composer was playing. Liszt stopped, and the Tsar asked him why he had done so. 'When Nicholas speaks,' replied Liszt, 'music herself must be silent.')

I must, in all fairness, add that during the war this pious and very talented lady organised some splendid Celebrity Concerts at which I was privileged to provide, with her as my accompanist, a group or two of *Lieder* as padding while the star performer relaxed.

Even more memorable was an evening when Grizel and one or

two of her guests, myself included, had wandered off – in the snow, she reminded me – with her golden retrievers across the meadow into Luxmoore's Garden; apparently her dogs had 'small Latin and less Greek', for they ignored what Mr Luxmoore had had inscribed at the entrance: 'ἔξω οἱ κύνες . . . καὶ οἱ φονεῖς.'[3] As we emerged from it, we were greeted by a remarkable sight which was also being eagerly watched by half the boys in the house from the windows of their rooms: Hubert was lowering another of the guests, 'Mogs' (Lady) Gage – who had one of her legs encased in plaster – on a rope from the window of the first-floor drawing-room. It seems that she and Hubert had had an argument as to whether a knot she had tied would hold. He said it wouldn't; she maintained it would, and had insisted upon its being put to the test – which, happily, it survived. This was typical Hubert.

Grizel, in a letter to me (21 August 1981), recalls another occasion which showed him in a very characteristic light. Almost to the end of his life, and long after he had retired from teaching in 1956, he would ride recklessly on a ramshackle old bicycle along the towpath, coaching boats on the river. While doing this 'he rode right over a couple – rather occupied in being a couple – in a dip by Brocas Clump. He said "I couldn't stop, because it was a race. But I went back afterwards to see if they were all right." ' And, incidentally, who but Hubert would have sprung out of bed in the middle of the night and thrown his wife's jewel box – the first object that came to hand – at an amatory tom-cat that had woken him? The window overlooked the road, and some of the jewels were never recovered. Those retrieved were to be stolen in 1983.

I forget how it came about, but someone had bet Grizel that she would not deliver, in a traction-engine driven by herself, a bunch of forget-me-nots to a member of the staff on his birthday. Somehow or other she managed to borrow a traction-engine, and successfully executed her potentially lethal journey up the High Street, through cheering crowds of boys, to fulfil her crazy mission.

She always fell for a 'dare'. Once when I was with her the

[3] Revelation xxii, 15. 'Without are dogs . . . and murderers' – which might very loosely be paraphrased, 'No dogs or murderers admitted.'

telephone rang, and I said, 'I bet you won't pick up the receiver and say, "Darling!"' She did, and in her most dulcet voice. Then came an embarrassed 'I'm most *frightfully* sorry! I was just expecting a call from a very old friend . . .'. It was, unluckily, a very snob parent whom she hardly knew. There was, perhaps, a grain of truth in what Grizel herself had overheard one boy saying to another on the playing fields, 'That's Mrs Hartley. I believe she's awfully nice, but absolutely bats.'

It must be admitted that she could, on occasions, be unwisely kind: was it, for example, sensible to give a new boy a catapult? I met her one day in the High Street, carrying a very large medicine bottle labelled in her meticulous, microscopic hand, 'One tablespoonful to be taken after *all* meals'. It was for 'poor old Mrs –. Actually, darling, it's brandy – but of course she doesn't know it. She says it's working wonders.' It was: two months later the old lady died – of cirrhosis of the liver induced by chronic alcoholism.

Another of Grizel's reminiscences. In that radiant June of 1940, while France was falling, the boys ('Alas! regardless of their doom . . .') had more important things on their minds; for a large pike had mysteriously found its way into Barnes Pool, a small piece of water opposite Baldwin's Shore. The 'Tommy [now Viscount Trenchard] Trenchard' she mentions was then a boy in Hubert's house. In reply to a letter from me asking for details, she wrote:

Baldwin's Shore and Barnes Pool in winter

Tommy Trenchard's PIKE. 3 ½ lbs. It seemed as if half the school was hanging over Barnes Pool bridge. He killed it – took it across to Rowlands to weigh – was photographed by my Dame holding it up by its tail. (This little photograph Hubert kept in his wallet all through the war!) Tommy then took it to Mrs Heath [her cook] to put into the larder until such time as he could have it for his tea.

It had an interesting sequel. An hour or two later, passing the kitchen door, I saw Heath and the maids all kneeling round a huge tin bath in which was the pike, in luke warm water. In spite of its having been killed, and weighed, and lying in the larder for over an hour, Heath was endeavouring to bring it back to life! For he was the son of a Thames Conservancy man. Not only had it been killed out of season, but it was a lady pike, and what's more, in an interesting condition.

After what seemed hours of what Heath said, 'stroking it in a peculiar way', signs of life returned. Then, he and I carried the bath – it weighed a ton – down to the bridge by Mr Luxmoore's garden. Here I took off my shoes and stockings, clasped the pike to my chest, and waded into mid-stream. She sank like a stone. We stood on the bridge for a long, long time. Then suddenly, she gave an enormous heave, and away she went! I was just about to tell Heath how nice it was to have a butler who was fond of fish, when he said in a laconic way, 'Pity to kill it now. It'll give a rare lot of sport later on.'

When Tommy heard the news he was absolutely furious!

When Hubert gave up his boys' house in 1951, he and Grizel established themselves in a gloriously dilapidated early Victorian house in nearby Dorney, where she remained until she moved to Marlow in 1980. She is therefore a mine of miscellaneous information about her beloved Eton over a span of almost sixty years, and Richard Ollard's dedication of his book to her was a very happy thought. After she had come to spend a weekend with me at Compton in 1982, I jotted down a further handful of unrelated bits and pieces, some new to me and some forgotten, that I managed to extract from her. Of certain things that she told me she said, 'Of course you *mustn't* put *that* in!' I saw her point; it would be impossible unless publication – like that of Government top-secret documents – was to be delayed for thirty years. Yet there were many innocuous titbits that seemed to me worth preserving.

I will begin by mentioning, *en passant*, that Grizel, though sadly she had no children of her own, has over the years accumulated forty-two godchildren – many the offspring of boys who had been in Hubert's house. This may not qualify for an entry in *The Guinness Book of Records*, but it is hard to imagine that her achievement of remembering all their birthdays with lavish presents that she could ill afford (for she was always recklessly generous) has often been surpassed.

The Bursar when I arrived at Eton was a great friend of Grizel's – Edward Marsden: a nice, simple soul, very different from his unloved brother, Bloody Bill. He had formerly been in the Imperial Forest Service in India, the kind of background from which bursars were often picked in those days. (Another and even more fruitful source of supply was the Army, and many public schools –, Haileybury among them – suffered from a retired major's lack of aesthetic sensitivity.) At that time the Eton Bursary was a small institution, which had not as yet appropriated a substantial part of the old College buildings.

Edward Marsden was famous for inundating housemasters with circulars of great length and of such complexity that often they were virtually incomprehensible. The impish in Grizel, which was never far below the surface, led her one day to send to all housemasters a bogus notice, allegedly from the Bursary, on the subject of the maintenance of boilers (I wonder whether a copy has survived). It seemed at first glance to be full of helpful information; but each successive reading made its contents more obscure and elusive. Marsden's most famous circular, however, was a brief one whose message was unhappily distorted by the carelessness of his secretary-typist. Most houses had several boys' rooms big enough for two brothers to share, and Marsden, ever eager for statistics, sent all housemasters a questionnaire asking how many rooms each had 'suitable for brothels'. Many stories are told of the typing errors of bursars' secretaries, but the prize must go to one at Wellington who circularised parents as to their willingness to accept an increase of school fees of £25 *per anum* – to which one father replied that he agreed, but would prefer to continue paying through the nose, as in the past.

Edward died in 1960; but his widow is still very much alive in her later nineties. Not long ago she told Grizel that she felt the time had come to divide up the family silver among her six children – 'just keeping back three dozen of everything'; and most of what she retained has since been stolen. When Grizel once drew her attention to a bull in a field they were about to cross, Mrs Marsden merely said, 'I thought they managed without them these days', and continued undaunted on her way. She must also have a good sense of humour, for only from her could the following have originated. Edward, who in his old age became confused, had woken her one night with a nudge and said, 'You must go now. I'm expecting my wife back at any moment.'

Grizel was wonderful at deflating the kind of parent who considers schoolmasters to be little more than paid ushers – people of whom somebody (was it Wilde?) once said, 'One might ask them to tea, but *not* to dinner.' A rather grand lady, lamenting the fact that one of her daughters had got engaged to a vicar, added, 'I'd always hoped that she'd marry a moor . . .' 'What, like Desdemona?' said Grizel. The lady ignored her and continued, 'and her sister a trout stream.' (Incidentally, the clergyman in question later became Bishop of London.) Nor did members of the staff always escape her shafts. Little Lord Chelsea had originally been entered for Hubert's house, but in the event had gone to Oliver Van Oss's. Oliver, proud of this aristocratic acquisition, had been extolling to Grizel the boy's many qualities. 'I suppose,' Grizel said, 'you've checked that he has an anchor on his bottom?'

Grizel missed nothing, forgot nothing. A parent who had come down to Eton with her daughter for her son's confirmation said, 'I was out East when Lavinia was confirmed, but I thought of her all day.' Lavinia overheard: 'Nonsense, Mummy, you know perfectly well you were at the Grand National!' Another story told me by Grizel was about Mrs Alington, wife of Dr Cyril Alington and mother-in-law of Sir Alec Douglas-Home. When Sir Alec rang Mrs Alington to tell her that he had been appointed Prime Minister, she replied bluntly, 'It ought to have been Rab.'

It was unusual for Grizel to make a *risqué* remark, and at the moment I can recall only one such occasion. There was a small sherry party, in the rooms of a bachelor colleague, at which a very prim widow had also been present. Grizel said suddenly that she had just heard that a servant attached to the Choir School had been sacked, and asked the company at large what he could possibly have done – stolen some of the College silver, perhaps?

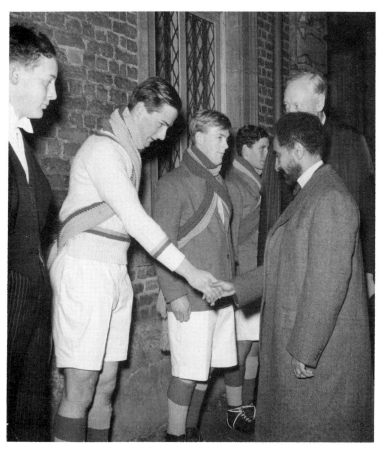

Visit of Haile Selassie, Emperor of Ethiopia, 16 October 1954.
The Emperor shaking hands with Lord Chelsea.

One or two of us knew the real reason, which Grizel eventually extracted from her embarrassed host: the man had been caught seducing a chorister. A moment of pin-dropping silence; then Grizel, no doubt to defuse the tension, said, 'But, darling, if you're a choirboy, isn't that all in the day's work?' A former colleague also remembers (but I do not) my once disputing – rather profanely – with Grizel the probable speed in miles per hour of the Ascension. No doubt alcohol was in part to blame for our ribaldry.

Hubert, too, could surprise. I remember his saying one evening (and of course his remark must not be misinterpreted), 'I can quite understand men preferring boys to girls: they're so much nicer.'[4] Hubert's own housemaster during his last three years at Eton as a boy had not stayed the full course – because, it is said, his talks on sex came to involve rather too explicit an approach to the subject. Yet the loyalty of many Old Boys to housemasters who did not always merit it is proverbial, and Hubert remained in close touch with the housemaster in question, and with the rich wife he had married after leaving Eton, until the end of their lives.

Grizel did not always realise how far-flung and unorthodox some of her admirers were. Visiting a cinema in Slough one evening with the handsome and smartly dressed wife of a colleague, she was embarrassed (yet also perhaps slightly flattered) to overhear a man in the foyer say to his friend, 'There's a couple of nice tarts.' 'Yes,' the friend replied, 'but too expensive for us.' During the war she was walking back alone in the black-out from Windsor to Eton when, opposite the Castle, a man drew up his car alongside her. 'Where are you going? Can I give you a lift?' 'To Eton.' 'So am I. Jump in.' 'How terribly sweet of you!' At the crossroads at the bottom of the hill he suddenly turned sharp right in the direction of Datchet. 'But . . . I said I was going to Eton!' The driver took no notice, proceeded at a spanking pace, shot up an unlit cul-de-sac and stopped. 'Now give us a kiss!' Those were the days before the rape of any female between the ages of five and ninety-five had become a common-place. The man was soon made to realise his mistake, apologised, and deposited his passenger undamaged at the door of her house.

Grizel's cocktails – except when their bank manager was in an uncooperative mood – were lethal. She would at the last moment add a tumblerful of orange curaçao or benedictine to a brew that was already perilous. All regular guests at her innumerable dinner parties soon discovered this and wisely bore it in mind, but rumour had it that once or twice her hospitality had been dangerously lavish. In 1949 there was certainly one such party – it was some kind of celebration, I think – at the Hind's Head Hotel in Bray, for I was one of the six people present at it. Hubert,

[4] cf. George Lyttelton to Rupert Hart-Davis (22 June 1960): 'How much nicer girls of fifteen are than boys of that age – so unshy and intelligent and friendly. Too strong perhaps. Boys can be very nice too.'

114

mercifully, was not; but among the others – and this really was the height of folly – was a very good-looking sixteen-year-old boy, still in the school.

A magnum of champagne contributed by one of the guests, in addition to other drinks both before and after the meal, was also undeniably an invitation to trouble. Though no one was actually drunk, we were all pretty unsteady when we staggered out afterwards into the hotel's large, moonlit garden. Here we were more or less 'paired off'; but since there were only two women, I found myself allotted the boy. He lay on the grass beside me, the two top buttons of his shirt undone, and soon we began to wrestle together. Such wrestling is, of course, a sublimated form of flirtation just tolerated because it masquerades as a *sport* and because nothing actually *happens*. On this occasion something did in fact happen – to me, for I am certain that I owe to it subsequent back trouble that still plagues me from time to time.

Grizel always lived dangerously; but she never exceeded the moral speed limit, for she was at heart a puritan. ('Isn't it lucky,' she once said to me, 'that we are both so under-sexed.' I don't think it ever occurred to her that I might in fact merely be 'homo-sexed'.) When driving a car, however, she was perilous at all times. Her sight was always poor, but vanity long prevented her from wearing glasses. (Hubert, I may mention, was even worse: a public menace on the roads.) I was thankful that after the party at Bray it had been agreed that we should return to Eton in two taxis, leaving the cars to be collected the following morning.

When Robert Birley, whom Grizel had known since the days when he had been a junior master at Eton, became Head Master in 1949, he no doubt remembered, or at all events had been reminded of, the lavishness of her hospitality, for on the first occasion when he dined with her after his appointment he rejected her proffered stinger with a 'No, thank you. I don't want any of your *stuff*.' This wounding and calculated rebuff was never forgotten or quite forgiven. Nor did she ever forgive Robert for converting his large drawing-room into a drawing-cum-dining-room, thus allowing the Bursary to take over what had formerly been part of the Head Master's house. How necessary this extra accommodation for the Bursary was, I cannot judge; but dedicated Old Etonians certainly deplored it, and bursars do

The Hartleys with (centre) their Dame, Olive Hempson,
at Ben Hervey-Bathurst's wedding, 1947

tend to enlarge their territories. Grizel remained, however, devoted to Robert's wife, Elinor.

Hubert retired from the staff in 1955, but he was still far too full of energy and curiosity to sit around doing nothing. He tentatively probed for a job as curator of some National Trust house, but – rather surprisingly, since he had so many connections in high places – none apparently came his way. Always a keen linguist, he taught himself Anglo-Saxon. He made history at chauvinistic Henley, where foreign competitors had traditionally been obliged to endure the massacre of their names at the hands of announcers, by discovering what was correct and insisting on that being used; a Soviet crew was, I have been told, both grateful and amazed. But what he needed was a full-time occupation, and this he eventually got in a shipping firm owned by the father of two boys who had been in his house. I gathered that it was not something that called for specialised qualifications; it needed principally a man of absolute integrity and incorruptibility, and in this respect one could have searched all England in vain for a better man. I always visualised it as the equivalent of 'counting the spoons' when the ships came in, but I am simply guessing; I never understand what businessmen do in City offices. At all events, it meant that Hubert had a *pied-à-terre* in London during the week, returning to Dorney to join Grizel for the weekends.

This really suited them both very well. It left Grizel free from Mondays to Fridays, and she therefore went, as a kind of deputy headmistress, to Hatherop Girls' School, housed in a large Victorian castle near Cirencester which had been my sister-in-law's family home. I had often stayed there in the thirties with her brother, Sir Thomas Bazley, who had eventually found it intolerably large and unmanageable and therefore disposed of it. Grizel was worshipped by the girls and was no doubt a liberating influence; but she was no Miss Brodie, and on reading Muriel Spark's book had been considerably shocked. One night, noticing a downstairs window open, she sat up for hours and so caught red-handed several girls who had been visiting a boys' school in the neighbourhood.

The headmistress, Mrs Fyfe, once suggested that Grizel might teach some science. Grizel replied, 'There's only *one* scientific fact that a girl needs to know.' 'Which is?' asked Mrs Fyfe. 'Darling, it's *so* simple – just that if you want to keep something cold you don't have to put the stopper back on the thermos flask.' When Mrs Fyfe retired, Grizel found the new regime unsympathetic and joined the staff of another girls' school – one which was only a few miles from Eton. Here, too, she was unlucky, for soon the retirement of the headmistress landed her with a trendy replacement who always referred to 'the kids'.

By now she had had enough of teaching, and in any case it must

26th January

My darling treasure - I forget how you know the bits about Fanny Burney at Kew and being chased round the trees by George III. If not I will try to find it - My history is like yours & they do not touch one the nice things - e.g that Prince Albert used to swing the babies about in table napkins.

Grizel's handwriting, 1977

have been soon afterwards that she began to have the recurrence of a mysterious trouble with her leg. Five specialists diagnosed five different causes and recommended five different treatments – none of which helped. From now on she was increasingly a prey to ill-health, but she brushed it all aside. There were two hip operations (on the National Health), one of which was unsuccessful. She had inexplicable black-outs, some lasting many hours. Every winter she had bronchitis. She became rather deaf. The sight of one eye had long been minimal; but to attempt to treat it would have involved a complicated operation with only a fifty-fifty chance of effecting any improvement, and since the other eye was adequate for general purposes it was decided not to try. Then, suddenly, she lost all sight in the 'good' eye (this was in 1983) and, as a last resort, the bad eye was operated on. Her luck was out; though not left totally blind, she could no longer see to read even large-print books.

But never was there a woman who faced adversity with more courage or less self-pity. Her wit was as sparkling as ever, and when one telephoned the hospital to ask how she was, one merely got her latest story:

How you would have laughed! I have to wait every day for hours on a hard chair, to see the surgeon. This morning, I noticed, on the other side of the room, a large, comfortable-looking blue armchair and asked if I could sit on it. The nurse said, 'I wouldn't if I were you; it's Mrs Murphy.'

Back home, she got on approval one of those machines that reads a book at you, and – needless to say – the sample book was a Barbara Cartland. Did she enjoy it? 'Darling, the man's voice was *absolutely heavenly*! I played it again and again.'

Recently her house has been burgled – twice. The first time, the thieves took (as I have already told) what remained of her jewellery, and all her silver; on the second occasion they got away with her silver plate and some lovely dining-room chairs which had been made for her family in Georgian days. 'Never mind,' she said, 'I've got some more chairs upstairs, and there's always Woolworths for the spoons and forks . . . and can you tell me – something I've always wanted to know – how – *how* do oysters "do it" ?'

9
Square Pegs and Round Holes

Some critics have said that the perfect autobiography
can be written only by a cad . . .

RICHARD CHURCH, *Speaking Aloud*

I have already mentioned that I arrived at Eton at a moment when
philistinism was rampant in high places, and inevitably there will
always be certain housemasters inclined to view with suspicion
boys who are by nature aesthetes rather than athletes. The ghost
of Rugby's Dr Arnold still haunts the public schools, which have
never been cosy incubators for the 'odd boy out'.

Nor is the 'garçon moyen sensuel' always ready to tolerate the
nonconformist. Of course things used to be far worse, and the
misery of Shelley's life at Eton is well known. Osbert Sitwell
recalls in *Noble Essences* how he met an octogenarian Old
Etonian who told him:

> I remember well when I went to Eton. The head boy called us together
> and pointing to a little fellow with curly red hair, said, 'Kick him if
> you are near enough, and if you are not near enough throw a stone at
> him.'. . . I have often wondered what became of him – his name was
> Swinburne.

Fortunately for Swinburne he was plucky, and learned to fight
back. But at first he found 'those dreadful boys' terrifying. In tears
he implored his housemaster to let him off going into school: 'Oh,
sir, they wear tailcoats! Sir, they are *men*!' His housemaster – a
clergyman, of course – read him a soothing Psalm and returned
him to his tormentors.[1]

Too many parents cherish the belief, or at all events the hope,
that their sons will inherit their interests, but the two most
prominent and militant aesthetes in my early days at Haileybury
were in fact the sons of an admiral and a general. Presumably they

[1] Henry S. Salt, *Memories of Bygone Eton* (1928), p. 125.

had battles to fight both at home and at school. Almost inevitably such boys tend to be 'difficult', and, should an unkind fate land them in an uncongenial house, then trouble is inevitable. Some, though only too well aware that the dice are heavily loaded against them, put up a resistance; others give in with barely a struggle and may never fully recover, while for a very few the discipline may prove their salvation.

That these square pegs in round holes occurred so frequently at Eton is largely the result of what, to my mind, was the regrettable system (now slightly modified) which condemned an infant only a few hours old to be entered on the list of a housemaster (or prospective housemaster) who might well have left, or even died, during the ensuing twelve or thirteen years. The Marlborough system, by which a boy spends several of his first terms in a Junior House, had enormous advantages in this respect, and saved me from the clutches of a militant athlete who might well have destroyed me. Eton masters who are themselves Old Etonians may disagree with my criticism, but I do feel that having inside knowledge of *three* public schools has its advantages.

Further, since the number of vacancies on a housemaster's list could not be forecast with any accuracy twelve years in advance, many parents were given only provisional places for their sons. I regret to say that, in the forties and fifties, juggling with the entries *did* occur fairly often. As I have related in *Married to a Single Life*, the Marlborough system was also open to abuse – but in practice only in a way that usually benefited both housemaster and boy. At Eton, a rejected boy was thrown to the wolves.

Another abuse – one connected with the admittance of scholars – was exposed by Freddie Ayer, who recalls in *More of My Life* how, with the support of Edward Boyle and Harold Macmillan, he was able to get an unjust regulation rescinded. This required the father of a King's Scholar to be British *by birth*, and had been introduced primarily to exclude the children of the many Jewish refugees who had fled to England from Nazi Germany; it would, incidentally, have excluded Ayer himself from College.

I propose in this chapter to examine a particular case history. The boy I have chosen – or rather, who chose *me* – was at Eton from 1936 to 1942 (I will call him 'O'), and his housemaster, Nichols

College Chapel in the Parish Church, 22 July 1959.
Services were held there while the Chapel roof was being rebuilt.
Nichols Roe (left) with the Head Master, Dr Robert Birley.

Roe, was a keen cricketer with a deep mistrust of aesthetes. What I write will inevitably be one-sided because Nichols Roe and his wife, Betty, Claude Elliott and Henry Ley – none of whom comes well out of O's account – are no longer alive to give their side of things.

It was by mere chance that I received a vivid account of what life in that house during the war was like for a boy who was an aesthete. I had heard nothing from O for forty years, but after seeing a photograph of myself and other members of my family taken after the cremation of my brother Anthony he wrote me a delightful letter; then, at my request, two extremely long ones about his time at Eton. As I said in my Foreword, the reader may well conclude that he protests too much, and certainly he was by nature a rebel; but when such venom survives in such detail after so long, it can hardly be without some foundation of fact. Of Nichols Roe and his wife I will say only that it is merely by the ill luck of the draw that they serve to illustrate a state of affairs that probably existed in other houses also at that time.

O, who now lives in Switzerland, wrote in his second letter:

> Your letter reminded me so vividly of happy times at Eton forty years ago now when you were really the only master who gave the slightest encouragement to me to become a musician. There was one other – Oliver Van Oss; but I well remember his farewell remark, when I was

Oliver Van Oss

leaving, that he did not think pianists were of any use to the world![2] Perhaps I was oversensitive; but I recollect walking away feeling completely destroyed. And there was the occasion when I spent my money from the Brinckman Divinity Prize on new Furtwängler records of Beethoven symphonies, and had as a punishment to take

---

[2] This seems quite out of character.

them back to Spottiswoode's[3] and exchange them for books, and stay behind a day at the end of the half and clean some floors at m'Tutor's – all rather unbelievable nowadays!

You started having gramophone evenings, at one of which you allowed (and actually encouraged!) me to give a piano recital, and Mrs Hartley offered me the use of her drawing-room. I still have the outrageously daring programme – Mozart, Brahms, Bach, Beethoven, Chopin, Palmgren, Liszt and Poulenc . . . and I remember to this day the sound of Mrs Hartley's dogs snoring while I was playing. The Roes had not been invited, and afterwards you asked us all to keep the whole thing fairly quiet for fear that the gramophone evenings might be stopped . . .

And of course you and Hugh Haworth introduced me to German *Lieder*, but I was so 'not allowed' to do music at Eton that it wasn't until Hamburg in 1946, during 4½ years having to be in the R.A.F., that I discovered Hugo Wolf when I gave a concert with Annelies Kupper.

I regret that dear old Henry Ley, Precentor (Director of Music) at Eton, had allowed himself to be won over by the enemy. Once, while waiting to speak to Elliott in Chambers, I heard Ley say to him, with regard to some projected unofficial music-making, 'I think we've scotched that one, Head Master!' In 1940 the Leys had had a miraculous escape when the two bombs fell on Eton. It was a time-bomb that destroyed a part of the Upper School, but that which hit the centre of the Leys' house in Weston's Yard exploded on impact, demolishing the dining-room where, two minutes later, Henry and his wife would have been sitting down to supper. Henry, very shaken, was never quite the same man again.

I replied to O's letter, asking for further details of his Eton concert, and he wrote again:

I seem to remember that the Roes were not invited because they did not like music, but I think they must have known about it because it was just before the concert, which in any case it was my duty to prepare for, that m'Tutor blew up because I spent *one afternoon* at the piano instead of playing in the Second Sine.[4] It didn't go down at all well when he told me that any playing I did was 'for the house' and I

[3] The school bookshop, now Alden & Blackwell. It did not stock gramophone records.
[4] Second Eleven house football team – I presume a game of minimal importance. 'Sine' is short for 'sine coloribus' – 'without colours'.

Henry Ley, simulating a casualty for the ARP

replied that I didn't quite understand as I thought that music was for the whole world. I'm sure I must have said it with a capital 'M'.

No doubt I was very tiresome and affected in the eyes of certain temperaments. I refused to learn all the house colours and games colours, for which I was beaten. On my first day I failed to salute a master because I was laughing so much at walking along the street in what I felt was fancy dress. I read 'Saki'. I *think* I called people 'my dear' fairly indiscriminately (this was only exuberance: one had such *joie de vivre* then), and one year I don't think I listened to the history lessons *at all* because I had fallen so totally in love with the Grieg piano concerto that I was listening to that in my head *all the time*.

I did not know until I read it two years ago that among the upper classes during the first years of the century to describe someone as 'musical' implied that they were probably homosexual, and this of course was the GREAT FEAR and perhaps inspired Claude Elliott's tirades against 'the fleshpots of effeminacy'... My mother was abroad most of the war, and my aunt Cicely went to tell Elliott that I wanted to take up music professionally. He replied, 'I'd sooner have heard that he'd taken to drink.' He also said, 'Would *you* be seen about with musical people?'

Curiously enough, I had chanced to run into his aunt, whom I knew well, just as she was coming away from seeing Elliott. She was seething with indignation, and quoted exactly what O wrote about music and drink.

125

There follows an account of his eager anticipation of his first (twenty-minute) music lesson at his prep school, only to find himself kicked out of the room for having his nails too long. The following week they were pronounced to be too short, 'and to this day I can feel his kicking me out of the room again'. He continues:

At Eton I was first taught by poor Ceddie Borgnis who, as rumour had it, lost his job when he begged the Head Master for more time for music and then *cried* when his request was refused. Perhaps this was not true; but he was marvellous and inspiring, as was Mervyn Bruxner who advised me to make a career of music and then left – leaving me to a teacher who only said, 'I can't concentrate on the football (there was a football field outside) if you play wrong notes.' . . .

I had two great friends at Eton – Tom Marshall, with whom I shared a passion for music and flying, and John Killick with whom I shared a passion for music and architecture. The three of us used to play Louis Kentner's records of Chopin and Liszt, and we thought it would be a marvellous idea, and full of praiseworthy initiative, to try and get him to come and give a recital. (This was fairly courageous as the only concert I had ever been given permission to go to, chaperoned by m'Dame, had been a Solomon recital in Slough – *on condition that we left in the interval!*) There followed the most extraordinary behaviour on the part of Henry Ley. Of course I admired him tremendously as a musician, but he put every possible obstacle in our way.

Having got a guarantee from us that we would pay any loss from the ticket sales, we set to work hard for a large audience in the Music Schools. Meanwhile Henry Ley went to London to ask if anyone knew of Louis Kentner (who was playing at the Proms almost every night!), and was he any good. [5] And then, every time a date was fixed he found some way of postponing it. After eight weeks a date *was* fixed, and one of the people most looking forward to the concert was Miss Stevens, the Dame at m'Tutor's, who adored music. In the afternoon John got permission to pick some flowers in Luxmoore's Garden to put on the stage. You cannot imagine the row when Daddy Ley heard about it – 'flowers for a *man!*' – and poor John had to *take them back* to Luxmoore's Garden!

And then – about an hour before the concert – a bombshell from Ley: 'Not more than thirty boys are to be present at the concert, on account of the blackout regulations.' We couldn't *afford* the financial loss this would have meant, and I wickedly (I wasn't at all wicked at Eton) pretended I hadn't received the message, so that the financial

[5] This seems hardly credible.

loss was very small . . . But most disturbing of all was what happened to m'Dame. The Roes had known for weeks that the Kentner recital was going to be the high spot of the half for her, and yet, half an hour before she was due to go over to the Music Schools, Betty Roe told her they were going out to drinks and she must stay in and look after the house. She was in tears when we saw her later; she had followed every step of our battle to arrange the concert . . .

Whenever we could, Tom and I used to play records in the Music Schools, only to be faced by regular grilling from m'Tutor when he came to our rooms last thing at night. 'Now I want to know what you were doing at the Music Schools this evening.' We were playing the Rachmaninov concerto, sir.' 'But I want to know what you were DOING!!' Night after night. And then suddenly, to my pride, I was elected, relatively young, to the library in m'Tutor's – especially nice for me as we had discovered that there was a Brahms piano concerto, in fact two, as well as the Grieg and the Rachmaninov and the Liszt No 2, and there was a gramophone in the library. Imagine my humiliation when I was not allowed to become a member of the library until Tom Marshall had left (*three or even four halves later*) because we were great friends and he was a year and a half older than I. So for a year or more I sat on those awful dusty wooden stairs outside the library listening to the Brahms through a crack in the door whenever Tom could persuade the others in the library to let him put on some classical music. And we were so innocent – I really don't think it ever *occurred* to us what Nichols Roe must have been thinking!

My aunt was marvellous and arranged for me to go 'on trial' to Tobias Matthay for six months or so before I went into the R.A.F. (disapproved of: it was not the Brigade). So, after only one half in the library, I went to Claude Elliott to be given my leaving book. 'I hear you now think you're going to do music for some months,' he said. 'Well, I hope they call you up before you have time for any of that nonsense.' And that was that, and I'm afraid I never open Gray's *Elegy*.

I have wondered sometimes why one was so victimised, why I made Nichols Roe so suspicious. 'You were at the Willow Tree last night.' 'What's that, sir?' RAGE. I didn't drink, and truly I had never even noticed that there was a pub in Eton called the Willow Tree. 'This is from your bookie. Open it in front of me.' (I didn't know what a bookie was.) I opened a typewritten envelope from a tailor in London with instructions from my mother for trying on a new suit. 'What were you doing between three and four yesterday afternoon?' 'Writing letters, sir.' 'Who to?' 'Thank-you letters for birthday presents, sir.' 'Which side of the letter-box did you stand to post them?' 'I can't remember, sir.' 'You are an extremely bad witness. I know that you stole some stamps off another boy's letter from Canada. I will come back in a quarter of an hour and I shall expect you to confess.'

And then the day came when some of us tried to get up a Shakespeare play, and the Head Master would not allow it and said it would be better for us to pick potatoes. And a Mr [Robert] Graham had a play-reading society, and we read *The Ascent of F.6*, and we were all thrilled as we were mad about mountains [this surely ought to have pleased Elliott]; but the play-reading society was stopped. Auden and Isherwood, I suppose! And I actually got philosophy to be taught – but that too was stopped, after one half . . .

O, as his letters show, was not the kind of boy to make things easier by any compromise. Those who were athletes or aristocrats, or who surrendered unconditionally, got the best deal.

In fairness to the Roes I thought I should inquire how they appeared to a parent. I approached a friend of mine who had had a boy in the house – one whom I did not know well but whom I would not have expected to be 'difficult'. Her verdict, though much briefer, was even more hostile, as was that of a third witness – who conceded, however, that Roe's reports on the boys in his house were 'detailed, conscientious and acute. He had no charisma, but . . . I could have done a lot worse – Bill Marsden.' Yes, indeed! Finally I was reminded of a fourth boy whom I had known, and since he was a peer he might have found the Roes more conciliatory. He wrote, 'I think Roe was really a rather pathetic chap and a bad housemaster. I am not sure that anyone really liked him.'

This is the best I can do for the Roes, as seen by three of his boys and a parent, and I can do nothing at all for Betty's black French bulldog, which was said by boys in the house to resemble Nichols afore and Betty astern. Undoubtedly some of my colleagues would have a very different story to tell, for the Roes had many friends – especially among the bridge-playing set. But to my mind their testimony, based largely upon agreeable social intercourse, could provide us with little that is really relevant here. When I met the Roes socially I found them pleasant enough, and the fact that I was neither the heir to a dukedom nor a bridge-player did not preclude my being on a number of occasions a guest at their hospitable table. On their retirement from Eton, Betty opened a chic boutique in Bracknell.

I find it strange that, in general, music seems to be more suspect than the visual arts; for at least there are no nudes in the symphonies of Beethoven. An Old Etonian, unknown to me personally and well before my time, wrote to me after reading *Married to a Single Life*: 'In one of my reports, m'Tutor wrote – "All his many shortcomings must, I suppose, be attributed to his musical temperament" '; and Lord Harewood, who when at Eton helped me with my gramophone concerts at the Drawing Schools, likes to quote the remark made by his uncle (the Duke of Windsor): 'It's very odd about George and music. You know, his parents were quite normal.' Claude Elliott might well have said exactly that.

As a postscript I will add one other story that illustrates the intolerance prevalent in parts of Eton at that time.

My interest in the art and way of life of Islam led me, one year in the early forties, to attend the *Id el-Kebir* (Great Festival) in the Woking mosque – or rather in a large marquee set up beside it, since the building itself was far too small. After the service, during which I sat on one of the side seats set apart for spectators, I spoke with the officiating mullah, who asked me whether my interest in Islam was spiritual or purely academic. I hastened to assure him that it was the latter. But when I told him I was a master at Eton, he inquired eagerly whether I thought there was any chance of his making converts to Islam among the boys. None whatever, I said – and gave the matter no further thought.

It seems that, some weeks later, a proselytising Muslim appeared at Eton and distributed leaflets in the street, outside the School Library. I learned, too late to intervene, that a boy who accepted one was seen to do so by his housemaster, summoned by him, and subsequently ordered to be beaten. I hardly think it possible that such a thing could happen today; indeed, might not the time eventually come when Eton, in order to remain financially afloat, was compelled to admit enough offspring of Gulf oil sheiks to necessitate the provision of its own mosque and resident mullah?

10

Provost Quickswood and Others

An even odder fish in the local pond than Tommy Trenchard's pike was Lord Hugh Cecil (created Baron Quickswood in 1941) – Provost of Eton from 1936 to 1944, and a lifelong bachelor. It would have taken a brave woman indeed to have become Lady Quickswood.

The Provostship of Eton – a Crown appointment – can be no more than an agreeable sinecure: the emoluments are substantial, the official duties few and not onerous; each holder of the office may make as much or as little of it as he pleases. It sometimes happens that the Provost is the retired Head Master, who from his ivory tower looks down – more or less benignly, as circumstances warrant – upon the labours of his successor. The appointment of Quickswood as Provost, like that of Elliott as Head Master, was unexpected, for his career at Eton as a boy had been brief and his subsequent contact with the school negligible; to the staff he was then known, if known at all, merely as 'an eloquent politician of erratic but usually extreme views'. He soon revealed himself as a splendid eccentric in the best English tradition, and his presence among us did much to cheer us during those grim war years. He knew few masters and fewer boys, and it was characteristic of him that at the time of Munich he should have mistaken for 'an unusually rough lot of navvies' a group of masters who were patriotically filling sandbags.

The relationship between the Provost (more or less the equivalent of a resident Chairman of the Fellows, who constitute the Governing Body) and the Head Master, though their spheres of influence were fairly clearly defined, was not always an easy one, especially if the Provost had been the previous Head Master. Elliott did not suffer from this particular disadvantage, but Quickswood's proximity, marked whimsicality and total unpredictability must often have combined to make Elliott's job awkward. I was unlucky in that Quickswood was blind and deaf to the beauties of the arts and of nature, and Elliott of course no better. On Quickswood's attention being drawn one day to a sensational sunset, he considered it for some time with a puzzled expression and finally observed, 'Yes, extremely tasteful.'

It was in Chapel, Quickswood's particular preserve, that the school as a whole came to know its Provost. Here (I am told, for I was rarely present) could be seen the fabulous green 'editor's eye-shade' which he would don to read the lesson – a lesson cut to a minimum in order to make time for a long and droll introduction of his own devising. Richard Martineau wrote:[1]

> This began with what appeared to be a conflation of old-fashioned commentaries, read and imperfectly remembered from the night before. Of rival interpretations the oddest would be preferred. Then in a pitying tone 'the learned' would be dismissed, and the Provost would draw on the riches of his own imagination.

His sermons, though invariably preluded by an apology for his lay status, were delivered with all the authority of the priesthood. His anxiety to make the services palatable to boys, and to counteract an Etonian tendency to what he called 'bushido and ancestor worship', was laudable, and appreciated by the school. Sometimes Fate tricked him into making them more lively than he intended; yet even when, in a moment of aberration, he announced the 'Narcissus' by mistake for the *Nunc Dimittis* (a slip that would have interested Freud), none of the congregation was more entertained than he.

When he presided at a lecture, he revealed his unique gift for extempore public speaking. No lecturer was too important to be exposed to the genial but ruthless dissection that he often substituted for the conventional vote of thanks. On one occasion a speaker had become so tedious that eventually even he had become aware that he had lost the attention of his audience. Turning to the Provost, who was presiding, he said, 'I hope I'm not boring you, sir?' '*Not yet*,' replied Quickswood with what one who was present described as 'a tigerish grin'. His *obiter dicta* swiftly circulated among the staff – for example, his reported

---

[1] From his brilliant obituary in the *Eton College Chronicle*, 7 February 1957, of which I have made further use *passim*.

comment on a distinguished Eton lady: 'Behind a very pleasing exterior – she conceals – [voice rising] *the instincts of a harpy!*'

Quickswood, though he had joined the Royal Flying Corps in 1915 at the age of forty-six and had eventually even been awarded his pilot's wings (on condition that he never flew solo again), could not really bring himself to accept that England was once more in a state of war, still less that Eton itself might be bombed. When the time-bomb fell on Upper School he was observed poking it angrily with his stick, shortly before it exploded. (I, incidentally, was inside the building all the morning, completely unaware that a time-bomb was ticking away only twenty yards from me.)

The Provost strongly opposed the provision of air-raid shelters for the boys, especially for Collegers, maintaining that by the Statutes of the Founder the authorities were obliged only to educate and feed the 'seventy poor Scholars'. Elliott's riposte to this was that Quickswood could not carry out his obligations to the boys if they were all blown up. The Provost himself never went to ground during an alert, and when asked what he would do if a bomb fell on the Provost's Lodge replied, 'I would ring for Tucker.' Tucker was his butler, valet and indispensable factotum, without whom he would have been helpless as an infant in arms.

It was Tucker who sent out the Provost's dinner invitations – tails and white ties obligatory for adult guests, the host wearing knee-breeches. Five or six of the bachelor staff would be summoned, their names taken in alphabetical order from the school list, and to this often incongruous handful of beaks were added two or three boys whose fathers or grandfathers were, or had been, known to the Provost. These boys might be eighteen, or they might be only thirteen; but however young they were, their claret glasses were relentlessly topped up by Tucker – often with unfortunate results which Quickswood did not appear to notice – and port followed. Quickswood dominated the conversation – and who would have wished it otherwise? His talk was always brilliant, always unpredictable, usually macabre, and sometimes positively sadistic: for example, the ingenuity of medieval torturers might prevail from the claret to the port.

Though drink flowed (and presumably still flows) freely at the tables of the Provost and many Eton housemasters, and though

Caricature of Provost Quickswood by Humphrey Lyttelton

133

no connection had as yet been suggested between smoking and lung cancer, no boy was ever allowed to smoke. Drinking was a venial sin if one at all, almost expected of even the youngest gentleman and far less reprehensible than 'swotting' – or, as the cynical Henry Salt had put it in the 1880s, 'taking to drink was a much less serious offence than taking to think'. Yet in the reign of Charles II, when the plague was raging, smoking – believed to be a prophylactic – had been *compulsory* in school, and an Old Etonian related that 'he was never so whipped in his life as he was one morning for *not* smoking'. (*Autres temps, autres mœurs*! To take another example: in College until 1834, boys who wanted a single bed were obliged to pay the Lower Master a guinea a year for the privilege; today the cost of being discovered two in a bed would probably be expulsion.)

No one who dined with Quickswood was likely ever to forget the experience, and those who merely saw that tall, heavily built and slightly stooping figure, faintly suggestive of an amiable orang-utan, as he ambled apparently aimlessly across the playing fields, will at least be able to understand how he came to earn the family nickname of 'Linky' (the missing link). Siegfried Sassoon described him (in 1925) as a 'soft-looking man, but there was also a touch of a Picasso *Guernica* bull about him.[2] I encountered him thus one day, near Fellows' Pond, and although he had of course no idea who I was he came up to me and said, 'Do you smell an unpleasant smell?' I sniffed and replied, 'No, sir.' 'Just so. They always say the worst smells don't smell', and he passed on. Presumably the Bursar had reported some suspected effluent from a Slough factory.

Soon after Quickswood's retirement there was an outbreak of nocturnal vandalism at Eton. At first the Drawing Schools and other relatively unimportant objects were the targets of sabotage, and nobody was greatly worried: it was just youthful high spirits. Then some of the pipes of the organ in Lower Chapel were

[2] Humphrey Lyttelton, while a boy at Eton, made a brilliant caricature of Quickswood as a bull, the tail to be attached by blindfold competitors at some party or other for frivolous beaks. The caricature fetched up at Baldwin's Shore and was framed and hung in the guest bedroom, where it afforded much amusement to Lord David Cecil, Quickswood's nephew, when he spent the night with us. If it has survived, it should surely find a place in the new Museum of Eton Life. Fortunately, Humphrey has kindly provided me with another.

interchanged, with bizarre and amusing consequences at the morning service; I believe that one pipe actually fell into the aisle. But when two large may trees, removed from a row that had recently (and rather surprisingly) been presented by Quickswood and planted along the edge of one of the playing fields, appeared miraculously overnight in full bloom in the middle of one of the cricket pitches, then the true gravity of the situation was appreciated. Traps were set, and eventually four boys were caught red-handed. Three were obvious potential hooligans of the kind only too familiar throughout the country today, the fourth a seraphic infant who in fact proved to be the ringleader. In this child's room was discovered a list of the gang's future programme. It began, 'Break down the Provost's front door with a hatchet.'

I think we all instinctively felt that Quickswood had a 'past', but it was not until long after his death that we were able to read the following in Raymond Asquith's letters:[3]

29 November 1908   Avon Tyrell, Christchurch

Hugh Cecil becomes daily more entirely given up to all form of chambering and wantonness. He cares for nothing but eating, drinking, hunting and cards; lies in bed till eleven in the morning reading loose novels, and grumbled loudly this morning when he was driven off to church behind the white horses.

I wish I were a fanatical Christian of high birth. It is the only way to enjoy oneself.

In the past, Provosts had never even considered the possibility of retirement; but Quickswood had always said that he would go at seventy-five, and he was true to his word. He was probably the most brilliant orator of his day; it is therefore a tragedy that no transcript of his farewell address to the school from the Chapel steps was taken, and that only scraps of it have been imperfectly remembered. It should, of course, have been recorded on tape, for without the characteristic high-pitched Cecil voice, rising as each sentence approached its brilliantly contrived and wholly unexpected climax, much of the flavour would have been lost.

'I shall address the School after morning service from the Chapel steps,' he announced. 'I shall address them in a tone of

[3] John Jolliffe, *Raymond Asquith: Life and Letters*, Collins, 1980, p. 159; and see also Kenneth Rose, *The Later Cecils*, Weidenfeld and Nicolson, 1975, ch. 8.

Dr Alington making his farewell speech from the Chapel steps.
This was the customary place for such ceremonies, but no
photograph of Quickswood's leave-taking appears to exist.

persiflage.' He did; but of his speech all that remains in the collective memory of the staff is:

> I dare say that at fifteen the prospect of having nothing whatever to do is alluring. I can assure you that at seventy-five it is – *irresistible* . . . In these last weeks people whom I have met have addressed me in sympathetic tones, as though a death were imminent. But I have not been sure whether I was cast for the part of the corpse or the chief mourner – the corpse, I hope, for its position is more reposeful. And so I go to Bournemouth in lieu of Paradise . . .

And he did – or rather, to Boscombe, which is worse – hand-in-hand with the ever-faithful Tucker, to end, uncomplainingly, in 1956 in a hideous little red-brick villa a life that had opened in the splendour of Hatfield House; and Eton was immensely the poorer at his going. 'No man', wrote Madame Cornuel, 'is a hero to his valet.' What would one not give for the discovery of an uninhibited diary by Tucker!

When I first came to Eton, I heard so much over dinner tables about the recently departed that I soon came to feel that I had actually known them. One such was 'Monty' James – M. R. James, bibliophile and writer of ghost stories – Quickswood's predecessor, who had died (in harness) two years before I arrived; and in particular I would like to have overheard – as, allegedly, had some passer-by – his celebrated, desperate remark to a party of influential but bored and ignorant Americans whom he had felt obliged to show round the Library and College buildings. In the garden presented to the College in 1929 by King Prajadhipok of Siam, which adjoins that of the Provost, stands a bronze statue by the Hungarian sculptor Lajos Stabs, of Perseus holding the Gorgon's head: 'And that', said the Provost, 'is our blessed Founder, King Henry VIII, holding the head of his sixth wife.' A few cameras clicked, but no one protested. (As with most Eton stories, there exist many variants of this. Some attribute the remark to the school porter, referring to the statue in School Yard of the Founder, who holds an orb.)

Monty James, a bachelor, lived with his sister, Mrs Woolhouse, whom I also never knew. One who did spoke warmly of her, but remembered chiefly the hats she wore in Chapel. The *Eton College Chronicle*, having once mistakenly referred to her as 'Mrs

M. R. James speaking at the Eton v. Winchester Centenary Match, 30 June 1933. Left, Henry Marten and (with top hat) Dr Alington.

Woodhouse', apologised in its next issue for having, thanks to a printer's error, misspelt her name 'Woodlouse'.

A very different 'Monty' – Field Marshal Lord Montgomery of Alamein – came many years later to address the senior boys. I forget the title of his talk, which I did not hear, but it was presumably about how he won the Second World War. He also generously handed to the Head Master, for the Macnaghten Library, a signed copy of one of his books. The Head Master (Robert Birley) thanked him warmly and opened it to look at the title page, where to his horror he found a gloss had been added in a different hand – no doubt that of some disgruntled underling: 'This chap thinks too much of himself.' The book was hastily put out of sight.

One of Grizel Hartley's great heroines, though they never actually met, was Blanche Warre-Cornish,[4] wife of Francis Warre-Cornish who was Vice-Provost of Eton from 1893 to 1916. This brilliant, witty and sometimes malicious woman moved in literary circles (her brother had married Thackeray's eldest daughter), and though Grizel was never malicious I think she undoubtedly saw in her a kindred spirit and so made something of a cult of her.

Mrs Warre-Cornish

Mrs Warre-Cornish's most quoted *mot* was that made to a master's wife who had sung a French song in her drawing-room: 'Thank you, dear Mrs Chitty. And how wise of you not to have attempted the French accent.' Francis Warre-Cornish, a grandson of the Vice-Provost and for a time a colleague of mine at Eton, wrote to Grizel on my behalf:

[4] See Percy Lubbock, *Shades of Eton*, Cape, 1929, ch. 8–9, and Mary MacCarthy's *A Nineteenth-Century Childhood*.

The only tale about her I ever heard my father repeat was the one about her climbing into the signal-box at Dulverton (Exmoor) station, because she had seen Dr Warre[5] coming along the platform and couldn't face talking to him. A 'Dulverton signal-box' became a family expression for a place of refuge . . . Tales about her were not current much in the family, because I suppose people were shy of repeating them to her sons and daughters, so I only began to hear them when I came to Eton.

Did you ever hear of her handing her baby (one of my aunts or uncles) to a young master in the train at Paddington station, while she went to fetch something? On her return, of course, train and master and baby were gone . . .

Percy Lubbock once described Mrs Warre-Cornish as an 'exceedingly remarkable woman who baffled the categories familiar to plain man', and remarked that 'she couldn't write six words, asking you to dinner, as though there were any accepted style for such a communication'. Letters from Mrs Alington, wife of Dr Cyril Alington who was Head Master from 1917 to 1933, might also surprise. Grizel recalls one to a railway porter who had found and returned to Mrs Alington a purse she had dropped. It began, 'Dearly beloved but hitherto unknown friend.' I am very glad that I was taken by Hugh Haworth to a Sunday lunch with the Alingtons in 1932, followed by informal music-making which could not have happened under the regime that followed.

Another almost legendary woman was in fact still alive, and still living in Eton, when I arrived there in 1938: Miss Goodford. It should be explained that she was remarkable only for being a link with an immensely remote past: the daughter of Charles Goodford, Head Master from 1853 to 1862 and then Provost until 1884. She had known George Bethell, who had been Shelley's Tutor at Eton ('Ah, did you once see Shelley plain . . . ?'). Of course it was only Mr Bethell whom Miss Goodford had seen plain, and even about him she was disappointingly uninformative. 'Mr Bethell? He said such amusing things . . . but I can't recall any of them.' (Bethell was described by Henry Salt as idle, and 'a very stupid man'.) 'Do you remember X?' 'Yes, I do.' 'What was he like?' 'He was very nice.'

I don't think I ever spoke to Miss Goodford, but I was familiar

---

[5] Head Master 1884–1905, Provost 1909–18.

with her appearance, described by Grizel as 'tiny and always in black, and nearly always it was a very old black pony-skin fur coat. She attended every Chapel service, Sundays and weekdays alike.'

I am very glad that I arrived at Eton just in time to know Edward ('Toddy') Vaughan, who was still living there in retirement. He had become a housemaster in 1884, and his marriage, to an enchanting and no less eccentric Irishwoman, light as a feather and many years his junior, had been delayed for some thirty years because her father, Colonel Waller, thought it rather 'dowdy' to marry a tutor.[6]

A single sentence from what Kinglake wrote in *Eothen* about John Keate, the famous (or infamous) Head Master of Eton in the early part of the nineteenth century, might almost have been written of Toddy: 'He was little more (if more at all) than five feet in height, and was not very great in girth, but in this space was concentrated the pluck of ten battalions.' He had climbed the Matterhorn in 1879, only fourteen years after the peak's first conquest by Whymper. An inscription in Toddy's memory is to be seen in his stall in the Chapel, where he worshipped for more than seventy years. In it he is described as 'treading faithfully in Christ's footsteps . . . gay and brave through danger, illness and age'. Like Zacchaeus, a man 'little of stature' who climbed a sycamore tree to see Jesus,[7] Vaughan (continues the inscription, which was obviously composed by his widow) 'sought to see Jesus . . . and Jesus saw him.'

By my time Toddy was in his eighties, and I do not recall a characteristic that had particularly struck A. C. Benson thirty years earlier: his laugh – described as 'a strange writhing or convulsion accompanied by a series of harsh dry sounds like wooden machinery'. Perhaps age had mellowed it; or perhaps I have forgotten. But certainly nobody who had a meal at Willowbrook could ever forget *that*. Toddy would ring up: 'Vaughan here. Come to breakfast tomorrow?' (This barbarous

[6] A phrase actually used by Lavinia Talbot when she heard that her half-sister, Hester Lyttelton, was to marry Cyril Alington, then Master in College. Lavinia Talbot pronounced the word 'tooter'.
[7] Luke xix, 3.

E. L. Vaughan

custom still obtained then.) 'I'm very sorry, but . . .' 'Come on
Wednesday?' 'I'm afraid . . .' 'Come on Thursday?' There was no
escape. There were luncheon and dinner parties too, when Mrs
Vaughan, gloriously hospitable and equally unpredictable, might
fill one's claret glass to the brim with vintage port, or answer,
truthfully if improbably, to a question as to what part of Ireland

she came from, 'I come from Paradise; my mother was a Henn.' Grizel, who was devoted to her, recalls how Mrs Vaughan would be pouring sherry all over the table on one side, and talking to someone on the other, and Edward would say from the far end of the table:

'Dorothea, Dorothea – do look what you're doing!'

'Don't interrupt me, Edward dear; I'm talking to this gentleman about Ireland' – and she would go on pouring.

One day Mrs Vaughan took me to her loft – a perilous ascent up a flimsy ladder – to see 'some old flower pictures' she didn't want and which, from her description, sounded like plates from Thornton's *Temple of Flora*. We did not find them;[8] but a worse disappointment awaited me: a solander box labelled 'Original Drawings by Rowlandson, Box I' proved to hold only a faded photograph of a painting by Burne-Jones, and no further boxes were visible. More macabre was a tin trunk allegedly containing her late husband's uniform, for on opening it a cloud of moths flew out, revealing nothing but a sheathed sword, and – dust.

Almost to the end of her life Mrs Vaughan continued to drive recklessly, and usually on the wrong side of the road. Stopped on one occasion for this in Knightsbridge by an elderly policeman, she was found also to have car and driving licences that had expired years ago; she was saved from prosecution only by the fortunate chance that the officer had once been a Boy Scout in Toddy's troop at Eton Wick, and worshipped his memory. She ignored the onslaught of old age and its attendant troubles, finding the necessary support in regular visits to a Turkish bath. I know precisely what her ailments were, because her annotated copy of *Black's Medical Dictionary* came to me after her death, when some of her books were distributed among friends. I also possess a beautiful little mirror, backed with mother-of-pearl, which she had bought in Constantinople fifty years earlier. She had lovely things and was always giving them away. Much else I was also forced to accept, and surreptitiously returned later; but I wanted to have one thing to remember her by.

---

[8] They *were* from Thornton, and I later discovered that she had given two of them to John Lally, her delightful Irish butler. What became of the remainder I do not know.

I I
Some Senior Colleagues

Eton housemasters, I soon discovered, differed from their opposite numbers, at such other schools as I knew, as sharply as do Englishmen from Frenchmen. Of course they also differed from one another, yet some highest common factor of Eton Tradition seemed present in them all. It was as though they were all descended from some perfect prototype; and just as an expert, presented with various corrupt transcriptions or copies of a lost manuscript, might reconstruct a close approximation to the original, so I think one could roughly reconstitute the ideal Eton housemaster – the type to which all the best of them aspired, and which (I gathered) was almost personified in C. M. Wells.[1]

Our housemaster should of course be (and once would have been) an Old Etonian; but if he is not, then he will become the faultless imitation of one. He is a distinguished cricketer or rowing Blue, and of course a double First – preferably in Classics. His hobby is probably climbing, where he shows himself to be completely fearless, even reckless. He has private means which he lavishes on his house, and a fine cellar with which to entertain his colleagues. He is a confirmed bachelor. He has a simple, unquestioning faith in Eton and God (in that order). He rises in term-time – or should I say, 'half'-time? – at a quarter to seven, and works without sparing himself until two o'clock in the morning. He is, in fact, a superman.

But he should also, preferably, have some amiable and harmless little foible or eccentricity by which he will probably be remembered long after his real virtues are forgotten. One housemaster was famous for his catch-phrase, 'You must *contrive*', with which he would puncture every excuse a boy might make to avoid carrying out an order. Another – 'Tuppy' Headlam

[1] Eton master from 1897 to 1926, died in 1963 at the age of 92. I never knew him.

– relied on his sequence of whimsical drawings entitled 'Father Coincidence', which portrayed monks with one gigantic fiddler-crab-like arm. Tuppy also earned notoriety for having entertained Anna May Wong in his house. He retired in 1935, but came back during the war to find that what had amused an earlier generation was not found so funny by recent additions to the staff, myself included.

No colleague of mine fulfilled all the conditions required of the perfect Eton housemaster; but a few came close to doing so, and the majority lived at a tempo that until now I had associated with business tycoons and factory workers rather than with schoolmasters. I wondered how they could survive the pace. One of two did not.

Julian Lambart was a housemaster when I arrived at Eton, but became Lower Master in 1945 and in 1959 Vice-Provost. He was twenty-one when the First World War broke out, and for a time acted as ADC to his father – a fire-eating general whose full-length portrait in his hall was so alarmingly lifelike that one almost sprang to attention and saluted as one entered. Julian had a gentle nature and must, I suspect, have been overawed by his father, who – it is alleged – sent him up the line in Flanders with an order to another officer which he delivered in homely language: 'Daddy says you are to advance immediately.' 'Oh does he! And what does *Mummy* say?' (Mummy, as I recall her, was hardly less formidable.)

Julian had the most memorable dame at Eton, Nora Byron[2] – a niece of the 8th Lord Byron. She was of gigantic girth, stupendous energy and unbounded kindness, seven years older than Julian, whom she seemed almost to mother after his own mother's death. The house was lavishly fed, but the comment of a beak invited to boys' dinner, 'Oh Miss Byron – *what* a spread!', could perhaps have been more happily worded. When Julian gave up his house he lost (and was lost without) Miss Byron; he therefore established himself in Weston's Yard with old Tom Cattley. But Julian needed the dominant influence of a strong-minded woman. He was very musical (there lay perpetually on his piano a volume

---

[2] See Nora Byron, *Eton – A Dame's Chronicle*, William Kimber, 1965.

145

entitled *Seven Virginal Pieces*); and thus, at the age of fifty-five, he came to marry the widow of Sir Walford Davies. Tom remained to provide the male company he also needed, and the ménage seemed to work well enough. However, soon after Julian's marriage I chanced to sit just behind him in the Green Line bus to London, and observed not without interest that he was reading a book entitled *The Private Life of Henry VIII*.

Julian Lambart

No one at Eton was kinder to me than Julian. He was the sort of person to whom one could turn to for advice that was always sound, and when in any difficulty I went to him or Conybeare – another charming and sympathetic man renowned for his *innocently* 'encircling arm', who was in my day at first Lower Master and subsequently Vice-Provost. Possibly Claude Elliott's counsel – on matters non-aesthetic – would have been equally sound, but it would never have occurred to me to ask it. Julian was the totally respectable aesthete. His devotion to Eton was challenged only by his devotion to the stained glass at Chartres, and I would not care to hazard a guess as to where the greater loyalty lay. Had Hitler said to him, 'I will destroy either Chartres Cathedral or Eton Chapel; which is it to be?' he would have been hard put to give an answer.

George Lyttelton, father of Humphrey, was in every sense of the word a 'big' man, in his day a distinguished athlete and an inspired teacher of English when he joined the Eton staff in 1908, though English did not officially become even an optional subject in the curriculum until 1925. As a boy, George had been fortunate in his Eton housemaster, A. C. Benson,[3] who shrewdly wrote of him in his final report that he had been

> . . . a great comfort – so strong, paternal, reasonable and truly loyal. It has been a great pleasure having him – though his mind is still flaccid and he is very indolent – almost incapable of hard pointed work. I am sure that his physical development is too pronounced . . . He is humorous and incisive in speech – but he neither reads nor works, only moons.[4]

When I first came to know George, he was already fifty-five; the days of his greatest glory, to which Rupert Hart-Davis and many other of his former pupils have paid tribute, were already behind him. His schoolboy indolence had over the years been transformed – in part, at all events – into an endearing lack of ambition. On Alington's retirement as Head Master he had been sounded about the possibility of becoming his successor. He modestly replied that if he were to be offered the post he would feel it his duty to accept it, but that he would much prefer not to be considered. I wish he had been appointed: not only would he have looked the part, as did Robert Birley later, but like Birley he would also have befriended the arts and at the highest level of authority. He was in any case a staunch ally and very good friend to whom I owed much.

[3] See Newsome, *op. cit.*
[4] Quoted by Ollard, *op. cit.*, p. 118. The book contains an admirable account of George, the six volumes of whose correspondence with Rupert Hart-Davis (John Murray, 1978–84) are also delightful reading.

George Lyttelton

Like Queen Mary, George, in later middle age, waged relentless war on the vegetable kingdom. The Queen campaigned against ivy; George, I regret to say, cut down a magnificent Banksia rose which over fifty or so years had laboriously climbed the full height of his Victorian house (Warre House), and I think a wisteria also. But rumour had it that nature took her revenge: one day, when he was sawing off the branch of a tree, he allegedly made the elementary error of sitting on the branch and cutting it at a point between himself and its juncture with the main stem, thus falling and breaking a leg. (As his doctor observed, 'People will always *say* that this was how it happened, so you had better make up your mind to it.')

I remember another story that George told me. Going round his house one evening he surprised a boy dressed in pyjamas but wearing his cap. '*Why* the fancy dress?' (I can still exactly recall the rich, Johnsonian tone of his voice). 'I'm saying my prayers, sir.' George had momentarily forgotten that the boy was a Jew.

On his retirement, George and his wife, Pamela, went to live at Grundisburgh, in Suffolk. Over the years I received from him more than seventy letters which I treasure to this day, but which will in due course be returned to his family. He had a delightful,

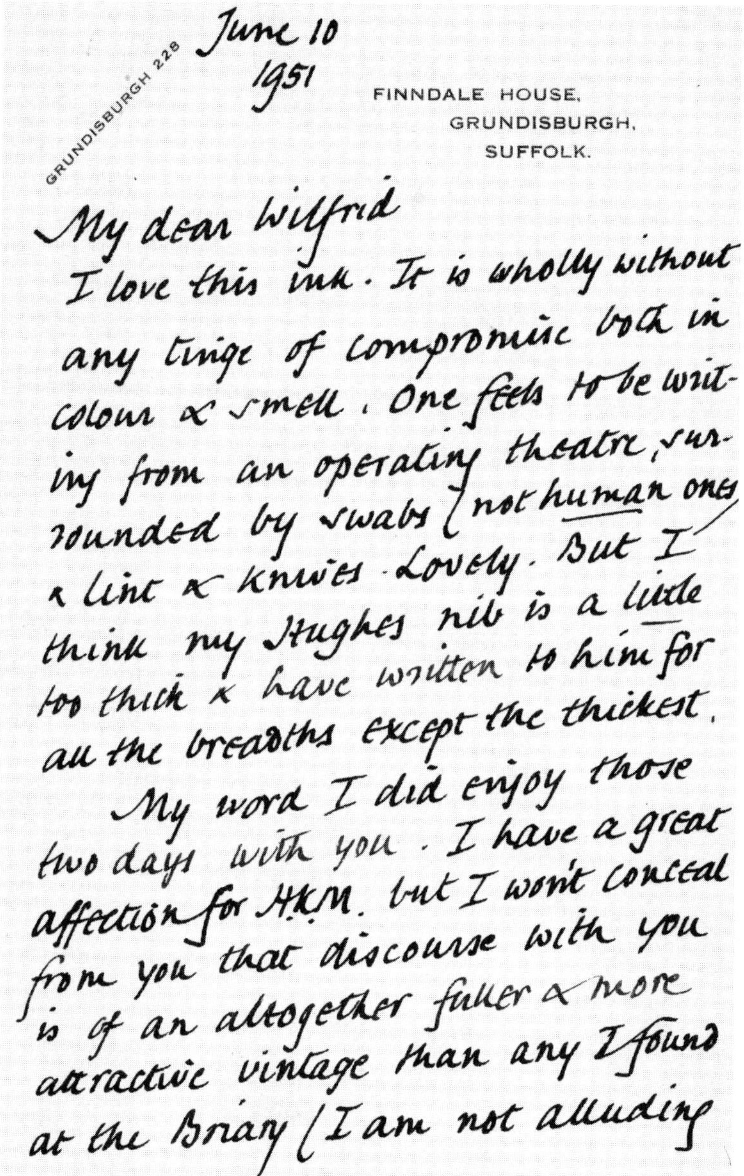

June 10
1951

FINNDALE HOUSE,
GRUNDISBURGH,
SUFFOLK.

My dear Wilfrid

I love this ink. It is wholly without
any tinge of compromise both in
colour & smell. One feels to be writing from an operating theatre, surrounded by swabs (not human ones)
& lint & knives. Lovely. But I
think my Hughes nib is a little
too thick & have written to him for
all the breadths except the thickest.

My word I did enjoy those
two days with you. I have a great
affection for H.K.M. but I won't conceal
from you that discourse with you
is of an altogether fuller & more
attractive vintage than any I found
at the Briary (I am not alluding

George Lyttelton's handwriting

149

though at times perhaps rather too contrived, wit, as all who have read his published correspondence will know. Like myself, he was forty when he began to reform his hand, and by so doing also incurred the disapproval of his mother. Incidentally, his son Humphrey is as brilliant a calligrapher as he is trumpeter, and has done much to promote the italic script.

I visited George at Grundisburgh not long before his death in 1962. I found him sitting in his revolving summer-house, a leaving present from the boys in his house. His conversation was as ebullient as ever. He was a splendid man, though I do not know if he would have made a great Head Master.

If in this chapter I include A. C. ('Timothy') Huson, a housemaster from 1927 to 1941, it is solely on account of my sudden recollection of a single and memorable evening in 1941. I hardly knew him, but I found myself invited to a stag dinner party at which all the other guests (the Head Master was among them) were ripe old men whose very shoelaces I was not worthy to untie. It proved to be a Lucullan banquet; the choicest wines flowed freely, and at the end of the meal our host said, 'I think – I *think* – that this may be the moment to open – my *very last bottle* of the *real* green Chartreuse.' Like Pavlov's dogs, we all salivated at the prospect of what was clearly to be almost a religious experience. Then Huson hesitated: 'Well – perhaps after all I'd better keep it to celebrate the peace.' We all unsalivated. Next day, while bicycling to investigate a bomb that had allegedly fallen somewhere in our neighbourhoood, Huson had a heart attack and died very soon afterwards.

Knowing the tricks that memory plays on one over a time-lag of almost half a century, I began to wonder whether I might have dreamed the whole thing. But Helena Lawrence, who was then living with her father, George Lyttelton, in the house almost opposite Huson's, assures me that though she cannot confirm that the heart attack occurred the *very* next day my story is basically correct. Very possibly her father was among those present at the party. And the historic bottle? Let us hope that it has been preserved.

The recollection of Huson's famous last supper set me wondering how knowledgeable these elderly connoisseurs of wine *really* were – for there must be almost as much pretentious nonsense talked about ancient vintages as there is about modern art. In reply to a letter on the subject, a former colleague wrote:

> The people I think of as wine connoisseurs were Huson, Routh and 'Sam' Slater . . . Richard Martineau used to speak of some ancient beak or other who said, 'When Sam came, we thought he had a very promising nose; but it never got any better.' In our time, you remember, it was a rich purple.

I do not, for he had retired before I arrived.

Peter Lawrence added Tuppy Headlam, Gow, and C. M. Wells. Richard Ollard[5] relates a nice story about Gow and Wells. An obituary notice of Wells, destined for *Salmon and Trout*, was submitted by its author, for checking, to the octogenarian but still acidulous Gow. The notice concluded, 'As all his friends will remember, C. M. Wells was a great judge of claret, burgundy and port.' The draft was returned with the word 'burgundy' deleted.

Certainly most of my younger colleagues knew little about wine, and I of course absolutely nothing. It so happened that, after the war, an Old Etonian wine merchant, eager to promote South African sherries, arranged a wine-tasting party for the staff. We were asked only to enter 'S.A.' or 'Spanish' on our cards. The senior beaks absented themselves, and I went purely to get a free drink. All I now remember is that the majority of those present mistook Tio Pepe for a product of South Africa. Quite recently a friend of mine at Compton, a delightful but naïve elderly spinster, told me in all innocence that a Belgian wine called, she believed, Château Plonque had been warmly recommended to her as both potable and economical. I said that I knew it well.

I think, however, that we were all capable of appreciating the excellence of the food provided by hospitable housemasters before those lights went out again over Europe, and the often witty conversation that even wartime fare and the black-out could not extinguish. Forty years earlier, when 'Piggy' Hill had arrived at Eton as a young assistant master, he had observed that 'at certain dinner-tables the conversation invariably turned on the follies and futility of someone who was not present. His

[5] *op. cit.*, p. 114.

character was torn to shreds, and he was held up to general ridicule.' By the time of his retirement in 1926, however, the badinage had become less malicious, and in general was to remain so; but I do recall one fairly senior housemaster describing a portly colleague as 'legs by Burroughs and Watts, fingers by Palethorpe's'.

A verse addressed to the author by Tom Cattley, having got his initials wrong.

The name of J. C. Butterwick, a housemaster from 1926 to 1944, will always be remembered in connection with a sensational bibliographical *coup*. In the school book-pound, where unwanted and unclaimed books are put on sale at bargain prices, he acquired a first edition of *Paradise Lost* for – tuppence! Tom Cattley, the epigrammatist of Eton, commemorated this triumph in a neat quatrain that has often been quoted:

> O J.C.B., too penny-wise
> For the pound-foolish Pound,
> How dearly lost is Paradise,
> And oh! how cheaply found![6]

[6] T. F. Cattley, *Anonyma*, Eton, 1941. The epigram is dated February 1921.

Cyril Butterwick

Cyril Butterwick had contrived to build up a successful athletic and aristocratic boys' house. He was also a great authority on silver, making shrewd purchases (and resales) in this metal, and on his retirement joined Sotheby's as their expert on the subject. The story is told that, dining one evening with another housemaster, he observed to him, 'That's a nice pair of candlesticks. What did you pay for them?' His host who had in fact bought them from Butterwick a few years before, thought this was a joke and quoted the figure. But Butterwick had forgotten. 'A pity,' he said. 'You were swindled.' In 1966 Butterwick dropped dead at a garden party at Buckingham Palace; he would not have wished for a more fitting end. His widow, Désirée, is still alive and flourishing in her nineties.

Claude Beasley-Robinson was an Old Etonian of pre-First World War vintage and a not altogether successful housemaster from 1930 to 1946. 'A kindly, sentimental enthusiast who would never have thought of punishing anyone for anything [wrote Ollard[7]], he lived for fox-hunting and high churchmanship' – his piety being openly proclaimed by a shrine, equipped with a crucifix and 'Palm Sunday' palm, in a corner of the schoolroom where he taught mathematics. Later he converted a whole room in his house into an oratory which, since it had been officially blessed, had to be deconsecrated when his successor took over. He was also for a long time in charge of the Eton Scouts. But Ollard does not mention his chief claim to fame – his *two* canary-yellow 30/98 Vauxhalls, known to all as the 'yellow perils', which created a noise rarely exceeded in peacetime Eton until the construction of Heathrow Airport.

On Beasley's retirement there came a conflict of loyalties: present pleasure (hunting), or future bliss via the austerities of the monastic life. He settled the matter by electing to hunt for a season with the Fernie and then become a monk. Both the Almighty and the fox will have approved his decision; but the bitterly cold winter of 1946/7 put paid to all hunting, and both were obliged to wait a further year before the Cowley Fathers at Oxford welcomed 'The Revd Father Claude' into their community.

Chaucer, in the Prologue to his *Canterbury Tales*, had already in one respect anticipated Father Claude in his description of the Monk – that bold rider who 'lovède venerie'. (It should hardly be necessary to point out that of the two definitions of 'venery' given in dictionaries – 'hunting', and 'sexual indulgence' – the former is to be preferred here.) But whether or not Father Claude loved 'a fat swan . . . best of any roost' I am in no position to hazard an opinion; certainly I cannot recall ever having eaten it at his table, where oysters and salmon usually greeted his guests on fast-days. Chaucer's Monk, however, would certainly have driven a vintage Vauxhall had it been invented in his day; Father Claude eventually replaced his two with a bicycle.

George Tait, a year younger than myself and an Eton housemaster from 1941 to 1957, was a delightful man: a born enthusiast and the best kind of amiably eccentric schoolmaster. 'Few could ever have been as good a tutor or surrogate father as

---

[7] *op. cit.*, p. 193.

George Tait

he was,' wrote an Old Etonian of him. He had a passion for archaeology and did sterling work in the Myers Museum – an important collection, principally of Egyptian antiquities, which had been presented to the school by Major W. J. Myers – where he trained his disciples in his chosen field. (Incidentally, I contributed to the collection a handsome Egyptian alabaster jar – I forget its dynasty – which I had bought in a junk shop in Kingston for threepence, a further threepence winning for me at the same time an unusual seventeenth-century wine-bottle which I presented to the London Museum.)

The Myers Museum now also houses a discovery that I chanced to make in the basement of the School Hall – a repository of miscellaneous bric-à-brac. Beneath a pile of assegais, brought back by loyal Old Boys from long-forgotten African wars and then dumped by bored descendants on the Old School, I stumbled one day upon a bronze from Benin[8] – a trophy, no doubt, of the British punitive expedition of 1897. I took it to Claude Elliott and suggested that it deserved a better home. He stared for a moment at this heathen idol with incomprehension, then told me to do whatever I liked with it. Forty years ago I dare say it would not have fetched more than a couple of hundred pounds in the saleroom, and I put it in my room at the Drawing Schools; but when the value of Benin bronzes rocketed, I thought it best to pass it on to George Tait for the greater security of his Museum.

Unless a school museum has the good fortune to be in the charge of a knowledgeable enthusiast, it is usually neglected or vandalised, and no school can count upon always having a George Tait or a Peter Lawrence around. Further, there are other objects of interest and value about the place which are in the care of no particular individual. What treasures Eton must have lost over the years through theft, carelessness, ignorance, prudery or religious bigotry! When I came to Eton a life-size bronze statue of a naked youth, arms outstretched come-hitherly, welcomed visitors to School Hall. This agreeable object was later removed, ostensibly to make space for an enormous terrestrial globe which had been presented to the school; but quite recently it re-appeared in a London saleroom where it fetched a five-figure sum. I know no more than that. And where now are 'a finger-joint and part of the Spine of John the Confessor, formerly Prior of Bridlington',[9] which were presented to the College by the Founder, King Henry VI? Probably the Reformation put paid to them – or may they yet eventually surface in some long-unopened drawer in the Bursary?

George Tait was an Old Haileyburian and, like my friend Francis Thompson[10] (whom he knew well), Head of the School in his day. He was a very loyal Old Boy, and even those of a much earlier vintage often looked in on him. One night in the late forties he had already locked up and gone to bed when he was woken by the pealing of the front-door bell. He came down – pyjama-clad,

---

[8] Reproduced in *Treasures of Eton*, ed. James McConnell, Chatto & Windus, 1976, pl. 131. No mention is made of the circumstances of its discovery, for which I am told others claim – quite mistakenly – to have been responsible.
[9] This versatile saint (d. 1379) could raise the dead, walk on water, and fill empty granaries by prayer alone. For his other achievements see the *DNB*.
[10] See *M.S.L.*, pp. 258–9, 296–7.

bleary-eyed and rather angry – to find a man whose face seemed familiar: it was that of the Prime Minister, Clement Attlee, also an Old Haileyburian, who had been addressing the Political Society.

Oliver Van Oss ('OVO') during the war looked after the boys' house of an older man who was serving in the Army, took it over in 1945 and was still *en poste* when I left Eton in 1959. He had three great qualities: enthusiasm, generosity and impeccable taste. His was one of the relatively few drawing-rooms at Eton where one's fingers did not itch to rehang or even carry away and burn the pictures, and he was an excellent gardener. He also had a very pretty, though dangerous, wit. On leaving Eton he became Headmaster of Charterhouse and subsequently Master of the Charterhouse[11] in London – a position which fitted him perfectly but from which he has now retired. It is sad that his long-projected *magnum opus* on Dutch art has never materialised.

As a gardener he was excelled only by Lionel Fortescue. During the First World War Fortescue had, it was said, driven a large consignment of unusually stubborn mules across Persia, an experience that stood him in almost too good stead when he came to have charge of boys. In 1933, after the tragic mountaineering accident in which three housemasters lost their lives, he found himself virtually pressganged, at no notice at all, into taking over E. V. Slater's house. It did not work, and the following year he reverted to being an ordinary member of the Modern Language staff.

This gave him sufficient leisure to indulge his passion for horticulture and so make a memorable garden at his house at Willowbrook. During the Second World War he pioneered a scheme for breeding rabbits on a large scale to help feed the school. A number of housemasters subsidised the venture, some of whom were far from pleased when disease killed off the rabbits. On his retirement Fortescue searched all England for a house and substantial established garden with perfect soil. This he eventually found at Buckland Monachorum in Devon, purchased it, and then proudly introduced his wife and family to his new acquisition. Here he created and ran a highly successful show

[11] Founded in 1611 as an almshouse for eighty male pensioners ('gentlemen by descent and in poverty', etc.) and a school. The school was moved in 1872 to Godalming, in Surrey.

garden and garden centre until his death in 1981. It is now looked after by the Fortescue Charitable Trust.

Norman ('Nigel') Wykes – a housemaster from 1944 to 1960 – was dark and very good-looking: as a young man almost another Ivor Novello, and later a Malcolm Sargent (I always thought), though I heard somebody once describe him as 'like the nicer sort

Hugh Haworth and Nigel Wykes, c. 1930

158

of snake'. He was exceptionally talented and versatile – another accomplished gardener, a music-lover, a skater of almost professional standards, a good classical scholar, and an efficient (if rather insensitive) botanical draughtsman. George Christie, son of John Christie of Glyndebourne, was in his house, and Nigel contrived to make timely room in it for the two sons of Niki Sekers, a wealthy silk manufacturer and generous patron of the Glyndebourne Opera Company. Sekers (now Sir Nicholas) printed fabrics from Nigel's designs, and on the latter's retirement from Eton employed him for a time in that capacity in his factory in Cumbria.

Kelsall Prescot – 'the Doctor', for he was a PhD – was a housemaster of charm and great wit. A member of the classical staff, he also taught some history, and some English in Extra Studies.[12] George Lyttelton, his predecessor in the latter field, described him as 'a man I always found rather gloomy. He was apt to talk about Chekov (spelling?)'[13] He may well have liked Chekhov, and probably George did not; but I find it incomprehensible that anyone could have called him 'gloomy'. Above all, however, the Doctor was a man of mystery. Nobody, to the best of my knowledge, ever discovered anything about his background – his parents, the school at which he had been educated, how it was that he had not come to Eton until he was over thirty, the reason why he never touched a drop of alcohol. Did he study for a time at RADA, as somebody once told me? It seems quite possible. To a request for him to send me his *curriculum vitae*, and a threat to invent a highly discreditable one if he did not, I received an answer telling me nothing, but naming a former colleague whom he alleged to be a far greater mystery.

Kelsall retired to the old family home at Kings Pyon in Herefordshire, sharing it at first with a brother and two sisters, all of whom have predeceased him. At eighty-six he now lives on there alone, doubtless in acute discomfort; but I have never heard of any of his innumerable friends having been invited so much as to set foot in Kings Pyon House. I know nobody of his age who is

---

[12] 'Three periods a week in school done by Specialists in almost any subject they care to choose, other than the main subject in which they specialise.' (B. J. W. Hill, *op. cit.*, Glossary). They are a particularly valuable feature of Eton education.
[13] *The Lyttelton Hart-Davis Letters*, vol. 5, p. 17.

so wholly free, both mentally and physically, of any trace of senility as he is. At Eton he shared Richard Martineau's passion for local gossip, but he was never malicious. He claims to be the oldest living Eton master (though I have been told that Monty Evans challenges this); and since he will certainly still be around when this book appears, I trust that I have not libelled him.

Kelsall was always known as 'the Doctor'. Being a non-medical doctor has its dangers, especially when travelling in remote places. A friend of mine, another bachelor schoolmaster, who had proudly had his luggage inscribed 'Dr X', told me of his hideous experience in a long-distance Moroccan bus when, vehemently protesting, he had been forced to act as midwife to a peasant woman who had suddenly gone into labour, miles from anywhere. He didn't, he confessed, really quite know where babies 'came out'. In such remote places *any* European is expected to have at least a modicum of medical knowledge, as I myself had found to my cost in Afghanistan. But it *can* happen to anyone, anywhere. One night, as I was returning to Eton by train from London, the only other occupant of my carriage – an Eton groundsman – embarrassed me by a sudden and highly detailed account of the state of his bowels; it transpired that he had mistaken me for one of the school doctors. I have no knowledge that any such fate overtook Kelsall; but then, he would not have told anyone if it had.

Writing of Kelsall inevitably reminds me of Francis Cruso, for they, together with Richard Martineau, Oliver Van Oss and one or two others, formed a kind of exchange and mart for Eton gossip. Francis was the sort of man nobody could have disliked – which possibly makes him hard to write about. Short in stature, genial, perpetually smiling, he had more than a touch of Mr Pickwick in him. He was very musical, an excellent housemaster, and a talented mimic who used that gift so extensively that eventually 'he had a hundred voices, none his own'. His mother was, appropriately, *née* Robinson, though why she named her somewhat formidable daughter 'Thalassa' I never discovered. A rather rough sea? Only quite recently – since his death a year or so ago – did I learn that Francis had been an Apostle at Cambridge, where he was an exact contemporary of my brother Anthony.

When he retired from Eton in 1968, Francis set up house in

Fred How and Kelsall Prescot, 1963

Bury, Sussex, with another bachelor housemaster, Fred How, who retired at the same time. This caused, I was told, much sorrow to Richard Martineau, who had hoped that Francis would join him in his spacious Old Rectory in Hampshire. But Francis chose wisely, for Richard would not have proved an easy stable-mate. Fred died before Francis, and by the merest chance the house at Bury has just been bought by one of my Hunt cousins – a grandson of my unloved Aunt Mabel whose tenacious pursuit of Queen Mary I have described in *Married to a Single Life*. I do not know enough of the workings of heredity to understand how this tiresome woman came to produce children, grandchildren and great-grandchildren so uniformly delightful; no doubt some very happy marriages played their part.

Tom Brocklebank had been a contemporary and an intimate

Tom Brocklebank

friend of my brother Anthony from Cambridge days onwards, and nobody sprang more swiftly or more courageously to his defence in 1979. My brother Christopher and I can never be grateful enough to him and to his wife Jane for all the support they gave him during the last three or four distressing years of his life, providing him in their house in Dorset, where they had settled after Tom had retired from Eton, with sympathy, affection and a secure hideaway from the importunities of the press. They also went with him several times to France and Italy.

Tom was a distinguished rowing man and mountaineer, and had taken part in Hugh Rutledge's Everest expedition of 1933, though illness prevented him from going beyond the base camp. But he was also a lover of the arts and of literature, and an ally in my periodic battles with Philistia. On my very first visit to Tom at Eton I might well have blotted my copybook with him for good. I had been carelessly flicking the ash of my cigarette into the log-basket beside my chair, not realising that it was serving as a cradle for their infant son and heir until a loud shriek betrayed that I had scored a bull's-eye. Much as I liked Tom and his wife,

I always felt that to them I was really 'Anthony's brother' rather than a friend in my own right. Tom died suddenly on 11 April 1984, aged seventy-six.

Finally – for I cannot prolong this list indefinitely – I will mention Bob Weatherall ('Botany Bill'); but I include him principally because of the colour added to our lives by his delightful and improbable bluestocking Czech wife, Mica (pronounced 'Mitsa'): 'Czechmate!' a colleague had remarked when he heard of their engagement. (A different story, current among the boys at the time, was that Bob had said, 'I've married a Czech: I wish I had more of them.') I confess that I have made some use in my book, *Of Flowers and a Village*, of this charming eccentric. Botany Bill was a kindly man and an enthusiastic botanist. It was he who showed me where to find woad (*Isatis tinctoria*), the plant which produced the blue dye that served the ancient Britons for concealing their nakedness. I did experiment with it, but decided it to be safer – and warmer – to continue to wear school dress.

Mica, with the help of her husband, translated nearly a dozen of Karel Čapek's works into English, and I was privileged to read and comment on her rough draft of one of these. It left me with the impression that when she came upon a word for which she did not know the English, she wisely consulted her Czech-English dictionary, then – unwisely – selected haphazard the longest or most bizarre she found there. I remember suggesting to her that 'Gongoresque' would convey little meaning to the average English reader. 'But it is in my dictionary! Come – I show you,' she replied indignantly, implying that I did not know my own language. Indeed it was; but so, too, was '(of style) affectedly elegant'.

So surrealist was Mica's conversation that after talking to her I always came away feeling slightly, but very agreeably, tipsy. She was a great friend of the Birleys and of Grizel, and it was at Grizel's dinner table that she produced her most memorable *mot*. Somebody had said that smells recalled past events more vividly than anything else. 'Yes,' observed Mica, 'I have loved always the smell of sex.'

A shocked silence; then Grizel, 'Darling . . . !'

'Yes,' repeated Mica without a shade of embarrassment; 'especially of secks of corn.'

12

Sport, Religion and the Corps

> At Eton [Lord Ronald] had made a splendid showing
> at battledore and shuttlecock, and at Cambridge
> had been first in his class at needlework.
>
> STEPHEN LEACOCK, *Nonsense Novels*, 'Gertrude the Governess'

It takes a brave man to write about Eton in terms other than of unquestioning worship. A brave man – or a fool?

> A friend, on learning that I proposed writing a little book about my life at Eton, and to include therein a few criticisms of some of its institutions and activities, remarked: 'More fool you! Nobody cares twopence what you think. You had much better leave it alone. But if you do shout from the house top, don't forget to take refuge in the cellar.'

So wrote M. D. ('Piggy') Hill, an Old Etonian and a housemaster from 1906 to 1926, in the chapter entitled 'Games' in his delightful and unorthodox *Eton and Elsewhere*.[1] He was particularly warned about criticising athletic activities: 'Let the man say what he likes about work, it doesn't much matter; but when he begins to fool about with games he must be suppressed.' Hill's views on religion were also suspect and, since he thought it was 'best to try to forget' about the First World War, it may be presumed that he was no ardent supporter of the Corps. Where work was concerned, he held the heretical view that biology (his own subject) was as important as the classics, and handicrafts possibly more valuable than either. He criticised school dress, dark and ill-ventilated schoolrooms, and much else that was sacrosanct. He pleaded for compulsory remedial physical training for those in need of it. That he survived at all is evidence that the old Eton was at last beginning to give place to the new. *E pur si muove!*

---

[1] John Murray, 1928. Ollard makes no mention of Hill or of his book.

It might be thought that what follows ought really to have provided me with enough material for three long chapters; in fact, it is only with some difficulty that I have stretched it to fill a short one. It must be borne in mind that my book is an autobiography, not about Eton only; and further, I do not set out to describe the Eton scene as a whole, only those parts of the school's activities which interested or diverted me, or in which I was involved. As an agnostic, unathletic, unmilitary, non-Etonian, although I was on the staff for more than twenty years I felt wholly unqualified to do more than that; in any case, the task has already been admirably performed by others. To be honest, I never, for example, quite discovered what the Field Game was; there is mention, in William Horman's *Vulgaria* (1519), of Etonians playing a game 'with a ball full of wynde', and for all I know it may be that.

Sport, Religion and the Corps: odd bedfellows, you may think – and all crowded here into one small single bed! Yet there is a highest common factor of worship in all three, for at every public school sport *is* still a religion, while Chapel services at Eton, though perhaps basically pagan, have at all events warranted description as 'Eton worshipping itself'. As for the Corps – surely preparing to defend one's country from enemy attack is a *sacred* duty. Where sport is concerned, I have always believed that the physically fit don't need to take exercise and that the unfit shouldn't. I was among the latter, with feeble knees that had never been confirmed (see Isaiah xxxv, 3). My only active sporting involvement at Eton was a little very mild and incompetent tennis during my first summer or two. My one recorded appearance on the immortal playing fields was in the capacity of a reluctant umpire in a cricket match between the Drawing Schools and the Music Schools. If I had ever known the rules I had forgotten them, and thus gave the captain of the opposing team unjustly 'out lbw' on his first ball. The field had shouted 'How's that?' with such unanimity that I felt sure I had made the correct decision. I can only hope the victim (who, as I write, is our Ambassador in Luxembourg) has forgiven me.

Conversation at dinner parties often turned eventually to sport, though to a far lesser extent than at Haileybury. If only I had been rather deaf I would have invested in a hearing-aid like

After the Wall Game: St Andrew's Day, 1954

Laurie Lee's, which has the curious habit of 'going dead' whenever the word 'football' is mentioned. I hardly ever watched a game of anything, though occasionally I caught a passing glimpse of one. I was never to be found among what A. C. Benson called 'those listless beaks' on the touchline, 'incapable of walking, talking or even smiling, looking drearily on in aquas-cuta, like opium eaters'.[2]

Most mysterious of all is, of course, the Wall Game, which, wrote Bud Hill, is 'the greatest fun to play' though often 'agonisingly painful'.[3] Almost any brutality short of actual murder is allowed, for in a real crisis anyone about to die may cry 'Air!' and so, if he can make himself heard in time, escape death. I realise how much I have missed in life through not finding pain 'fun'. The rules of the game and the esoteric jargon used are equally incomprehensible to almost all spectators other than the

[2] Quoted by Ollard, *op. cit.*, p. 86.
[3] *Eton Medley*, Winchester Publications Ltd., 1948. Though (or perhaps because) the work of a non-Etonian this remains, in my opinion, the best guide to the arcane mysteries of life at Eton, while the two volumes of Peter Lawrence's *An Eton Camera* (Michael Russell, 1980 and 1983) provide the perfect visual accompaniment. Bud Hill died in August 1985.

very few who have ever played it, and these are mostly past or present Collegers. In both the Wall Game and the Field Game a lot of 'furking' is involved – a word that proof-readers need to watch carefully. Playing conditions are considered ideal for the Wall Game when the ground is a foot deep in liquid mud which soon transforms the participants into mobile Rodin or Henry Moore sculptures. It is a game which, to a non-Etonian, appears to be played by masochists for the delectation of sadists.

So much for games.

'There can be no doubt', wrote Hill, 'that Chapel is, as the Founder intended, the very essence of Eton life.' I seem to have heard this before, somewhere. True, the building was always packed to overflowing, but this was hardly surprising since attendance (in my day) was compulsory.

It was a fortunate 'perk' of drawing masters that they were not obliged to take their turn of duty in Chapel, and, as I have explained in *Married to a Single Life*, where religion was concerned I share the views of the young man of Dijon, so eloquently described in a famous French limerick.[4] I agree with Goethe that 'to be uncertain is to be uncomfortable, but to be certain is to be ridiculous', and with Tennyson that 'there lives more faith in honest doubt,/ Believe me, than in half the creeds'. In a nutshell, I have 'no invisible means of support'. Unless I was a soloist in some oratorio or other I rarely set foot in the building; thus it came about that when, during my second half, I was showing rather pious prospective parents round Eton, I led them by mistake into what proved to be the Chapel boiler-house.

I once gave a recital from the organ loft, with Henry Ley at the organ. He was a masterly performer on the instrument, and it was marvellous to watch his tiny legs leaping with chamois sureness from pedal to pedal. The oddest feature of services was the punctual, funeral-march entry of 'The Ram' – a dignified procession of twenty members of Sixth Form which advanced

---

4   Il y avait un jeune homme de Dijon,
                 Qui n'aimait de tout la réligion.
                   Il disait une fois,
                    'Je déteste tous les trois –
                 Et le Père, et le Fils, et le Pigeon.'

Since the fourth line does not scan, the limerick is presumably of English origin.

The Corps: recruits passing out, 1939

like a mourning multiped up the aisle under the adoring eyes of lesser mortals. Here, at least, was Eton worshipping itself. I am told that today the Ram is no longer a special feature – not, indeed, always in operation, and briskly moving when it is.

Of the Corps I have nothing to say beyond that the fiercest battles I had to fight at Eton resulted from the already-mentioned unhappy juxtaposition of the Drawing Schools and the Parade Ground. It was as rash as placing a mosque cheek by jowl with a synagogue. There was a gate which gave access to the Parade Ground and afforded the only approach by car to the Drawing Schools. This gate was constantly being padlocked by officious sergeant-majors, whose infantry could reach their drilling-pitch between a line of concrete posts. I would rather have had as my neighbour the remains of the old gasworks, which in any case would today probably be a listed building. Better a nasty smell than a nasty noise.

All these monstrous sentiments I of course kept to myself; had I not, I would doubtless have lasted no longer than a single half.

Rowing: the Eight below Corporation Steps, 1933

And I suddenly realise, to my shame, that I have forgotten even to mention rowing. But I had had my fill of that at Oxford where I had established beyond any doubt that I would always be 'slow on the feather', and at Eton the river – or at all events that part of it which was rowed over – was no more to me than a snapshot as I crossed Windsor Bridge. 'Happy river of Eton-Windsor!' wrote Cyril Connolly.[5] 'I have always been very vague about its name, but I often pictured it winding away past Reading Gaol and into the great world somewhere – the world of the Ballet and the Sitwells, of Cocteau and the Café Royal.'

In short, a large part of Eton life – to many boys the most important part – passed by me unnoticed.

---

[5] *The Condemned Playground*, 'Where Engels Fears to Tread', George Routledge & Sons, 1945 – a dazzling parody of the career of an Etonian aesthete.

13
A New Regime

When Claude Elliott retired in 1949 and became Provost, he was succeeded as Head Master by Robert Birley, until 1947 Headmaster of Charterhouse, and at that time in Germany as Educational Adviser to the Military Governor.

In September 1948, when it was becoming obvious that Elliott's reign as Head Master was drawing to its close, George Lyttelton had written to me:

> There is no doubt it is high time old Mutton was hashed – from Eton's point of view. What can you all do but mark time till he goes? He is dried up; out of his belly rivers of water no longer flow . . . I hope you will get Birley, but the G[overning] B[ody] is packed with Habakkuks, & you may easily get Nichols Roe.

A year later, when Birley's appointment was announced, he wrote again:

> I *am* glad the G.B. really has made the right appointment. He may make his mistakes, but he is a man of intellect, ideas & personality & you will all feel a freshness in the air . . . Birley has a quickish way with dead wood or fungi.

Elliott stated in *Who's Who* that his recreations were 'climbing, shooting,[1] rowing'. Birley listed 'none; but it may be safely assumed that, had he done so, these three would have found no place among them. He was an ardent bibliophile, a lover of the arts, an inspiring teacher, a tireless worker and a man of boundless curiosity. He always had the courage of his liberal (and sometimes unpopular) convictions; but the legend that it was this that had earned him his sobriquet of 'Red Robert' is denied. It is believed that it was derived from a portrait of the aged Brahms,

---

[1] Incidentally, why *shooting*? I have found nobody who can throw any light on this. Even during the First World War, in which he served in a Red Cross unit in Flanders in 1915 and subsequently had a temporary job at the Admiralty, he cannot have had much opportunity to fire at anything.

Dr Robert Birley in the Cloisters, 1959

hanging outside his office when he was in Germany, being mistaken for that of Karl Marx. He was never more than palest pink. His decision in 1935 to leave Eton, where he had only narrowly missed being appointed Head Master in 1933, to become Headmaster of Charterhouse was in part due to his finding the new regime uncongenial. He immediately became both an ally and a friend, and since a full-length biography of him has been published,[2] I will principally confine myself to putting on record my personal admiration and gratitude.

However, there is one point that I do not think Hearnden has sufficiently stressed: Birley's immense and always utterly genuine enthusiasm. This, combined with the fact that even *his* day ran only to twenty-four hours, led him at times to promise what he was physically incapable of carrying out. I give a single example involving the Drawing Schools (in which Birley took much interest though Hearnden nowhere mentions its existence). I thought it might be possible for me to organise there a small exhibition of Impressionist paintings – not, of course, works of major importance – and asked Birley whether this met with his approval. He was – I use the word again – enthusiastic: 'Look here, Wilfrid; I know Lord Sandwich very well. He's just your man. I'll write to him today. And I'll also try . . .'

A fortnight later I approached him in chambers to see if he had had any response from Sandwich *et al.* He was full of apologies; he would write to them that very day. Another fortnight passed, and I tried again. He was even more apologetic: those Confirmation classes had been taking so much of his time. But he would write at once . . . I did not trouble him further, and abandoned the project. What I want to stress is that he was *genuinely* eager to help, but that he simply could not fit everything in. As Hearnden does make clear, he did not always get his priorities right (not that I would for a moment dare to suggest that the Impressionists were more important than Confirmation). For example, to a letter from a member of the Eton staff he replied in seven or eight delightful pages in his own hand, but became so carried away that he quite forgot to answer the simple question on which his

[2] Arthur Hearnden, *Red Robert*, Hamish Hamilton, 1984. But Birley is unlikely to have pointed out to his travelling companion in Italy the exact spot *in Venice* where Savanarola was burnt at the stake in 1498 – see p. 55.

opinion had been asked. He could not dictate, and he could not delegate.

Birley was largely responsible for getting Evie Hone to design the new east window for the Chapel, and incidentally I am probably the only person who can throw some fresh light on one particular feature of it. I was privileged to attend the meeting in College Library when Miss Hone displayed her design to the Provost, the Head Master, and a few members of the staff. Miss Hone was a daunting woman, who did not hesitate to make full use of her lameness to establish her dominance. It may, of course, have been no more than an accident that she dropped *all* her papers as she came into the library with the Provost and the Head Master, who had to go down on hands and knees to recover them. (What a picture that would have made for Peter Lawrence's *Eton Camera*!) Thereafter she was in total command of the meeting.

There was some comment, by one of those present, on the supernatural length of the arms of the crucified Christ, which recalled Tuppy Headlam's drawings of 'Father Coincidence'. It was her intention, she told Birley, for them to seem 'to stretch over every boy in the congregation'.[3] This interpretation was either a brilliant improvisation or a prepared reply to an almost inevitable question. I managed to get a few words with her alone as she was leaving, and ventured to suggest that, had she *not* extended the arms, the hands would have been concealed by two of the mullions. She was much amused, and admitted that she had indeed discovered, too late to alter without a major upheaval, that she had made a miscalculation. We artists, Ma'am, stick together, and I told nobody at the time; thus the myth was perpetuated, and the inspired symbolism of the all-embracing arms became the universally accepted explanation, much quoted when there was a need for moral uplift.

At the time of Birley's arrival, I was having difficulties with my assistant colleague at the Drawing Schools.[4] It had so unsettled me that I even put in for another job, that of the curatorship of Kenwood in Hampstead, which was controlled by the London County Council. I was one of two finalists out of seventy-eight

[3] Hearnden, *op. cit.*, p. 166.
[4] He was a friend of Denton Welch, who, I understand, made use of him fictionally in two of his novels. (See Michael De-la-Noy, *Denton Welch*, Viking, 1984 – in which he is referred to as 'Gerald'.)

Evie Hone's east window, 1959

applicants, and we were interviewed in turn in the vast conference hall of the LCC, across the Thames from the Houses of Parliament, where five years later I was to find myself lecturing on italic handwriting. The Councillors – some fifty of them – sat in a great semicircle, the interviewee at its centre. It was an alarming experience, and I was thoroughly put through my paces.

Why, I was asked, did I want to leave Eton when the salary offered was slightly less than I was getting at present? Because, I said, my job at Eton meant retirement at sixty, whereas at Kenwood I could carry on until I was sixty-five. In sixteen years at Kenwood I would earn a good deal more than in eleven at Eton. (This was true, but it was not the real reason.) Further questions followed; then, suddenly, a formidable-looking woman about fifty yards to the south-east of me said, 'I expect you know, Mr Blunt, that there is a proposal to hold concerts at Kenwood? [I didn't.] Do you approve of the period presentation of music?' I was not quite sure what she was getting at. 'If', I said, 'you mean that only eighteenth-century music should be played in a house mainly of that period, I would much regret it. If you mean performances in period dress I would deplore it even more.' This frankness gained me at all events one supporter – an ancient, bearded gentleman due east of me who cried, 'Hear, hear! We don't want any of that nonsense!'

But I did not get the job – and, in retrospect, I see how wonderfully fortunate it was for me that I did not. The flat was at the very top of the house. I would have been uprooted again at sixty-five. Further – and perhaps this would have proved worst of all – I could have published *nothing* without the permission of the LCC. With the departure of my assistant and the simultaneous advent of Robert Birley the sun shone again.

The forty-ninth year (seven times seven) is termed the 'lesser climacteric' – for men the equivalent of the menopause in women – and 1949 was a time when for various reasons I had been under a good deal of stress. I felt bruised and in need of a complete change of scene. One small additional shock had been delivered on the occasion of a recent visit to Austin Reed's, where I had eventually succeeded in finding an off-the-peg jacket that fitted me. 'What size', I asked the salesman, 'should I say if I want another at any time?' He looked at the label and replied, '46

Outsize Portly.' Now 'portly' is an offensive euphemism for 'fat'. I looked in the triple mirror and did not much care for what I saw of myself, from front, back or side. I was growing middle-aged and rather gross, and perhaps I ought really to have asked for sabbatical leave; but I didn't – until later.

However, in the Christmas holidays I sailed to the Canary Islands, where with a Czech woman named Mrs Low-Beer and her Gordonstoun son (inevitably nicknamed 'Dregs' at school) I ascended the 12,200-foot volcano, Mount Teide: an exhausting sixteen-hour expedition. There was no mountain railway then, so it meant car to 7,000 feet, then mules till they stuck in a snowdrift, and finally a battle on foot through a blizzard to the

Mount Teide

base of the sun-scorched cone of hot ashes on which one slipped back half a step for every step taken. Or more – and I am glad that I did not then know that one of Alexander von Humboldt's companions had thus slithered to his death at the very spot in 1799. I had in fact been warned, for my guidebook stated that in mid-winter the ascent 'is only to be undertaken by very strong and experienced climbers'. I was neither. Today I can hardly climb a short flight of stairs, and certainly could not reach the summit of Europe's notorious butter-mountain – not even if it 'came to

Mahomet'. But at least, unlike the Low-Beers, I was spared mountain sickness – so far as I know, I have been sick only once in my life (in 1915 or 1916, during an appalling Channel crossing in the *Sussex*, which was soon afterwards torpedoed and sunk by the Germans with the Spanish composer Granados on board).

Robert Birley, like John Talbot at Haileybury, looked every inch a headmaster (and he had half a dozen more of them than Talbot); but I never had occasion to test whether he could be equally terrifying in his wrath. Elliott certainly could not, and after one of his unsuccessful attempts to register indignation at a masters' meeting George Lyttelton was overheard to whisper to his neighbour, 'Exactly like the milk boiling over.' With two such very different men as Elliott and Birley at the helm, occasional friction was inevitable, and I blessed my good fortune that the Provost's sphere of action was mainly confined to College matters, the Chapel, and the College estates which he managed with great efficiency.

Birley had immediately given me permission (refused by his predecessor) to start an art society, which I named the Alexander Cozens Society in honour of my most illustrious predecessor, a natural son of Tsar Peter the Great, who had taught drawing at Eton from 1763 to 1768. Whether or not there had been such a society in the time of any of the four generations of the Evans family – Samuel, William ('William Evans of Eton'), Samuel II, and Sidney – who had successively been drawing masters from 1798 to 1922, I do not know. At all events, Sidney, as Anthony Powell makes plain in his *Infants of the Spring*,[5] had created, in his private studio in Keate's Lane, a salon and a refuge for aesthetes such as I had attempted at both Haileybury and Eton.

The demand for an art society at Eton had arisen in 1922 as the result of a sudden post-war flowering of artistic and literary talent which included Brian Howard, Robert Byron, Oliver Messel, Alan Clutton-Brock, Cyril Connolly, Anthony Powell, Noel Blakiston, Henry Yorke ('Henry Green') and Harold Acton. Two or three years later a similar upsurge had occurred at Marlborough, with John Betjeman, Louis MacNeice, Ellis Water-

[5] Heinemann, 1976, pp. 103–15.

house, Graham Shepard and my brother Anthony as the leaders of a revolt against the current tyranny of athleticism.[6]

In 1922, when Eric Powell became drawing master at Eton, an 'Eton Society of Arts' was founded, Brian Howard being the prime instigator, and the *Eton College Chronicle* mentions a meeting on 22 October of that year to discuss 'Post-Impressionalism' (*sic*).[7]

At both Eton and Marlborough there was a great deal of affectation and athlete-baiting, but Etonians being in general richer were able to be more aggressively 'difficult' than Marlburians. At Marlborough, Anthony unearthed some old but never-repealed statute entitling members of the Sixth Form to bowl hoops in the Court, and with his fellow aesthetes proceeded to take full advantage of it. The extravagances of the Etonian *jeunesse dorée* are fully recounted by Brian Howard and Harold Acton.

Among the meetings recorded by Howard (in a letter to a friend) was a lecture by Edith Sitwell

> to a tiny audience containing all the bloody Eton intellectuals – Gow, Lyttelton, Butterwick, Lubbock, Whitworth, the Vice-Provost [Macnaghten] etc., etc. She whispered her speech into a table, and as a result it was horribly difficult to hear anything at all. Ostensibly lecturing on Modern Poetry, she went on for hours about Stravinsky ... I heard that Gow and Lyttelton – Lord God damn and shrive their smelly souls! – kept nudging one another and grinning ... and at the end, and just when I'd finished 'thanking the audience for listening with such courteous attention', the beastly old Vice-Provost got up and advised Edie to *speak louder in future*! Eton is a queer place, isn't it? I nearly smacked his face.

There must have been many occasions when beaks would gladly have smacked Howard's.

It appears that the Eton Society of Arts survived for only two years. Possibly interest lapsed after the first band of enthusiasts had left; possibly Eric Powell, when he realised that he was about

[6] For an account of aestheticism at Marlborough in the mid-twenties see Louis MacNeice, *The Strings Are False*, Faber & Faber, 1965, and 'From Bloomsbury to Marxism' by Anthony, first published in *Studio International* in 1973 and reprinted in *Art Monthly* in Dec 1979/Jan 1980, immediately after his exposure as a spy.

[7] For the Eton Society of Arts see also *Brian Howard: Portrait of a Failure*, ed. Marie-Jacqueline Lancaster, Anthony Blond, 1968, *passim*, and Harold Acton, *Memoirs of an Aesthete*, Methuen, 1948, pp. 91–5.

to become a housemaster (which he did, in 1925), foresaw that he would then be too busy to sustain it. None was in existence when I arrived at Eton in 1938, and for more than a decade I was prevented from reviving the Eton Society of Arts – to some extent by the machinations of a senior colleague who ran the Archaeological Society and anticipated possible rivalry and defection of his members.

The Archaeological Society did in fact have occasional lectures on subjects more fittingly describable as 'art' – in order, no doubt, to attract boys who would soon have tired of a pabulum of archaeology pure and simple. I recall Sacheverell Sitwell (on 'The Baroque'), who arrived somewhat ill-prepared and expecting to find a large collection of appropriate slides from which to make a last-minute selection:

'Now this painting is . . . I *think* is . . . in a church in . . . in Rome . . .'

Voice of helpful boy working the lantern: 'It says *Naples*, sir.'

'Oh well – they're all very much the same.'

Sachie was always charming, but he was not always accurate. When his *German Baroque Sculpture* appeared in 1938, my brother Anthony reviewed it rather scathingly in the *Spectator*, pointing out that it was full of errors. Sachie wrote to him to protest, asking for a few examples of these. On receiving a list of about eighty of them, Sachie replied tartly, 'Since you seem to know so much about the subject, why not write a few books on it yourself?'

The Right Reverend Herbert Bury, Bishop for Northern Europe in our Paris days and author of various autobiographical volumes such as *A Bishop among Bananas*, wrote somewhere a memorable sentence which began, 'Among the nicest Emperors I ever met was . . .' (I think, the Kaiser). This is a warning to the reader that some name-dropping lies ahead, and may perhaps excuse my writing, 'Among the nicest princes I ever taught at Eton was . . .' PROG – or so he signed his pictures.

Prince Richard (now Duke) of Gloucester had considerable artistic talent, and in addition a delightful sense of humour and that particular brand of engaging pertness which (just) never overstepped the mark. He was exactly the sort of boy I like. I left

Eton before he did, and being well aware that the constantly returning retired beak is a bore, I strictly rationed my visits there. It chanced, however, that one half I did come twice, and each time found Prince Richard in the Drawing Schools. On the second occasion he looked up from the picture he was working on, and said, 'What, not *again*!' I much regret that *force majeure* has prevented my keeping in touch with him, as I still do with a number of my best 'Drawing Schools boys', and that because of the death of his elder brother he has not been able to pursue his chosen career as an architect. I am also full of admiration for the unobtrusively conscientious way in which he carries out public duties which must often seem tedious chores.

It was very characteristic of him that when he came to leave Eton in 1962 he gave Geoffrey Engleheart, a keen philatelist, not only a specially taken signed photograph of himself with his dog, but also a very valuable album of Australian stamps that had been presented to his father. I will not, however, drop the name or even disclose the nationality of another 'royal' who flung a pan of powder colours at the unfortunate and at that time shamefully overworked and underpaid Geoffrey, permanently ruining his shirt and not so much as offering to replace it. The only prince who ever threw paint at *me* was Alexander of Yugoslavia – and he missed: he was presumably a 'wet-bob'. He did not survive for long. And the only prince whose portrait I painted was a Haileyburian – the Maharaja of Dhrangadhra. The picture was found unacceptable: I had not realised that I was expected to bleach the agreeable *café au lait* colour of his skin, and he was too polite to warn me.

I last met Prince Richard at a literary drinks party given by Hatchards, to which I had gone with my friend Richard Brain; it must have been about 1971. I was sitting on a sofa with Brain when I felt a hand clapped firmly on my shoulder, and heard a loud and familiar voice saying, 'Don't get up.' Of course I did, and presented Brain. Then the Prince's fiancée joined us. After they had moved on, Brain said, 'Just *who* was that Richard Foster?'

Prince Michael of Kent (for I am still in a royal mood) I remember for one incident only. He was at the time a rather bewildered new boy, obviously using the Drawing Schools as a refuge. 'Come and see my floral painting, sir!' (What, a potential botanical artist in the royal family?) He led me into another room and proudly showed me a rather childish daub of a house and two trees which he had painted in powder-colours on the parquet. I imagined he was pulling my leg, but apparently he was not; if a picture painted on the wall was a mural, then surely one on the floor was a 'floral'.

Perhaps the most gifted artist to pass through my hands at Eton was Rory McEwen, whose suicide in October 1982 was a tragedy. He was also extremely musical. His versatility as an artist was astonishing: at one moment he was painting on vellum a single flower or a dead leaf with a finesse that Redouté might have envied; at another he was producing abstract three-dimensional work that meant nothing to me. The Basilisk Press published a sumptuous folio of his paintings of tulips, three times lifesize *lineally*, for which I revised and added to my *Tulipomania* (1950) to make a book to accompany the plates. Robin, an older brother of Rory, was also a born draughtsman, as the illustrations he made for Gavin Maxwell's *Ring of Bright Water* testify; but he did not pursue art as a career. Of the six McEwen brothers, all very talented and all but one at Eton in my day, only two survive.

Edward Plunkett was another boy who became a successful artist, but who has lived and exhibited chiefly abroad. He is a grandson of old Lord Dunsany (an Irish barony created in 1439), whose short stories had fascinated me in my youth. Eddie took me to stay with his grandfather at Dunstall Priory in Kent, his home when in England, and I am very glad to have known, if only slightly, this glorious eccentric who always brought his own salt-cellar (rock salt) with him when he dined out, and who still used a quill pen.

Dunsany was an ardent admirer of the poetry of my unspeakable litigious kinswoman, Judith, Baroness Wentworth – daughter of Wilfrid Scawen Blunt and great-granddaughter of Byron. I met her once only. I had found myself staying near Crabbet Park, her house in Sussex, and rang up to ask whether I might call on her.

'This is Wilfrid Blunt speaking . . .'

'No, it's not! He's *dead*!' And she banged down the receiver.

I knew, of course, of her bitter quarrels with her father, of whom she had once written that he was 'as unscrupulous a villain as could be found outside Dartmoor', so I rang again to explain. Thus I was allowed to visit her – in the incredible squalor in which she lived, by day and by night, in the library of that vast house, with her bed behind a curtain and her 'smalls' hanging up to dry on a clothes-line strung across the room. She proved very affable, and gave me on leaving an inscribed copy of her wartime verses.

DUNSTALL PRIORY,
SHOREHAM N° SEVENOAKS,
KENT.

Aug:10.1957

To Lady Wentworth.

A poet to Parnassus goes
Whence none has recognised her rhyme,
But to be welcomed among those
Whose lyrics have outlasted time.

Dunsany

Lord Dunsany's farewell verse to Lady Wentworth

Two days after her death on 8 August 1957, Dunsany wrote to me enclosing 'a farewell verse that I wrote today . . . My admiration of your cousin's poems is almost a one-man heresy.'

Eddie once invited me to lunch with him, somewhere quite modest in Soho. When we had finished, the waitress handed me the bill, which I passed on to my host. The good woman was

Eddie Plunkett, 1957

horrified: 'What, you're not going to let the *little one* pay!' The heir to the barony of Dunsany, whose glittering sports car had brought us to the restaurant, and whose mother owns, I believe, quite a large slice of Brazil, was well able to afford it.

Eddie, when still a boy at Eton, did a very good portrait of Grey Gowrie[8] who used it as a 'leaving photograph'; it was an excellent likeness, but the photo is not good enough to reproduce. Grey had just arrived at Eton when his grandmother – a very kind friend to me – asked me if I would take this unknown infant over to lunch with her sister near Aylesbury. It was an expedition that I shall never forget, for Grey had just bought a volume of Victorian verse at 'Ma Brown's' bookshop in the High Street, and, all the way there and all the way back, read the poems out loud to me. I was fascinated, and so distracted that I nearly killed him by stupidly

[8] The Earl of Gowrie, one-time Arts Minister in Mrs Thatcher's Cabinet.

trying to overtake a car when going uphill on a too narrow road. He was far too absorbed in his book to realise the danger.

Howard Hodgkin is another of a handful of Etonians of my day who have made an impact on the art world. I find his sense of colour lovely, though I must confess that I cannot make head or tail of his pictures. Recently he was chosen to represent Great Britain at the Venice Biennale. And yet another, had he not died so sadly young, might well have been Jeremy Cubitt, whose picture of a nun, hanging in the summer exhibition of Boys' Work at Eton, was bought by Geoffrey Agnew in the teeth of strong competition from Kenneth Clark.

If I am a snob, I believe myself to be only quite a mild one; it just so happened that a number of my most talented as well as nicest pupils were titled. So were two of the most repellent parents who came, my way – both women from the upper echelons of the aristocracy who treated me as a servant paid to educate their hardly less objectionable offspring. I remember one of these women mentioning casually a visit she had paid to 'Maud Norway'; and I, who had not been brought up to refer to queens thus, longed to ask who Ms Norway was.

But to return to art. Alexander Weymouth, eldest son of the Marquess of Bath, was a potentially very gifted painter; he could also lay claim to being the most handsome Etonian of his day. Evelyn Waugh, after meeting Alexander at the age of twenty-four, wrote to Lady Bath, 'I think he is the most enchanting creature of either sex I have met for twenty years . . . I see his mother's lovely mad eyes and I said what cocktail and he said gin & tonic. That was really all I saw of him but goodness I fell in love . . . Goodness he is a beauty.' Waugh was then in his fifties, his so-called 'homosexual phase' thirty years behind him. Alexander was, indeed, extraordinarily beautiful, and I find that I can write about him thus because, for reasons that I cannot explain, I was not in the least attracted to him physically. He was to me like some exquisite Greek marble statue of an *ephebos*: it was nothing more than this. At Baldwin's Shore he was always referred to as 'the pleasure peer'.

It is hard to imagine the gentle, elegant, sensitive, almost epicenely beautiful youth I knew (or *thought* I knew) at Eton developing, as he has done, into the unconventional, hirsute,

184

Alexander Weymouth, 1950 and 1979.
'Look here, upon this picture, and on this.'

bare-footed, exotically dressed, dreadlocked, hang-gliding giant of today – the 'hippie lord' of the gossip-columnist, champion of the restoration of the Kingdom of Wessex, and painter of vast acres of remarkable murals at Longleat and elsewhere, in some of which the eroticism must strike many who see them as indistinguishable from fairly hard porn. Yet even the Karma Sutra bedroom at Longleat, a sexual free-for-all painted in 1969, seems – as he shows one round it – so honest in intention that it does not provoke a snigger; one feels more like a voyeur at some strange oriental religious rite. His motivations may, I dare say, be more clearly understood when his 'personal journals', which have now reached volume 77, come – if ever – to be published; but in any case I shall no longer be around.

Meanwhile he has produced a small guide entitled *Lord Weymouth's Murals* in which, incidentally, he thanks me very handsomely for my 'encouragement' while he was at Eton, and for taking him to Burlington House to see an exhibition of French Impressionist paintings which made 'a lasting impact' on him. (One of my best pupils confessed that, in the foreword to a catalogue of an exhibition of his paintings, he had not dared to mention Eton or myself for fear that a public school connection might damage his reputation.) My 'encouragement' of Alexander

185

did not, I may add, influence the subject matter of the Karma Sutra bedroom, the inspiration for which, he writes:

> naturally comes from India. I had seen photographs of these Hindu temples where erotic couplings have been sculpted to poetic, or even religious effect. It struck me that Western art is curiously devoid of any candid eroticism. Where copulatory scenes have been depicted here in Europe, they have all too frequently been engineered in an atmosphere of pornographic smut . . . [Titillation] was not my intention . . . To my eyes, this mural is a poetic expression of man's joy in womanhood, and vice versa. I sincerely hope that tourists will be able to view it in the same spirit.

So, perhaps, might Gauguin have written. And what might not Gauguin have achieved had he returned from Tahiti to be given free rein at Longleat?

At the end of every half one had to write a report on each boy's work, and though it was only of the really talented that one could hope to find anything worth saying three times a year, it was agreeable to have the opportunity to take revenge on a few persistent thorns in the flesh. Weary of writing various permutations of 'Has no aptitude for the subject, but does his best', I eventually got permission to use a short printed report for those who were hopeless but harmless. (Aldous Huxley, during his brief spell on the Eton staff, had devised an ingenious form at the head of which was printed 'He talks too much, but . . .' – and then completed it by hand.) Every housemaster had also to send at the end of each half a long letter to the parents of his pupils and of boys in his house – a chore which, if conscientiously performed, knocked the best part of a week off his holiday, but which was usually much appreciated by the recipients.

Mones's famous report on a boy's 'drawers' had to be returned to him from the housemaster for emendation, but some even odder reading was provided by those members of the music staff who came only one morning a week to teach an instrument outside the scope of the resident musicians. Boys press-ganged by parents to 'do music' in some form or other soon discovered that if they opted for an instrument that necessitated a visiting teacher they need never turn up, though the teacher would still be paid – an arrangement that suited all concerned. In the unforgettable March of 1947, when all Eton was under water, a little man who

The floods of 1947: outside Baldwin's Shore.
The author to the right of the left-hand group, Tom Lyon (left)
in mortar-board, Grizel Hartley in riding breeches in the distance.

had swum in from Slough to give his weekly lesson on the trombone to a pupil who had not as yet ever put in an appearance was much excited to hear a sort of knock on his door. He opened it, and there entered – sheer *Lohengrin* – a swan! These poor chaps never quite got the wavelength of Eton, and it is alleged that one of them once wrote in an end-of-term report on a trumpeting peer (who actually did turn up for his lessons): 'His Lordship has the most beautiful lips.'

I cannot leave the Drawing Schools without a further word about our attendant there, Geoffrey Engleheart, for loyalty and dedication such as his are rare today.

Geoffrey is descended from the famous George Engleheart, miniature painter to King George III. His father, a sergeant in the 10th Royal Hussars, won the VC in the Boer War, receiving it from the hands of the Queen at her last investiture at Windsor Castle in October 1900. On his retirement he was appointed a gatekeeper at the Castle, where his two sons – identical and virtually indistinguishable twins, of whom Geoffrey was the elder – were enlisted as playmates for the unfortunate epileptic Prince John (1905–19), the youngest son of King George V. Geoffrey, after a short spell as a laboratory assistant at Eton, was transferred in 1934 to the more congenial atmosphere of the Drawing Schools where, but for his wartime service, he remained for forty years. He was called up in August 1940, but his war was largely spent, safely if draughtily, in the Orkneys; in December 1944, however, he was drafted to the Far East. He arrived too late to be involved in any fighting, but not too late – as he constantly told us – to catch a glimpse of 'a great big pagoda' before also catching malaria, which was to plague him intermittently after his return to England.

Because it is so characteristic of the man, I quote from a letter to me (30 March 1982) in which he described his return to his beloved Eton after the war, and the welcoming letter he had received from Mones. Geoffrey wrote:

> Here I give his famous signal for my return.
>
> He said. Mr Blunt & I both regard you as an Old Friend & want to consider your Interest, as we would our own.
>
> Well Sir, these kind words from Him to me. Have always inspired me to serve my very Best to all you Good Gentlemen at Eton College and I may say I have never regretted the day, I started work for Eton Colledge Masters. This is an honest statement, on Masters at the Drawing Schools & is still right, to the Present Day as they are always inviting me to Look at any exhibitions. Which I greatly appreciate.
>
> If I had my life over again I would choose exactly the same Job again to work with such nice Masters & Boys.

Geoffrey did not – as he had hoped – win the VC, but he *presented* his father's to the 10th Royal Hussars. Many a man in straitened circumstances would have sold it – and for a sum that would have meant for Geoffrey and his fireman brother substantial extra comfort and security in old age; but such a thought would never have crossed his mind. He should at least have been made an honorary O E ;[9] he would have worn the famous tie day and night for the rest of his life. I take this opportunity to thank him and to salute him.

Some time in the late seventies Geoffrey retired from the Drawing Schools to take on the far less arduous task of looking after the rather depressing School Natural History Museum.

[9] At Haileybury, two such lifelong loyal servants of the school were made honorary OHs.

Over the years Mones and I had had to fight every inch of the way to get him the occasional rise in his very meagre wages, and my successor, Oliver Thomas, had managed to persuade the authorities that in his new job there would be no reduction of the pittance he had been receiving. One Sunday morning a small sherry party was held at the Drawing Schools at which Geoffrey was to be presented with a watch and a cheque – the former in no way reflecting on his punctuality, since he always arrived two hours early and left several hours late. I came over from Compton to be present.

Oliver made a short and appropriate speech, then handed over the gifts and left Geoffrey to reply. Now Geoffrey had the weakest head in the world: a tablespoonful of sherry affected him as a double scotch would most men. And by this time he had had at least *two full glasses of sherry* . . . If only his speech had been recorded on tape! He began with a paean of praise of Eton, of its masters, its boys. Then the alcohol took over, and he suddenly changed tack to embark upon a vicious onslaught on the unnamed beak who, on Geoffrey's arrival at Eton (when he had worked briefly in the Science Schools), had allegedly bullied and maltreated him. We well knew to whom he was referring. All the bitterness borne in silence over nearly fifty years had broken the dam that had for so long contained it; Hitler could not have bettered his invective. It was extraordinary, pathetic – yet sublime. Eventually Oliver discreetly steered him to a chair into which he slumped in total silence.

But how tricky even recent memory is! Oliver, on being asked to check this passage, wrote:

> I don't believe that that onslaught had anything to do with Geoffrey's weak head. I think it was made in the same vein of sudden inspiration as when he once said to me, 'Sir, don't you think – I hope you don't mind my saying so, but my brother and I sometimes talk about it – but, don't you think, sir, it's extraordinary how quiet the Zulus have been lately?' At the time this seemed so true that one wondered why one hadn't thought of it oneself. *excellent*

When Geoffrey presented his father's VC to the 10th Royal Hussars, the Regiment gave a dinner in his honour. I would welcome an eye-witness account of that evening – and no doubt it will reach me from a former pupil, too late for inclusion.

14

Younger Colleagues and Some Holidays Abroad

Most Eton masters join the staff in their mid-twenties, but I had not come until I was thirty-seven. Colleagues who were roughly of my own age group were therefore already well established, with their own circle of friends, while those who were of my standing on the staff list were usually a dozen or so years younger than I. Thus I had at first found myself neither fish nor fowl. Not that this really mattered: my contemporaries welcomed me into their coteries, while I soon began to build up agreeable friendships among the younger beaks and, over the years, with still younger additions to the staff, some of whom had been boys in the school at the time of my arrival.

After the war I resumed travel abroad – usually at first with my former Haileybury colleague Francis Thompson, though occasionally with my brother Anthony, with my mother, or alone. But in the fifties I generally went with Eton friends, among whom were Raef Payne, Giles St Aubyn, Anthony Caesar and Richard Brain. All were bachelors. So often a friend who marries becomes half a friend lost – tied henceforth to domestic chores and restricted to the annual family month at the seaside. I could write a chapter on each of my trips abroad – indeed there was a whole book, *A Persian Spring*, about a sabbatical four months I spent in the Middle East in 1956. But I must confine myself to a single sample for extended treatment here, and I have chosen a holiday I spent in Italy with Giles in April 1955.

Giles, then thirty, was a fascinating and complex character, a delightful man whose amiable eccentricities, enthusiasms, allergies and phobias must present an irresistible temptation to any biographer. Unlike most schoolmasters he was both well off and well born – his father was the late Lord St Levan, owner of St

Anthony Caesar and Richard Brain, August 1954

Michael's Mount where I once spent a very pleasant week as his guest. When accused one day by a colleague of extravagance, Giles replied simply, 'I'm not extravagant, I'm just *rich.*' I think of him first and foremost as all legs and golden retrievers – the former reminiscent of Lytton Strachey's in Henry Lamb's well-known portrait of him in the Tate, the latter characteristic appendants to a confirmed bachelor. At sixty he has just retired from Eton to go and live in another island – the tax-haven of Guernsey.

In a 'rich' gesture Giles rashly bought a gigantic Mercedes-Benz which had formerly belonged to some important Nazi – perhaps von Ribbentrop. (He never really *owned* the car: he was owned *by* it, just as the besotted pet-lover is the slave of his adored cat or dog.) Since it proved too large for any Eton garage, it had to be stabled in a barn about half a mile away; and this of course involved a second and smaller car to enable him to get to the barn. The monster turned out to be a dipsomaniac, drinking a gallon of petrol before it would condescend to do nine miles, even on a long run, and was soon sold – no doubt at a considerable loss – and replaced by a Bristol (of which more later). A somewhat similar

Giles St Aubyn and the author, April 1953

situation arose when Giles decided to buy a tiny uninhabited
island and former lighthouse-keeper's house about half a mile
offshore in Cardigan Bay. Since it was impossible to land on it in
bad weather, a house on the mainland had also to be bought to
serve as a hospice for marooned guests.

It was from Giles that I bought my first typewriter – an ancient
machine that had been passed on to him by his uncle, Harold
Nicolson. Giles had no need of it since he had recently acquired
the latest de luxe model. The old wreck was historic because it
had, allegedly, been used by Harold to type the first draft of *Some
People*, and a memory of the part it had played in the creation of
that little masterpiece seemed still to prompt it when I got stuck
for a word. Eventually it became afflicted with so many of the
distressing ailments that old typewriters are heir to that I had to
have it 'put down' – i.e., sold for ten bob. (By now it would
probably qualify as a collector's piece.) Also from Giles came, just
before I left Eton, my first (black-and-white) television set. He
had bought it a week or two earlier, but having decided that it did
not 'go' with his period furniture, he put it on offer at a very
reduced price. At Compton I immediately became a TV addict,
and replaced it later by a colour set.

Among Giles's passions was the bull-ring; among his allergies were lifts, aeroplanes, small babies, and eating liver. In 1955 I went with him to stay a week with a friend of Grizel's who had a tobacco farm in Puglia, the uttermost heel of Italy, beyond Lecce – a desolate part of the country which all Italians from Naples northwards like to pretend does not exist (for Italy is really *two* countries – the relatively prosperous north, and the poverty-stricken south). We travelled by train; it was too far to go by car, and Giles would not entrust his precious life to an aeroplane. At Genoa we struck a trade fair, and it was only after trying half a dozen hotels that we eventually got a double room on the seventh floor of the kind of establishment to which Giles was not accustomed. I confess that it was with a certain *schadenfreude* that I entered the prehistoric lift while I watched him begin his Everest ascent on foot; but between the fourth and fifth floors the lift stuck . . . And there I remained, bored but perfectly safe, for a full half-hour, while Giles implored me, up from the fourth floor, to be brave and, down from the fifth, to remain steadfast. The hotel manager was summoned, and advocated patience: the fair was making exceptional demands on the city's electricity. At last there was a sudden jerk, and I was in motion again. Giles was badly shaken, and ate little that evening. I made a hearty meal, and drank a whole bottle of my favourite Lambrusco.

Next morning we secured comfortable seats at one end of a long compartment in the Rome Express. Just as it was due to start, a peasant woman with a tiny nut-brown infant in her arms clambered in at the other end, a good fifty feet away. The child was not being breast-fed or anything shy-making; it was not even crying; it was obviously sound asleep. But Giles instantly sprang to his feet, seized his luggage and jumped out onto the platform. Of course I had to follow suit. He could at least have used the corridor, and we were nearly left behind.

Grizel's friend, Costanza Gargasole ('She'll *adore* to have you, and take her a large Georgian silver soup-ladle because I know it's what she wants'), was a spinster in, I would guess, her mid-forties. She had taken a degree in Medicine at Bari University, but had not made a career as a doctor. Her father (by this time dead) and mother were intensely pro-British – as was she – and in their town house in Bari had shown Hubert Hartley much kindness when our armies were advancing through Italy during the Second

World War. It resulted in a lasting friendship between Grizel and Costanza, which both much valued. (Nearly thirty years later, when Costanza wrote to say that she was about to have a mental breakdown, Grizel replied by return, 'Darling! Come and have it here!')

In 1955 Costanza, now in charge of the family tobacco business, was living with her mother in the new *castello* at one end of the village street of Uggiano la Chiesa, while her enchanting centenarian grandmother and one of her aunts occupied the *castello vecchio* at the other end. Its walls were twenty feet thick, and within them the old lady sat all day long doing crochet-work of a delicacy which would have taxed the eyes of many women half her age.

Uggiano la Chiesa was – and doubtless still is – another world. We were back in the Middle Ages, or perhaps almost with Alice through the looking-glass, and so intensely Catholic is the deep south of Italy that Costanza, when told by Grizel that I was a clergyman's son, observed coyly, 'We call them nephews here.' Even the ubiquitous scarlet pimpernels are blue in Uggiano. Time, as we understand it, did not exist. Lunch might be at midday, or at half-past four; apparently it had once been at seven o'clock, but that, as Costanza admitted, made dinner so late. I half suspect that the natives still used sundials. On going to my bed I found it seemingly already occupied by an immense woman. I pulled back the sheet and blanket, thus nearly overturning a very large saucepan of red-hot cinders, covered with a lid, and inevitably setting fire to the bedding.

On our first evening Costanza had said, 'What shall we do tomorrow? Would you like to go to Castel del Monte?'

'That would be lovely.'

'Or would you prefer Lecce?'

'Whichever you like. I want to see both, if it's possible.'

It was finally decided that we should set out for Lecce at ten o'clock the next morning. We were both ready on time, but there was no sign of Costanza until noon.

'Where shall we go today? To Otranto? To Castel del Monte? Or would you like to go to Lecce? But I must go to look at the tobacco first. Come with me; we can decide after lunch. Come with me.'

A tobacco factory needs no description, and shall get none. I will record only that at the door of it sat, face to face, two ancient men: the one, a Government official to check that nothing escaped without duty being paid; the other, Costanza's agent, to prevent theft. It might have been said of either of them, 'Sometimes I sits and thinks, and sometimes I just sits.'

Lunch was at a quarter to three. 'It will be too late to go to Taranto now.' Taranto had never been suggested. If stress is the cause of duodenal ulcers, they must be rare in Puglia.

Girl with Asphodel: *Pompeian mural, 1st century* AD
(Museo Nazionale, Naples)

Asphodelus microcarpus *at Compton, 1984*

Every Italian family seems to have a botanically orientated *zia* (aunt), and it was Zia Giulia who offered to show me a very secret spot where an incredibly rare yellow iris grew. I eagerly consented. After driving a good thirty miles over an uninhabited plain we eventually reached a marshy spot where, after much searching, we found three leaves (no flower) of the common yellow flag iris that grows in every English water-meadow. However, I did bring back from Castel del Monte, one of Frederick II's splendid medieval castles, several huge bulbs of *Asphodelus microcarpus*, the asphodel of the ancient world, which have flowered regularly for nearly thirty years in my garden at Eton and subsequently at Compton. (When in Italy with two friends in May 1966 I collected another species, the unbranched *A. albus*, in the hills above Genoa. This also still flowers at Compton.) I cannot understand why these handsome and obliging plants are so rarely to be seen in English gardens; perhaps the reason is that the leaves smell of tom-cats.

A week of my holiday with Giles was spent at Agropoli – a little coastal townlet about fifty miles south of Naples whose unspoiled charm my brother Anthony had discovered a year before and whose identity he begged me not to reveal. My trips were often in part paid for by a subsequent broadcast, and Agropoli provided the material for a talk, entitled 'No Regrets', on the Light Programme.[1] I have thought it best to give it in full in the chapter that follows as a sample of many such scripts I produced over the years.

Other Continental trips, some earlier and some later than that to southern Italy with Giles, must be treated more briefly. In particular, there was an Easter holiday in 1953 with Giles and Raef Payne, whom I have already mentioned as a one-time member of our Baldwin's Shore colony. Raef became my closest friend at Eton. As a boy he had been a classical scholar, one of the best painters of his generation, and in 1948 Captain of the School. After four years at Cambridge he joined the Eton staff, living with

---

[1] Published in *The Listener*, 25 August 1955. To simplify the talk, I made no reference to Giles, who was with me all the time. I would also add, as a warning to anyone thinking of going there, that Agropoli's peculiar charm has, I am told, now completely vanished.

Raef Payne: picnic on Simplon, April 1953

us at the Shore until he was appointed Master in College in 1957. Ten years later he took over a boys' house, moving into Evans's in 1974.

The Master in College is usually chosen from among the most promising of the younger masters: he is, as it were, the housemaster of the seventy King's Scholars, and the job is an exacting one, as there is inevitably a larger proportion of highly strung boys among the cleverest. (One Master in College in my time was woken at midnight, after his first day in office, by a boy announcing he had just discovered that he was Jesus Christ, and what ought he to do about it.) When in due course a Master in College became a housemaster, by the end of his fifteen- or sixteen-year stint he would probably have had well over twenty years of particularly difficult work. Since my time this has been changed. Today the Master in College ranks as an ordinary housemaster, remaining *en poste* for thirteen years unless, as has twice happened, he leaves to become a headmaster before his time is up.

Raef has just given up his house, and I am delighted to learn that he has decided to stay on at Eton until he reaches the retirement age. He is now my principal surviving link with the school. His house was one of the best; for not only does he understand boys, he has wide interests (in particular, the drama) that are not always to be found in classical scholars.

The holiday with Giles and Raef in 1953 was made in Giles's Bristol and took us as far as Naples. It began inauspiciously. Giles was taken ill the day before we were due to leave, but since the passage for the car had already been booked, Raef was obliged to drive me through Germany to Venice, where the terrified Giles joined us *by air* a few days later. Giles, a historian and author, was working at that time on a book about Garibaldi, and in Ravenna we pursued his hero to some remote forester's hut in the pine forests where he had taken refuge in 1849. It was very like any other forester's hut, and the pine forests remarkably like most pine forests.

Giles's nerves were still so shaken by the terrors of his flight to Venice that when we reached Rome he panicked and refused to take any left-hand turns against the traffic. I could sympathise, having once driven my own car in Turin. I suppose that the AA, duly forewarned, could have provided us with right-turn-only routes to our hotel, and from it to the principal sites; without its assistance, some of our journeys were to prove extremely circuitous. Soon after entering the city we found ourselves at the end of a cul-de-sac, with a garage where in desperation Giles decided to leave the car. The garage attendant, noticing the word 'Eton' on the car's papers, was in ecstasy: he had just seen *A Yank at Eton* in his local cinema, and now he was seeing three representatives of the famous school in the flesh.

We reached Naples safely, though on the return journey northwards the furious driving of the Italian Jehus finally forced Giles to abandon the perilous winding coastal road. Raef and I were both rather relieved when we drove out of Dover on an English road, and not a little amused to observe, in a ditch a few miles outside the town, an Italian sports car which had swept past us in the main street. A policeman stood beside it, notebook in hand.

Over the years I paid a number of brief visits, either alone or with a friend, to Percy Lubbock, author of *Shades of Eton* and other books well known between the wars, at his magically beautiful house, Gli Scafari, on a small promontory on the Gulf of Spezia near Lerice. He was in his early seventies when I first went there, but already his sight was troubling him and by the time of his death he had become almost completely blind. I was never more than a passing guest, but soon there was always some resident young man or other to read to him and act as his secretary and factotum. It must have been a difficult job, for it was so easy to put a foot wrong.

Though a keen lover of music, Percy deplored the gramophone as an invention of the devil; he had, of course, never heard a decent one. One day he was amazed by the sound of a superb pianist playing Brahms in a room in the house in which he knew there to be no piano. He flung open the door, to find his current reader playing – a gramophone! From that moment he became an enthusiast for the hitherto condemned machine, and each evening two or three hours were set aside for a 'concert' – 'Tonight we will listen to the first and last acts of *Die Walküre*' (or whatever) – and no guest was ever invited to offer a suggestion. He worshipped Kathleen Ferrier, and I was thoroughly carpeted for saying that I did not always find her diction clear. Nor was the slovenly or colloquial English of a guest tolerated (he would not have passed 'thoroughly carpeted'!) – and my mention of someone being 'a Wagner fan' was succeeded by an ominous silence, broken eventually by 'I *suppose* I know what you *mean*.'

And then, an unlucky slip of the tongue: 'I so much enjoyed your *Roman Portraits*.' 'You cannot have read it with much attention. My book is entitled *Roman Pictures*.' Useless to explain that I had also just been looking at *Roman Portraits* – a different book, on Roman portrait sculptures. (It is curious how many people get book-titles wrong. When Michael Russell published *Married to a Single Life* he received a number of bizarre orders, including a request for *One Man and His Single Wife* – 'the one', he supposed, 'who meant to mow a widow.')

As Percy's sight continued to deteriorate, life became an increasing burden to him. One morning, through the open door of his bedroom, I heard him talking to himself: 'Oh, *another* day . . . *another* day!' He died in 1965, at the age of eighty-six. I doubt whether many people now read his *Shades of Eton*, or even *Earlham* – to my mind his best book. But they need to be taken in small doses because the very perfection of his style tends, after a while, to cloy. It is like eating spoonful after spoonful of Hymettus honey.

On my way home from one of my visits to Percy I looked in, at his suggestion, on Max Beerbohm at Rapallo. It was in April 1954, two years before Max's death, and Derek Hill, a fellow guest at Percy's, kindly gave me a lift in his car. Elisabeth Jungmann, who tended the old widower devotedly and finally married him, regretted that he could see nobody; but when I gave my name she said that he was at that moment on the terrace reading my *Sweet Roman Hand*, and relented. I shall never forget the wonderful gentian blue of those tired old eyes with their vermilion lids, though foolishly I made no note at the time of what he talked about. I also now realise, with a shock, that he was then exactly the age that I am today.

There were many other holidays abroad; but of one bitter-sweet week in Venice I cannot bring myself to write, for it was made in the company of the second of the two friends – no, lovers – I mentioned in an earlier chapter. In fact, Venice, which I have so often visited, was by curious chance to play an important role in my life. My parents spent their honeymoon there, and – as I have told elsewhere – since I was born nine months later it seems probable that I was conceived there. It was there, in 1929, that I had fallen in love for the first time; and it was there, more than twenty years later, that I was forced to accept that a physical relationship with the greatest love of my life had finally come to an end.

That was *my* 'Death in Venice'.

15

'No Regrets'

A RADIO BROADCAST

Castelrovinato – do not look for it on the map, for I have changed the name – is a little one-horse town in south-east Italy. Its cool, white houses cling to the sides of a rocky headland that juts out into the blue Tyrrhenian Sea. When you have scrambled up and looked at what time and the Saracens have left of the Castle, when you have scrambled down to the tiny beach with its handful of brightly painted fishing-boats, when you have failed to discover the miraculous imprint of St Paul's feet upon the shore, you may say you have 'done' Castelrovinato.

In fact, there seems no obvious reason why anybody should ever go to Castelrovinato at all. But I had been told by my brother Anthony that I should find there a simple, clean, cheap hotel with a terrace overlooking the sea, a few orange-trees to scent the air, and white doves for mealtime company. I wanted sun, I wanted the sea, I wanted wine. I wanted peace to write. And I did not want to be robbed. So, a few days before Easter, I found myself at Castelrovinato.

I had not been misled – except on one point. It turned out that the terrace of the hotel did *not* overlook the sea; it looked upon the playground of the local school. This was a blow. I remembered the village school at home, with its bright-voiced teachers, its perpetual hymn-singing, and the unbelievable, shrill clamour of small children 'letting off steam'. But the boys who were playing netball at that moment seemed quiet and well-behaved enough. I walked past the open window of a classroom. Within, about twenty youths, most of whom seemed to be about seventeen or eighteen years old, were taking down notes. Though I could sense that they had seen me, they never looked up from their books. I thought: in an English country grammar school a passing stranger looking as ridiculously foreign as I did would

Agropoli

have caused something of a stir. I was reassured. But in any case I need not have worried, for I discovered that the Easter holiday was due to begin on the following day.

I woke to a golden morning. In order to get a general impression of Castelrovinato, I went down to the harbour and found an old sailor who agreed to take me out for an hour in a rowing-boat. When I came to pay him, he thrust the notes back at me: he had known my brother, he said; he could not take my money. I went back to the little *piazza* and selected four or five postcards of the castle; the shopman forced me to accept them as a souvenir of my visit. I stopped an ice-cream seller and asked for an ice; he handed me one and said that as it was the opening day of the ice-cream season there would be nothing to pay. Fresh as I was from the brigands of Naples and their endless extortions, I began to wonder whether I was suffering from some kind of softening of the brain. I went into the Bar Nazionale and ordered a cup of coffee. 'There is no charge,' said the proprietor when I tried to pay him. 'Today, your first day in Castelrovinato, you are my guest.' It is the sun, I thought. I must be more careful in future.

Just as I was getting up to go, two students of about eighteen came in and sat down at the table next to mine.

'You are a foreigner?' said one of them.

'Yes.'

'Dutch?'

'No.'

'German?'

'No – try again.'

'Then you are English! Churcheel! Churcheel! Churcheel *è un grande statista* – a great statesman. May we talk with you? Would you like to meet our friends? Would you like to go for walks with us? Do you play billiards? Do you play cards? Do you shoot lizards? Will you bathe with us? Will you teach us English? Will you teach us French? Will you teach us German?' And before I could answer, they had drawn up their chairs to my table.

I thought again of the Neapolitan robbers who had cheated me so often, and wondered what the catch could be. I offered the two youths cigarettes, but they firmly refused: 'We are too young,' they said. I offered them coffee: 'Thank you, we are not thirsty.' This meant, as I afterwards discovered, 'We are too poor to buy these things, and too proud to accept them as gifts.' For the bar, it seemed, was a club where all might sit and none need buy; except for a few lire which changed hands when a game of billiards was played or a single sweet purchased, the little money that was taken came chiefly from the sale of groceries. To the proprietor, these 'chair-warmers' – as he called his unpaying clients – seemed the most natural thing in the world.

Soon the 'bush telegraph' that operates in simple communities had announced the presence of a foreigner in the bar. In rapid succession, a dozen or more youths arrived. Introductions were effected. 'This is Gaetano; his father is a barber. This is Mario; his father is deputy-governor of the district. And this is Tonio; he sells ice-creams.' (But he does not, I thought to myself; he gives them away.) I was struck by the fact that the difference of their stations in life apparently embarrassed no one; in England, such revelations would have made everyone feel uncomfortable.

'And now,' they said, 'let us walk to Quarantove.'

Quarantove, they explained, was a small beach about a mile from the town, and so called from the legend that a local hen had once laid forty eggs there simultaneously. ('It is only a fable,' they said. 'You must not believe it!')

Student group, Agropoli, April 1955
Top, left to right: Mario, Pietro, Tonio, Franco
Below: Fernando, Gaetano, Carmine, Giuseppe

I felt more like lunch than a country walk, but it would have been churlish to have refused their invitation. So we set out, in the hot April sunshine, towards the crest of the hill that separated the two bays.

'What do the English think of Ariosto, Professore?'

Though there was, in the days of my childhood, an eccentric English peer who used (it was said) to read through the whole of

Orlando Furioso every year, I would be prepared to wager that if one were to collect together all the inhabitants of the British Isles who had ever really *thought* about Ariosto, they would not unreasonably crowd a moderate-sized drawing-room. So I replied that we revered his name but that, to be perfectly honest, his works were not much read nowadays.

They seemed disappointed. 'He is a great poet,' they said. 'Do the English think Dante as great a poet as Shakespeare? Tell us about England. Is the Regina Elisabetta very much beloved? Is Vembley Stadium as big as the new stadium in Rome? What are the best English cars? Is Sir Anthony Eden the most handsome man in England? Is there work in England? Is there always fog in London? What caused the sudden darkness in London in January? Is the Opera House of Coovent Garden as big as the Scala in Milano? Why are there strikes in England? How great is Chowser?'

'Chaucer? Do you read Chaucer?'

'Certainly we read Chowser – in our fourth year of English. Chowser is a great story-teller, like our Boccaccio. Chowser came once to Italy. Have you read Victor Hugo? Have you read Lamartine? How do you say *capello* in English? And in French? And in German? How old are you? How tall are you? "Ohl tings brate and biutifuool, all creajers great and smohl" – is that O.K.? I will gather some flowers for you. We will find you some *gamberi* [shrimps]. How do you say *gamberi* in English? In French? In German? Do you love London as we love Castelrovinato?' We were pausing for breath on the brow of the hill. Below us, slipping from terrace to terrace, fell the shimmering olives, the golden-fruited, glossy-green orange trees, down to an immaculate sea. That old grey widow, London, seemed suddenly very remote and very unlovable.

'What do you want to be when you grow up?' I said to Pietro, a dark-eyed boy of about sixteen who appeared to be the youngest member of the party.

'*Una lucertola*,' he said, pointing to an emerald-green lizard that was basking on a nearby rock. Then he snatched the communal air-gun from Mario, approached to within about a yard of the lizard, and fired. The wounded animal sprang into the air, fell, then crawled away into a crevice in the rock to die.

Hoping that he did not know the things we do to hares and foxes in England, I tried to reason with him. But Gaetano was the only one to come to my support. 'It is not good,' he said. 'Let us rather aim at trees.'

We spent the afternoon searching for shrimps, little crabs, sea-urchins (male sea-urchins – for the females, it seems, are not edible), and *frutti di mare* which are like very small limpets. These, eaten raw, constituted my only lunch. Then, as the sun dropped down into the silent sea, we returned, hungry but happy, to Castelrovinato.

In ways such as this I passed the days that followed. There is something infinitely affecting in finding oneself accepted, naturally and on equal terms, by the members of a community so wholly different in every respect from one's own. (So it is when the shy robin alights on one's finger and is not afraid.) These youths were friendly, affectionate even; but they were never familiar. They were gentle, considerate, courteous. ('Do not walk on that rock, Professore; it is slippery.' 'Do not step in the water; it will spoil your shoes.') And among themselves they were just the same. ('Let us wait for Fernando; he is tired.') They were completely innocent. 'I do not read *libri gialli* [sexy thrillers],' said Aldo, 'they would corrupt me'; and he was not being the least bit priggish. But the quality in them that I found most remarkable – and they all possessed it – was that curious and rare combination of childish enthusiasm and adult poise. They were mature, but they were absolutely unspoilt: Rousseau's 'noble savages'. And though most of them were poor, and some of them very poor, they seemed to be without a care in the world.

In the evenings, I played billiards or ping-pong with the fishermen in the bar; and though I did my best, it was not always possible to prevent them from paying. Giuseppe, the fourteen-year-old boy who served behind the counter, challenged me to a game of ping-pong, paid for it himself, and then stood me coffee. One or two of the men would occasionally accept a cigarette, but never a drink of any kind. I thought: eleven years ago, almost on these very beaches, we were fighting their fathers and their brothers . . .

On Easter Day I went to High Mass in the tawdry little Baroque church. Or rather, I tried to: but there were such crowds that it was impossible even to reach the door. That night there was dancing in the house of Tonio's father, the ice-cream merchant. I have been to smarter parties. I have danced on better and more spacious floors. For the room was perhaps sixteen feet square and, when I entered it, already contained more than a dozen adults, five babies, an immense family bed, and about as many pictures of the Madonna as there are in the Uffizi. And there was the additional hazard of a hole in the floor that went straight through to the room below. But it was an evening that I shall always remember. Nor shall I forget Tonio's four dusky, black-eyed sisters, with each of whom I danced in turn. I shall never dance again.

On my last evening in Castelrovinato I gave a concert – if anything so informal deserves the name – in the Piazza. I sang all that I could remember of Rossini and Verdi and Puccini, then fell back upon English and French folk songs. It was not easy – without a piano, and without a copy of the words and music. But though I was sadly out of practice, and my Italian accent anything but convincing, nobody seemed to be in a critical mood.

When I came to leave Castelrovinato, where so much work was to have been done, I found that I had written nothing: nothing but this. But I have no regrets.

16
'Cacoethes Scribendi'

Always scribble, scribble, scribble! Eh! Mr Gibbon?

WILLIAM HENRY, DUKE OF GLOUCESTER

While in Meknès during my visit to Morocco in 1939 I had become fascinated by the figure of the bloodthirsty and sadistic tyrant Mulai Ismail (1646–1727), the ruins of whose gigantic palaces dominated the landscape; but the local bookseller could provide no biography of him, and indeed maintained that none existed. Back in England I discovered this to be untrue, and managed to get from Paris a recent 'popular' French life of him – apparently the only one to have been published in any language for the last two hundred years. Research in the London Library, however, of which I now became a life member, revealed that much contemporary material was available in accounts left by ambassadors, missionaries and escaped slaves, and in the innumerable scholarly volumes of Henri de Castries's *Sources inédites de l'histoire du Maroc.*[1] Before the year was out, war had virtually put a stop to agreeable but time-consuming foreign travel;[2] I was therefore free in much of the holidays, and of course in leisure moments at Eton, to do what I liked, and my thoughts turned to making an attempt to write a biography of this Moroccan monster.

The Haileybury Buildings, which I had written and published privately in 1936, had been no more than an extended essay, and various friends had corrected the more outrageous grammatical errors in it. But I realised that I now needed more substantial help and criticism; that I had to learn a craft. In 1942, therefore, when

[1] Paul Geuthner, Paris, 1905 etc.
[2] Actually I visited Paris, as a civilian, and without any difficulty, in April 1940. I wanted to see how conditions compared with those during the First World War. I was lucky to have got out just in time.

Mulai Ismail

I had finished *Black Sunrise* (as I entitled my book), I sent the typescript to my former colleague at Haileybury, Lionel Gough, who gallantly worked through it word by word, marking clichés, unattached participles, mixed metaphors, pointless inversions, illogicalities, superfluous adjectives, careless punctuation, polysyllabic humour and jargon. He easily persuaded me to prune unnecessary footnotes by showing me a grotesque example in a school edition of the Four Gospels.[3]

Much of *Black Sunrise* was written at Bridestowe, in Devon, where I was frequently the guest in wartime holidays of my friend

[3] 'Now there was much grass in the place' (John vi, 10); *footnote*: 'From this we conclude that it was probably a very beautiful spot.'

of Haileybury days, Arthur Harrison[4] – he had moved his preparatory school there from Kent for greater safety. I wrote mostly in the greenhouse, whose sub-tropical warmth and exotic plants helped me to imagine myself back in Morocco. I had no literary agent, so I sent my book to four or five publishers, all of whom rejected it. I was naturally disappointed, but I had by now an irresistible urge to write and immediately started to work on a further North African subject – a biography of Abd el-Kader, the Algerian patriot who in the 1840s had heroically resisted the invasion of his country by the French. When it was half written, I began to wonder whether I was engaged on another fool's errand; I therefore submitted it in its incomplete state to Methuen, who to my astonishment immediately offered me a contract. Later I learned that the reader who had recommended its acceptance was Captain Cyril Falls, one of the most distinguished military historians of the day. Why I – most pacific of men – wanted to write about a long military campaign remains a mystery to me.

Desert Hawk, as I called the book, appeared in January 1947, and I frankly admit that opening the first copy of it was one of the most exciting moments of my life. About half a dozen more books followed while I was still at Eton, but it was not until I was over sixty, after I had retired to the greater leisure of the Watts Gallery at Compton, that I was able to produce a further twenty or so. Writing is certainly laborious; but I have never found it a chore, and it has given me untold satisfaction.

After *Desert Hawk* was off my hands I returned to *Black Sunrise*, some of whose major faults were now apparent to me; so I rewrote a good deal of it, and it was published – also by Methuen – in 1951. It achieved a mild and quite unexpected *succès de scandale* when *Reveille* gave it their front page, gigantically captioned: FATHERED 40 SONS IN 3 MONTHS. 'The Emperor leaned forward. His wicked eyes, bright with delight, watched the victim as the torturers set about their task . . .' By skilful selection and some wild distortion, the author of the article managed to convey the impression that the book was what is described as 'curious' in booksellers' catalogues. A thousand copies were sold almost overnight; but I fear that the purchasers

---

[4] See *M.S.L.*, *passim*. His wife Mary ('Muffet') is one of those close friends of very long standing who have somehow or other escaped mention.

must have felt as sadly swindled when they came to read it as did all those North-Country sheep-farmers who bought copies of Ruskin's *Notes on the Construction of Sheepfolds*.[5]

Mercifully my mother, who abandoned reading the book after a slave had been sawn in two, did not see this review; nor, I feel sure, did Queen Mary, to whom my Aunt Mabel Hunt had rashly given a copy for Christmas. One of her ladies-in-waiting reported that it was being read aloud to Her Majesty in the evenings, but I cannot imagine that she got very far with it. I am not proud of either of these books today, and there is much to be said for the advice to would-be authors that they should write for the first five years for their waste-paper baskets.

My method of work, even when attacking a subject of which I know virtually nothing, is to put pen to paper almost at once, though fully aware that almost all of what I write will subsequently have to be scrapped. I simply cannot study for six months, making nothing but copious notes and synopses. For example, when asked some years later by Lord Zuckerman to do a book on the London Zoo for its sesquicentennial, I wrote snippets as I browsed through the pages of a dozen 'popular' works with titles such as *Wonders of Animal Life* and *Happy Days at the Zoo*, only then proceeding to serious study. I also make much use of a technique that an artist would call 'peinture par touches', waking at five in the morning full of little ideas which surface spontaneously and have to be instantly jotted down on a pad beside my bed and then added later, like baubles on a Christmas tree, in an appropriate place in the text. This I have found particularly useful in these two autobiographical volumes, when something suddenly recalls a long-forgotten happening.

Though I could use the Green Line bus to London for writing a broadcast talk, for more serious work I need to be alone in my room, with reference books to hand and a general chaos prevailing. What I find unbearable is the presence of somebody who *might* be going to ask a question that requires an answer. Later, when I had discovered the indescribable pleasure of cats, I liked to have one silently around. There is, however, a snag here

[5] 1851 – a plea for a united Protestant front and an attack on the dogma of the Roman Catholic Church.

Wilfrid Blunt's Writing-Table at Compton
Oil painting by Oliver Bevan, 1982
The corner at which the author writes is further to the left
and is not included in the picture. The chaos has not diminished.

We are taught in childhood that THE CAT IS ON THE MAT. He isn't: to enjoy the warmth from my Anglepoise lamp he always prefers the sheet of paper I am trying to write on. I also like a background of non-vocal music – preferably something orchestral, meandering, romantic, unfamiliar and interminable: any good fat Bruckner symphony serves the purpose perfectly. I write, and rewrite, and re-rewrite – remembering Sheridan's salutary warning:

> You write with ease, to show your breeding,
> But easy writing's vile hard reading.[6]

I always use a ball-point pen, and quarto-sized paper – never what used to be called foolscap, and which still reminds me of exams at Marlborough.

Almost all my non-fictional books are what the French describe as *ouvrages de vulgarisation* and the English, more kindly, as 'popular'. I try very hard to avoid factual errors; but, unlike my two brothers, I constitutionally lack the true scholar's approach. I write for the general reader (as I sometimes make clear in a foreword), take it as a compliment if he is entertained, and generously forgive the criticisms of those scholars and pedants who, deploring the absence of weighty erudition, accuse me of failing to achieve what I never had the faintest intention of attempting.

In fact, in all of the fields into which I, improperly qualified, have rashly strayed, alone one or two British musicologists have shown a 'closed shop' kind of hostility. By opening my life of Mendelssohn with Alfred Bacharach's warning clerihew,

> The art of biography
> Is different from musicography.
> Musicography is about 'cellos
> But biography is about fellows.

I thought I had made my approach plain. But apparently I had not, and I had made matters worse by suggesting that many musicologists, when allegedly addressing the layman, were quite unaware that they had lost all touch with their audience. When writing about the London Zoo I faced a different hazard: the

[6] *Clio's Protest*, i, 55.

Colchicums: *quick study on grey paper by the author, 1947, showing two different shapes of petals.*

authorities seemed terrified of even their forty-year-old dirty linen being washed in public. It was the botanists who proved the most generous, understanding, and helpful of all.

The merest fluke – a chance meeting at Kew in 1946 with John Gilmour, the botanical editor of Collins's 'New Naturalist' series – led to my being invited to write a book which was to become a standard work of reference: *The Art of Botanical Illustration*. I had no qualifications whatever for undertaking it beyond a fondness for flowers, and an art training; I hardly knew a style from a stamen. But I was on the lookout for a new theme, and had not Ruskin himself said that the best way to get to know a subject was to write a book on it? Somehow or other, I bluffed my way through a rather tricky catechism by the editors, and the contract was signed. I also made some indifferent flower drawings in order the better to appreciate the problems botanical artists have to face.

Over the research for the book I received much help from that brilliant botanist (Professor) William T. Stearn, and from my

Campanula latifolia: *watercolour by the author, 1947*

picture researcher, Joan Ivimy. I also approached Dr Agnes Arber, the rather formidable world authority on herbals, asking if I might come to Cambridge to see her. I received a chilly reply, addressed to 'Miss Winifred Blunt', grudgingly offering me a few minutes of her valuable time. I replied accepting, and pointed out that I was in fact 'Wilfrid' and not 'Winifred'. A cordial letter came back by return: 'I am *so* thankful. I thought you were yet another of those "herby women"!' Thus I came to receive VIP treatment and an invaluable three-hour discussion with her.

My research, though it also involved visits to Germany, France, Italy and the Netherlands, was mainly carried out in English public and private libraries and institutions, most especially at Kew, which was so conveniently accessible in the holidays. At that time the library there was crowded into two or three rooms of a handsome eighteenth-century building whose shelves might have been expected to afford shelter to the humanities rather than to science. But the tempo of those who worked there was, I found, that of the anthill rather than of the cloister, for there was the perpetual scurry of feet of those who came and went between the library and the herbarium proper – a succession of vast echoing Victorian prisons stretching away behind the Georgian façade towards the mud-banks of the Thames.

To flower-lovers, as opposed to botanists, a herbarium is one of the most depressing places in the world, for it is no other than a botanical cemetery where ten million vegetable dead await Judgement Day in their browned paper shrouds. As I surveyed its hundred cells, each complete with its imprisoned botanist and its sheaves of plant-folders, I found it almost possible to believe the old story of the botanist who, straying one day by chance among the lilies of the field, failed to recognise in the common daisy the familiar *Bellis perennis* L. of his *hortus siccus*. But the *genus* Botanist was – indeed always is – kindness itself: always ready to interrupt his labours to show me where to find what must to him have seemed no more than a pretty picture-book of flowers, a work long since devoid of all scientific value.

These men were kind, charming, but remote as Chinese. I would often go for lunch to a small tea-place on Kew Green, decorated excruciatingly in orange and magenta and much frequented by the botanists; and, since I ate alone, their talk

Queen Mary with the author
at the Flower Books Exhibition, National Book League, 1950

entwined itself around my tepid sausages and mash. I can recollect two men disputing, for a full hour, the most suitable kind of watercress to introduce into Trinidad – disputing it with the fervour of theologians at variance over a dogma of the Church, or schoolmasters in disagreement about an umpire's decision in a housematch. I suppose the truth is no more than this: that after a time we all grow parochial, and therefore blind to our own professional absurdities, while we rarely come close enough to another profession to observe and take warning from theirs.

The Art of Botanical Illustration, published (at a guinea) in 1950, was awarded the Veitch Memorial Gold Medal by the Royal Horticultural Society. At the same time I organised an exhibition of Flower Books for the National Book League in London. Queen Mary, then in her eighty-fourth year, honoured it with a visit, and my mother greeted her on arrival with a bouquet of gentians, unluckily kicking a fire-bucket in the hall as she curtsied. (Badinage about 'kicking the bucket' etc. broke the ice.) At the same time, being aware of Her Majesty's amiable tendency to cadge, I presented her with a copy of my book, hoping thereby to forestall any raid on exhibits from my own collection. But she was in an acquisitive mood. 'And to whom do those two pretty paintings of heather [by Franz Bauer] belong?' 'To me, Ma'am.' 'They're *very* pretty.' 'Yes, Ma'am.' 'Very pretty *indeed* . . . ?' I did not yield; but seemingly she bore me no grudge, for in due course she sent me the signed photograph reproduced opposite, as well as a Christmas card.

It was Sacheverell Sitwell, an enthusiastic flower-lover, who in the mid-fifties introduced me to George Rainbird and suggested that I might contribute to a sumptuous folio, *Great Flower Books* (1956). This kind act was to lead to my having a handful of my later books superbly produced by George, to whom also I am eternally grateful. Many people refer disparagingly to 'coffee-table' books, assuming that anything richly illustrated will be poorly written. I have always tried, though others must decide with what degree of success, to take as much trouble as possible over both the text and the choice of relevant pictures to accompany it.

There was a further by-product of *The Art of Botanical Illustration* which, though it occurred only after I had left Eton, it seems appropriate to mention here. In 1962 I was invited by Roy Arthur Hunt, the Pittsburgh aluminium multi-millionaire, and his wife Rachel to become one of the three European advisers to the splendid Hunt Botanical Library, now incorporated in the Carnegie-Mellon University there. The Hunts had built and endowed it at a cost of $9m – I suppose the equivalent of about $100m today. No expense had been spared, and it was alleged (I did not have any opportunity to check it) that the taps of the basins in the ladies' powder-room were of solid 18-carat gold, and the armchair 'throne' to rival Solomon's.

The kindness and hospitality extended to me on my four visits to Pittsburgh were prodigious, and at the time I was quite unable to repay it. To put it frankly, I simply could not contribute anything at these highly scholarly conferences. Though my old friend John Gilmour, another of the European advisers, did everything possible to 'cover up' for me, my futility stuck out a mile. I had been invited only because Mrs Hunt had been enthusiastic about my book. She had come over to Compton to meet me (when – awful moment! – I had mistaken her modest and retiring husband for her chauffeur), had approved me, and asked that I be included in the team. Her slightest wish was a royal command.

There was one conspicuous gap in the Hunt Library's wonderful collection of flower paintings: it contained nothing by Franz Bauer – perhaps the greatest of all botanical draughtsmen. It so happened that, fifteen or twenty years earlier, I had spotted, tucked into an odd volume of Henry Andrews's *Coloured Engravings of Heaths* in a second-hand bookshop, those two Bauers which Queen Mary had coveted. I had bought the book, and the two pearls hidden within it, for a song, and later – almost by way of conscience money – I presented the paintings to the Hunt Library.

Life in Pittsburgh was at a pace that is, I presume, familiar to all businessmen; it was undeniably fascinating, but it was also killing. From a working breakfast at the University Club, where the three of us were put up, until our return there at midnight, we hardly surfaced from a ceaseless round of conferences and parties. I found myself – no doubt as the result of Mrs Hunt's propaganda – mysteriously lionised: one Pittsburgh dowager, when asked if she would like to meet me, replied that she would be thrilled to do so, but added, 'I'd no idea he was still alive.' Perhaps she had confused me with my far more distinguished kinsman, Wilfrid Scawen Blunt (b. 1840). Nonetheless it made me feel suddenly very old – *and* very bogus.

All I achieved for the Hunts was, I am sorry to have to confess, to organise and contribute an introduction to an edition of Walahfrid Strabo's famous *Hortulus*, for which Raef Payne provided a felicitous English translation. An elaborate project for establishing at the Library a reference collection of photographs of plant drawings in the principal extant manuscript herbals and florilegia was politely scrutinised and no less politely shelved. I still think it was rather a good idea.

Finding myself on each visit already in America at no cost to myself, I seized the opportunity to see something more of the States. Thus I came to visit New York, Washington, Philadelphia and Boston and – most memorably – several cities in California. In Los Angeles I was the guest of Dr Mildred Mathias, Director of the Botanic Gardens, who drove me for a whole unforgettable day through the Mojave Desert and also arranged for me to give several lectures. Now, in gratitude for so much undeserved kindness, I try to make American visitors to Compton particularly welcome.

I flew home from California 'over the Pole' (in fact, you go nowhere near either of them). My neighbour in the plane, who arrived breathless and in tatters at the very last moment, proved to be an Englishman who for a few days had captured the headlines in all the papers as 'The Man in the Crate'. He had emigrated to Australia, found he hated the place and wanted to return to England. But he was penniless. He had therefore got a friend to nail him up in a crate labelled for London and put him on a plane. It disgorged him in Cairo, left him (more or less upside down) on the runway for three days, and then packed him off – to Los Angeles and a week in hospital. 'My great mistake', he said sadly, 'was not having been labelled "THIS WAY UP WITH CARE".'

17
Further Books and Travels

It was thanks to an introduction from old Lady Gowrie, wife of the Governor of Windsor Castle, that I came to know Captain Neil McEacharn, and was thus on several occasions a guest at his villa on Lake Maggiore.

Neil was an enormously wealthy Scot whose grandfather had made a fortune in Australian gold mines. In 1930, while on his way from Venice to London, he had noticed by chance in *The Times* an advertisement of a property for sale on Lake Maggiore. For the past two years he had been thinking of making a garden in Italy; when, therefore, his train reached Verbania-Pallanza he jumped out, saw the place, and bought it as casually as I might purchase a packet of cigarettes. Within twenty-five years, and in spite of the war and the necessity later of dispensing with the services of fifty of his hundred gardeners, he had extended and converted the grounds of the Villa Taranto into the finest botanic garden in Italy.[1]

He was one of the kindest, simplest, most genuine, most generous men I have ever known; his shyness was almost pathological. He had been twice a widower when I first met him, and his second wife, Emma, was a first cousin of Queen Wilhelmina of the Netherlands. ('I found it so difficult,' he said, 'when she told me to call her "Wilhelmina".') But he was wholly without class-consciousness. Consequently, when one stayed in his hospitable, comfortable but rather pretentious house – it had been built in 1875 in Belgian-baronial style, and Neil himself referred to it as a 'horror' – one might find as fellow guests a princess or two, a duke who owned a large part of Scotland, and a couple of working gardeners who had, one almost felt, hung up their spades in the hall. All were made equally welcome, and talk

[1] See Neil McEacharn, *The Villa Taranto: A Scotsman's Garden in Italy*, Country Life, 1954.

(over the champagne) was more likely to be of magnolias than of grouse moors.

On one occasion the Athlones were also guests at the Villa, and Neil told me of his acute embarrassment when Lord Athlone had asked him to tell him frankly whether it was true that people were saying that his sister (Queen Mary) cadged things when she visited other people's houses. Athlone was then old and getting rather senile, so Neil felt that a white lie was in order. I, too, had a difficult moment when Princess Alice learned that I had no dinner-jacket. 'When *I* was a gal, no Englishman ever went abroad without one! But Alge [pronounced 'Algy'] will be pleased; he hates having to dress now.'

In fact, I had many difficult moments. Athlone, who had known my mother when they were young, got it firmly into his head that they had been brought up together. Nor were meals easy when, as several times happened, I found myself placed beside him. His memory (and how I now sympathise with him!) frequently failed him, and this made him angry, not with himself – which is more usual – but with the person whom he was addressing:

When I was in . . . in . . . What's the name of that big place?'

'Rome, sir?'

'No – not *Rome!*'

'Paris?'

'No – NOT PARIS, you fool! . . . LONDON!'

Did he actually say, 'You fool'? I would not swear to it; but it was clearly implied, and I could see that Princess Alice was embarrassed for him. Nor could the servants ever do anything right. It was sad, for he was obviously very nice – and only in his seventies.

Since the death of his second wife, Neil had come wholly to rely on the support of 'Il Capitano' (I forget his name) – an Italian who acted as his buffer against the outside world. Neil's Italian was even worse than mine, and in the Capitano's absence I one day found myself obliged to act as translator and intermediary when the local mayor visited him on a matter of business. Without his Capitano he was helpless as would Quickswood have been without Tucker.

On his death Neil bequeathed his house and garden to the

Italian Government, to become the 'Kew Gardens' of Italy, and he had told me why he was doing this. One day in the thirties he had found himself inexplicably summoned to Rome by Mussolini, who immediately began to cross-examine him about his family. How was his sister? Was his aunt still alive? The mystery was soon solved: Mussolini had been having English lessons from the old family nurse, and since Neil and his relations had often provided the material for conversation, his curiosity had been aroused. It was thanks to the Duce's personal orders that throughout the war the untenanted Villa Taranto's garden had been looked after and the house left untouched; and Neil, who cared nothing for politics, never found the least embarrassment in speaking later of his gratitude to the monster for this particular kindness.[2]

The year 1950 was an exceptionally productive one for me, for besides *The Art of Botanical Illustration* and the organisation of the National Book League exhibition, there had also appeared, after four years of gestation, my King Penguin, *Tulipomania*. To celebrate their recent publications the firm threw a highly alcoholic party in the garden of its house in Bedford Square, towards the end of which I found myself in one-sided conversation with a very tiny guest in tails. The reason both for his small size and his lack of small-talk gradually dawned on me: my companion was one of a handful of penguins, hired for the evening, and released at what people call the 'psychological moment'.

I suddenly recall a further by-product of my botanical involvement that I should have mentioned earlier – an invitation to take over the gardening column in the *Sunday Times*. It was in many ways a pleasant job; for one could write a frisky article on, say, 'Haughty-culture' and then safely go on a holiday abroad, whereas the music critic had to attend a concert and then rush home (usually before the end) to do his piece. But it provoked a lot of correspondence from readers who only wanted to be told

[2] It was both unnerving and curiously touching when Winifred Wagner, interviewed in her last years, confessed that if Hitler were to walk through the door now she could not help being pleased to see him – because although she now *knew* all the terrible things he had done, or caused to be done, she had never herself *seen* him being anything but a dear, friendly man.

whether, for example, they were over- or under-watering their wilting cyclamens – and I never knew the answer. Kenneth Rose, who was living with us at Baldwin's Shore at the time, has reminded me of the innumerable packets of wilting flowers, diseased bulbs, and other miscellaneous and often moribund vegetable matter which arrived almost daily on my breakfast table for identification or advice. I was not altogether sorry when, after about eighteen months, my contract was terminated – mainly, I believe, to provide a job for a friend of Lady Kemsley. I have discussed, in my *Of Flowers and a Village*, the futility of repeating in an ephemeral article practical material readily available in dozens of standard gardening books. I wanted to write about how the first dahlia reached our shores, not on how to nurse it through an English winter.

One article, on tulips, involved me in a moment of embarrassment. I had praised in exaggerated terms the brilliant red *Tulipa fosterana*, urging readers to buy a dozen, a hundred, even a thousand bulbs if they could afford it. I myself had half a dozen in my cat-run at the Drawing Schools, and one of them had not come up. I was therefore taken aback when the secretary of a ladies' gardening club wrote to ask if she might bring two coachloads of her members to see my garden next spring when my tulips would be at the height of their glory.

Another article, however, which was exceptionally accorded the centre page and a photograph in the issue of 23 July 1950, bore unexpected fruit. It dealt with what were then known as the Woodland and the Valley Gardens in Windsor Great Park, the recent creations of Eric Savill, the Deputy Ranger, and concluded:

> His Majesty the King, who had shown a keen interest in Mr Savill's work, once expressed the hope that the Woodland Gardens would be known as the Savill Gardens. Only the modesty of their creator has prevented the suggestion from becoming a reality. But one day, perhaps, when woodland and valley gardens join hands to form almost a mile and a half of green swards and flowering glades, the Savill Gardens will be found to be a fitting name by which to commemorate an enterprise of genius and an act of faith.

A week later an order came from the Palace that in future the

Anthony Caesar, Istanbul, April 1952

gardens would be called by the name they still bear. I received no thanks from Savill – merely a reproach for one very small criticism I had made, namely that formal summer bedding seemed to me out of place in a garden that had no house attached to it.

Before I left Eton I wrote several other books, including *Pietro's Pilgrimage* (about a Roman patrician, Pietro Della Valle, who travelled extensively in the Near and Middle East from 1614 to 1626), and *Sebastiano* (the journey made by an unorthodox young Bolognese priest to Paris and back in the 1660s). Both these books, which were published by James Barrie, involved visits to the Continent, though for the time being I followed Pietro (with Anthony Caesar) no further than Istanbul. But writing about him strengthened my determination to get at least as far as Iran and Afghanistan before I was too old for rough travel. In 1956, therefore, I obtained four months' leave of absence and set out on the journey which I have described in *A Persian Spring*, a travelogue written in diary form and also published by James Barrie.

While I was away, my work was taken over by a very old friend, Maurice Percival, who was in his day art master at (among other places) Malvern, Harrow and Downside. He was such a success at Eton that I think the news of my death at the hands of an Afghan brigand – a very real possibility – would almost have been welcomed by some of my colleagues. I could, had I space, write at length about Maurice, whose life was something of a tragedy: he was always taking jobs, throwing them up, and then bitterly regretting having done so. His final folly – he said it himself – was to enter a religious house in the neighbourhood of Seville (he was an ardent Roman Catholic), where the austerity of the life eventually killed him. He had lost an arm in childhood – we never knew how; but he managed so skilfully that he could cope with almost anything except a boiled egg.

I am a timid traveller. I cannot claim to have been an explorer, and have never even plucked up the courage to go to the Costa Brava or to Butlin's. Admittedly one of my godfathers was Captain Scott's brother-in-law, but that was not enough to inspire me to join a polar expedition. However, in Afghanistan I

Market at Herat, Afghanistan, 1956

was a tourist in a land not yet open to tourism, and travelling alone there at the age of fifty-five did involve a slight element of risk. In Herat, with a native population of about 60,000, I had found only two resident Europeans: a German doctor (murdered ten days after I left) and his pregnant second wife – a recent replacement of his first, who had been killed on her initial flight with Afghan Airways.

In Iran I received great kindness from Dr and Mrs Coleman, then medical missionaries in Shiraz, who were later to be imprisoned after the overthrow of the Shah, and from old Bishop Thompson, Bishop in Iran, whose daughter was wounded and grandson murdered about the same time. On my way home I was arrested at Tortona, in Syria – on, as it happened, the Fourth of June – for having strayed unwittingly into a military zone without the necessary permit, held in prison for some hours, and then expelled from the country. I will quote from my entry for that day since it contains a thumbnail sketch of the way in which the birthday of King George III was celebrated at Eton before hooliganism put a stop to the fireworks:

Stuck in a flooded river in Afghanistan

As I lie in my not uncomfortable bed in the Hôtel Ambassadeur [at Aleppo], I think of Eton.

It will be almost lunch-time here when the first fine cars begin to park themselves on the giant NO PARKING sign beneath my windows at Baldwin's Shore. Closing my eyes, I seem to see those fresh, eager, overscrubbed Lower Boys, being worn (as Dylan Thomas might have said) by large, overpriced carnations, and waiting so hopefully by Barnes Pool Bridge for the arrival of tardy parents. Older boys, Fourth-wise boys, remembering the long hours that lie ahead, have fixed a later rendezvous. And though I am more than two thousand miles away, I think I hear a bright, brittle, upper-class voice saying: 'Ronnie dear, tell John to tell Angela that the caviare is in the boot of the Bentley.'

In Upper School, where it is rather uncomfortable and probably very hot, a Colleger in knee-breeches is now reciting Euclid in Greek. Although it has not understood much, the audience claps loyally and wonders how the match is going on Upper Club. I see myself, in imagination, at the Drawing Schools, talking to a parent whom I cannot place, about the water-colours of her son that I cannot remember. Someone is saying that the boys' work is too modern, and someone else is saying that it is too old-fashioned. A large Leanderthal man with a rather bushy moustache is asking why there aren't any pictures of Henley.

229

Fireworks: Fourth of June

It is one o'clock. In the Hind's Head and the Hôtel de Paris, corks are popping. Beside the river, under shady elms, the great luncheon cornucopias burst open to disgorge their treasures of salmon and strawberry. A happy satiety descends.

But how to bridge the broad gulf that stretches till night turns blue and the first golden rocket may cleave the darkening sky? There is always the cricket, sprawling on; and oh, how deck-chairs ease the aching feet! Green and white, green and white. 'Diana! How lovely! You know Michael? And Alistair? And this is Tom's sister. Where's Arthur?'

At last, a movement towards the river-bank, where the pale slim boats glide softly by and straw hats are wreathed with flowers. A crew is standing, swaying crazily, 'They'll go in! They're going in! THEY'RE IN!'

It is half past eleven; I can stay awake no longer. But in the night I stir. Now the rockets must be rising, to tumble in their golden rain. One! One, two! One, two, three! one, two, three, FOUR!! 'Sit down! SIT DOWN, CAN'T YOU!' 'Toby, what the devil have you done with the whisky?'

But before Toby can find the whisky, I shall have fallen asleep again.

So I mused, little guessing what tribulations the day had in store for me . . .

Through the kindness of George Lyttelton I became Vice-President, and in due course President, of the Eton Literary Society, thus meeting a great many of the most illustrious writers of the forties and fifties. It was interesting to observe that the more distinguished the speaker, the less trouble he had usually taken to prepare his talk – and yet, of course, the bigger the audience. Somerset Maugham, for example, after arriving half-an-hour late, merely read a ten-minute trifle he had broadcast the evening before. (It was the only time I ever met him, but I had once sent him – via my brother Anthony – a snapshot of a Paris cinema with its current attraction advertised in gigantic letters over the entrance as OF HUMAN BANDAGE.) And then there is the gift of holding an audience. The dreariest lecture I ever heard in my life was by Sir Arthur Evans, at Haileybury, on 'Crete'; the most lively, one at Eton on 'Precious Stones', by a man whose name I cannot recall, and to which I was unwillingly dragged. He scored his greatest success by circulating a priceless 'emerald' (probably a bit of green glass) among the audience, and, when it vanished, accused Lady Elliott of having pocketed it.

18

Retiring from Eton

At Eton in my day the retiring age, which had previously been fifty-seven, was raised to sixty, and is I believe in certain cases now extended to sixty-five. For some masters this is more than thirty years too late; for others, another decade would still be profitable to both teacher and taught.

In the thirties, housemasters, by keeping a watchful eye on the feeding of their boys, could count on putting by about a thousand a year, at that time a substantial sum which enabled them to retire in comfort – and most of them preferred to do this as soon as they gave up their houses. Then centralised financial administration was introduced, and housemasters without private means were obliged to stay on, as teachers only, until they could draw the full pension which, in the words of a sybaritic colleague, was 'barely enough to keep a man in cigars'.

Beaks with hobbies found retirement enjoyable and fulfilling. Some who had none – and this was so at Haileybury too – continued to haunt the place, battening on gossip and intrigue: at Eton 'Bloody Bill' was of course one of them. Others fought boredom by taking on relatively undemanding jobs such as setting or correcting School Certificate papers, coaching, or part-time teaching at a prep school. (I suddenly recall the sad story of a Haileybury housemaster without an interest in the world, who retired to darkest Dorset with his admirable wife, a keen gardener. All her efforts to involve him in the garden seemed to have failed; but one day, to her great satisfaction, she saw him heading, fork in hand, for the herbaceous border. An hour later he returned with a barrowful of her finest delphiniums. 'Great big whoppers!' he cried triumphantly. 'But I got them out in the end!' It took her all her self-control, she told me, to look on in silence as he carted them off to the bonfire. However, her policy paid dividends, and she gradually trained him to differentiate between a delphinium and a sow-thistle.)

In 1959, when I had only two more years to run at Eton, I began to keep my ears and eyes open for a suitable part-time job such as looking after a National Trust house. But those in need of a curator seemed mostly to be miles from anywhere – *and* in the Midlands or the North of England. The accommodation offered was often a flat at the top of the building, manufactured out of an agglomeration of servants' bedrooms and – as at Kenwood – approached by eighty or ninety stone stairs. Further, the retirement age was usually sixty-five, which would soon involve another upheaval. Although there was no immediate hurry, as the months passed I would have to become less choosy, till finally I would be obliged to accept gratefully any straw that was offered me.

Hardly had I begun my preliminary search when my brother Anthony rang up: Rowland Alston, Curator of the Watts Gallery[1] at Compton ever since I had succeeded him at Haileybury in 1923, had died, and the post was vacant; but Anthony hardly imagined I could want to spend the rest of my life 'among those dreadful pictures'. Unlike our kinsman, Wilfrid Scawen Blunt, who after sitting to Watts said he would rather have been painted by him than by Rembrandt, I could not but agree with Anthony: Watts was not my favourite artist. But in every other respect it was the ideal job, as I discovered when in due course Raef Payne drove me over to Compton, for the recollections of my visit there more than thirty years earlier had become vague indeed.

Compton is near Guildford: within easy reach of my mother (still living at Ham), of my friends at Eton, and of London. Sir Hugh Casson later wrote of the Gallery, 'Buried in foliage, its roof pulled over its ears, it looks like an abandoned gipsy encampment. Inside it is enchanting – sunny, empty, casual, with huge Watts pictures dozing on the walls above a sleeping cat.' The Curator's house, quite a substantial building, adjoined the Gallery and was virtually a bungalow, which appealed to me; and

[1] There is no space here to discuss the life and works of George Frederic Watts, OM, RA (1817–1904), who built a house, Limnerslease, in Compton in 1891 and a Gallery in 1903, or of Mary Watts (1849–1938), the artist's second wife, who designed and built the mortuary chapel and started the Watts Pottery. My biography of Watts, *England's Michelangelo*, was published by Hamish Hamilton in 1975, but is now out of print.

it had something that I had always longed for – a loggia where I could write in summer. The situation, garden and grounds were indeed delightful, and there were two acres of rhododendron-free woodland as well. Admittedly it was 'commuter-belt', but at least it was not the sandy-military Bisley Surrey that I so dislike.

Above all, there was no retiring age. Further, the job made no pretence of being more than half-time, the intention being that it would allow a creative artist or author to continue pursuing his own work. And not, it appeared, really even *half*-time. 'What', I asked old Bill Westbury, the custodian, 'did the late curator do?' 'I don't rightly know, sir.' 'I suppose he spent a good deal of time in the Gallery?' 'Oh no, sir; he hardly ever came into the Gallery.' Then, after a pause, he added, 'I think he used to order the coke for the central heating.' It should in all fairness be added that Alston, for the last years of his life, had been a very sick man (leukaemia), who earlier had done much for the Gallery. He was an accomplished ornithological and landscape artist and a keen countryman, much loved locally. He left behind him at Compton a rich legend of charm, vagueness and unpunctuality; of an icy sitting-room in winter, and a precocious parrot; and of a battered

The Watts Gallery: *watercolour by the author, 1961. The Curator's house is on the right.*

motor-bike and even more derelict 'banger'. His handwriting was illegible, and he adored fishing.

But there was one serious snag. On consulting the *Museum Journal*, Anthony told me that applications had had to be in by the middle of February, and it was now the end of March. He knew, however, that the post had not been filled, because he had just been asked by one of the Trustees whether he could suggest a suitable candidate. So I wrote at once, and by stages found myself on a short-list of three. In May we were summoned to the National Portrait Gallery and imprisoned in separate cells in the basement to be interviewed in turn. The chairman, Lawrence Powell, a retired architect with something of Mones's old-world charm, cross-examined me kindly, but I knew that the really dangerous question was still to come: 'I imagine, Mr Blunt, that at Eton you have often had occasion to talk to your pupils about Watts?' It seemed the moment for (almost) total truth. 'To be honest,' I said, 'I can't remember ever having mentioned his name except in connection with his *Sir Galahad* in the School Chapel.' I did not add that I had chiefly stressed its mawkishness. There was a sinister silence, and when I had left the room I was so certain that I had failed that I did not give the matter another thought. Next morning, on my breakfast table, was a letter offering me the job.

I was even more amazed when I later learned that my two rivals had been a very old friend of Alston's who had virtually promised him the succession that was of course not in his gift, and a well-known authority on nineteenth-century English painting. After I had taken up my new position a visitor to the Gallery, also perhaps perplexed, asked me how I had come to be its Curator. 'Perhaps', she added, 'you are an *ancestor* of Mr Watts?' That fearful old battle-axe Flora Russell (Bertrand Russell's cousin) was – as always – actively offensive, suggesting that I 'must have known Mr Watts very intimately'.

'But, Miss Russell, Watts *died* in 1904!'

'Well – and what of that?'

I had probably owed my appointment at Eton and at the Watts Gallery largely to the reputation in the art world of my brother Anthony.

By a lucky chance I was able to carry *Sir Galahad* away with me

Sir Galahad *(Fogg Art Museum, Cambridge, Massachusetts):*
Watts's first version, exhibited at the Royal Academy in 1862.
The Eton version was painted in 1897.

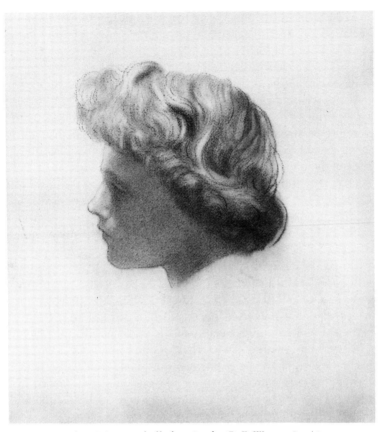

Arthur Prinsep: *chalk drawing by G. F. Watts 1855/6,*
used by the artist for his paintings of Sir Galahad.

to Compton on indefinite loan. True, I was far from devoted to
the picture, but I thought the gesture would make a good
impression on my Trustees. The picture had been taken down and
put into store at Eton in 1956, when the Chapel was closed for
three years while the roof was being reconstructed, and Elliott,
who hated the sight of this 'verray parfit gentil knight', jumped at
my suggestion. He always stoutly maintained, in the face of
irrefutable evidence to the contrary, that Ellen Terry had served
as the model, who was in fact the fifteen-year-old Arthur Prinsep,
subsequently a lieutenant general in the Bengal Lancers. About
ten years later, when Elliott was no longer Provost and a greater

interest was being shown in Victorian painting, *Sir Galahad* was reclaimed by the College and hung, not on the walls of the Chapel itself but, more appropriately, in the ante-chapel.

There is a rapturous account in the *Eton College Chronicle* (17 June 1897) of the reception accorded to the picture on its first appearance on the walls of the Chapel; so noble indeed was the conception of 'chivalrous, devoted and pure manhood' considered to be that another periodical assured its readers that Watts, at all events, could only have been an Old Etonian. As for the seemingly angelic Arthur (who, curiously enough, had been educated at Haileybury in the days when it housed the East India College) – he was, so his nephew informs me, a good deal less than perfect, having been prevented from reaching the very top in India by his passion for gambling and for the wives of junior officers.

Eton gave me a most friendly send-off at the end of the summer half. The Matron-in-College helped me to organise (i.e. organised) a farewell party at the Drawing Schools for masters, their wives, and the dames. Modesty forbids my quoting from an astonishing letter I received (sonnet enclosed) from a young Colleger I barely knew, saying that his one ambition was to model his life-style on mine. I trust he saw the light in time. I also sang at the end-of-half concert – 'Non più andrai' from *Figaro* and several *bergerettes*, my voice being no longer able to cope with more demanding pieces. At the close came, of course, the *Eton Boating Song*, with the 'swing, swing together' that set the whole audience – even the staidest beak – swaying from side to side. (There had, however, been in the forties a cleric, the Revd G. C. Stead, who always remained stiff as a ramrod throughout. 'I suppose,' a new boy once said to Grizel – 'I suppose he thought Jesus didn't swing.')

At Haileybury, Bonhote, in his end-of-term address to the school, had informed the boys that I was 'leaving to continue my missionary work at Eton' – a statement mistaken by many to mean that I was about to be ordained. At Eton it was not the custom for leaving masters to be speeded on their way in this fashion, but I record with pride that I was made an honorary member of the Old Etonian Association. I left with great regret and cherish many happy memories of my time there; and though not a rowing man I never hear 'Jolly Boating Weather' without a little pang of nostalgia.

So my thirty-six years of schoolmastering were over.

It chanced that I was at that very moment reading *The Grecians* by James Elroy Flecker, who at the age of twenty-three became, very briefly, a schoolmaster in Hampstead before taking the Golden Road to – Beirut (for he got no further). His father was headmaster of Dean Close School, Cheltenham, and he himself had been educated there and at Uppingham, so that his opinion of schoolmasters, however prejudiced, was at least based on inside knowledge. In 1907, after attending a service for schoolmasters in Dean Close School chapel, he had written the following:

> There, in a narrow space, were collected some two hundred head and assistant masters. A more tragic sight I have never seen . . . When I left the Chapel I nearly wept. Thank God one does not often see a congregation of schoolmasters. Those withered trees are usually surrounded by the fair and delectable shrubs of youth: they look ill in a forest by themselves. Usually, we see the usher's unromantic figure graced by the boys who flock round him; and to them he is so familiar and trite a thing that they pay no heed to his sagging trousers and rusty coat, to his surley [*sic*] manners and unkempt hair, to his unchanging cravat and rectangular boots. But when I saw that unearthly congregation of men who had failed, whose lips were hard, and their faces drawn and sallow, when I remarked the imbecile athletes who taught football, and puny scientists who explored the dark mystery of nature, the blighted and sapless scholars who taught Plato and Catullus by the page and hour, the little wry-bodied men in spectacles who trained their pupils in *King Lear* for the Cambridge Locals, I shuddered and felt faint; for I remembered that I, too, was one of these; I, too, was rusty – I effete – I growing old.

A yet more savage indictment of frustrated schoolmasters comes from the brilliant but vitriolic pen of Cyril Connolly:

> Ah, those Eton masters! I wish I could remember any of their names, for I was really sorry for them. What tragedies went on under their mortar-boards! Some of them were quite young, and one often got the impression that they were trying, inarticulately, to communicate; would have liked, in fact, to share in the rich creative life that already was centring round me. They used to teeter round my Baksts, and once I caught my housemaster sniffing at a very special bottle made up for me by Max of Delhez, and gingerly rubbing some on his poor old

pate. Worldlings, yet deprived of all wordly grace, of our rich sex-life how pathetically inquisitive! They are all there still, I suppose, and I often wonder, when I motor through Switzerland in summer, if one will not find a bunch of them spawning round some mouldy *arête*, in their Norfolk jackets, like eels in the Sargasso Sea.[2]

Were we really quite as bad as that? I hope, and believe, not; but even the more liberal-minded in our profession acquire by degrees the mark of the beast. A candid friend maintains that, even today and after only a few minutes' conversation with me, any observant stranger would – from a touch of pedantry, or impatience with stupidity, or a bullying tone of voice – spot that I had been a schoolmaster. As I have described in *Married to a Single Life*, my return to the Haileybury Common Room after a year's sabbatical leave had opened my eyes to much that I had not previously recognised as petty and absurd.

In the early forties I had indulged in a sudden orgy of writing sonnets, and when sorting papers recently I came upon a clutch of them. Several have already been quoted, but I think another might appropriately be included here. It must not be interpreted as thinly disguised autobiography, for on the whole my years as a schoolmaster – my spring at Haileybury and my summer at Eton – were very happy, and my even longer autumn at Compton was to prove a reward far beyond my deserts:

AN OLD SCHOOLMASTER RETIRES

For forty years those walls have been his prison,
But now his long, self-sentenced term is run.
He has thrown off his chains; he has arisen
To snatch a moment's warmth before the sun
Slopes down that grey decline the Dead call living,
The Living, death – that no-man's-land of age;
To breathe more liberal air, while yet forgiving
Fate that so long confined him to his cage.

But he has left too late the time for freeing
That tired body. Love is dead – and lust,
And, like the simulacrum of a being
That was a Pharaoh once, that painted crust
Of balanced molecules, deaf, dumb, unseeing,
He feels the light, one touch – and he is dust!

[2] 'Where Engels Fears to Tread'.

240

*John Christian's watercolour of the author, 1985,
surrounded by themes of some of his books*

19
My Brother Anthony: A Postscript

If I had the choice between betraying my friend and betraying my country, I hope to God I would have the guts to betray my country.

E. M. FORSTER

One late September day of 1979, when I was lunching with a friend in London, my host handed me a copy of *Private Eye*, and, pointing to an article in it, said, 'I don't suppose you've seen this; it doesn't actually come out until tomorrow.' Though what he showed me contained no positive accusation, the implication was clear enough: Anthony was as good as denounced as having been a Russian spy – the long-sought missing Fourth Man of the Burgess-Maclean-Philby affair.

The evidence seemed dangerously damning, but I simply did not believe it: the charge was preposterous. I had always considered us to be a fairly closely knit family; it was inconceivable that Christopher and I could have known *nothing*. I immediately rang up Anthony, who asked whether he might come over next morning to Compton to see me. Yes, he had, he confessed, been aware at the time of what was going on, but I did not gather from what he said – as he later assured me he had intended – that he himself had been *actively* involved. I asked no further; it was for *him* to tell me more if he wanted to. He looked worried, but I felt slightly relieved. It could well be that, from loyalty to friends, he had remained silent – only that – when he ought to have spoken out: that, for example, he had known about Guy Burgess but had said nothing. A few weeks later, however, the whole ghastly truth had been given to the world by the Prime Minister and an understandably gloating press. Anthony was denounced as a traitor.

I searched my memory, trying in vain to see whether, in the light of the disclosures, I could now identify anything (other than his close friendship with Guy) that should have forewarned me. I

Left to right: Christopher, the author, Anthony, 19 July 1981.
Taken at Ramsbury on the author's eightieth birthday.

have described in some detail the Russian trip we made together in the summer of 1935,[1] and so far as I can recall there was only one morning – that on which I visited a shoe-factory but he did not – when we were not together and in pursuit of architecture and art. I suppose he *could* have used it, or found some other opportunity, to establish contact with Russian Intelligence. He said later, referring to the way in which he had led a double life so successfully that not even those closest to him had suspected anything, 'You must admit I'm a very good actor.'[2] But contact with the Soviets could have been made just as easily in London. I still believe that it was not until the following winter that he was ensnared by the machinations of Guy Burgess[3] – who was not,

[1] See *M.S.L.*, pp. 295–6. In 1985 a former Haileybury pupil, who had been in our party and is now a Liberal peer, surprised me by saying that a frivolous little article which I published in *The Haileyburian* ('Caviar', 17 December 1935), debunking the propaganda to which we had been subjected, had opened his eyes and helped to save him from falling into the clutches of Communism. I had completely forgotten it. Bread cast upon the waters?

[2] A Cambridge friend commented on reading this: 'He *was* a good actor! I remember in about 1941 discussing with him how awful it would be if we found out that MI5 was investigating one of our Cambridge friends. We agreed that of course we would have to help the authorities, though in the case of somebody special it might be tempting to give them the chance to get away.'

[3] I had written 'the vile Burgess', but Anthony, to whom I showed a rough draft of much of this, begged me to remove the epithet. I have done so with reluctance. Guy seems to have exerted an almost hypnotic influence over people.

243

incidentally, in our party. I met Burgess four or five times in all, and although I do not deny that he was amusing company I disliked and mistrusted him from the first. For one thing, you could not believe a word he said. The photograph here reproduced of Anthony and myself bathing in the Starnbergersee was taken by him in July 1934. I never met either Philby or Maclean.

Anthony (right) and the author bathing in
the Starnbergersee, July 1934; photographed by Guy Burgess

After Anthony left Cambridge in 1936 I saw him all too rarely. He was busy and I was busy; he had his circle of friends and I had mine. I never visited him in the flat in Bentinck Street which he rented with Guy and two other friends in 1940, though I was not wholly unaware of the unconventional parties that took place there. At no time did we discuss political matters, which he knew did not interest me and which I believed no longer interested

244

Anthony as Elizabeth Barrett Browning: Trinity, Cambridge, c.1930

him.[4] Though after the war I went abroad with him and not infrequently had a meal or was his overnight guest at the Courtauld, for some reason which I have never quite understood he would not come to stay with me at Compton. I do not for a moment think this was due to any diminution of affection – not even to his intense dislike of Watts's pictures. I suspect that he preferred the domestic comfort that his innumerable married friends were only too eager to provide, for I know that, like myself and many other homosexuals, he found great support in the companionship of sympathetic and understanding women

For forty years Anthony had carried his dreadful secret ever with him, yet no member of the family had the faintest inkling that anything serious was amiss. He often, as my mother said,

[4] The already mentioned Cambridge friend commented after reading this: 'Don't you think in some way it was Anthony who was the ostrich and buried his head? Realising how he had become involved, and not, sadly, having the courage to leave and betray his friends, he somehow cut himself off from reality. I think that was why he never talked about politics.'

245

looked 'tired', and I accepted her verdict that this was the result of overwork. How thankful I now am that I suspected nothing. He was, however, never too busy (or, as I now realise, too much under strain) to make time to help me with a book I was writing, or to give me invariably sound advice when difficulties of one kind or another came my way. In many respects I grew to think of him as an elder rather than as a younger brother – almost as a guru – for I was a very slow developer and he had so soon far outpaced me. Whatever he did, and however much I may deplore what he did, I remain devoted and deeply grateful to the Anthony whom I knew for more than seventy years. That other Anthony I never knew and may never really understand.

He himself was never to tell either Christopher or me anything that was not given, with varying degrees of inaccuracy, to the world through the media, and though I have now read the 30,000-word memoir that he wrote, I found little meat in it.[5] I very much regret that he did not leave behind, to two brothers whom he knew he could implicitly trust, a confidential letter which would have helped us to understand. In the absence of any such document I can only speculate on how I *think* he may have argued to himself when he made his fatal decision to spy for the Soviets.

In the television interview he gave on 20 November 1979 Anthony offered his explanation of why, initially, he came to act as he did, and I am prepared to accept every word of the passage that I now quote from it. (I do, however, feel that he might have made it plainer that his decision had been taken, not merely to help to destroy Fascism, but also actively to promote a *positive* vision of Communism as the answer to social, economic and other troubles.)

> In the mid-1930s it seemed to me and to many of my contemporaries that the Communist party and Russia constituted the only firm bulwark against Fascism, since the Western democracies were taking an uncertain and compromising attitude towards Germany.

[5] This was valued for probate at the astonishing figure of £120,000. Anthony had said that he wanted my brother Christopher to have it and for it to remain in the family, but in the absence of any written bequest it passed to Anthony's friend John Gaskin, who presented it to the British Library with the proviso that it was not to be released for thirty years. Neither Christopher nor I would have dreamed of paying death duties of such magnitude on so dull a document, and doubtless he felt the same.

> I was persuaded by Guy Burgess that I could best serve the cause of anti-Fascism by joining him in his work for the Russians. This was a case of political conscience against loyalty to country: I chose conscience.
>
> When later I realised the true facts about Russia, I was prevented from taking any action by personal loyalty; I could not denounce my friends.

Nor, presumably, could he without jeopardising his own safety have got off the back of the tiger he had so recklessly mounted, though probably thereafter he did no more than the minimum necessary to protect his friends – and, of course, himself.

He now, he said, 'bitterly regretted' what he had done, admitting that he had been too immature to make that decision; but, as the press hastened to point out, he seemed to be sorry rather than ashamed. He has in consequence been accused by many people of arrogance, but I believe that to make such a charge is wholly to misunderstand his nature. I believe that he did not say he was ashamed of what he had done because he was not. He did what he honestly then believed to be in the best interests of his country (his contrasting of 'conscience' and 'loyalty' was an ill-judged one), and too late he saw that he had been both foolish and wrong: it was this that he now 'bitterly regretted'. What other motive could he have had? Not even the most venomous of his attackers has suggested that he might have acted for financial gain.

It has been alleged by some people that he must have derived a certain intellectual satisfaction from having contrived the perfect cover-up (his membership, in due course, of the Royal Household, his KCVO, etc.) for his espionage. I can well believe it. Undoubtedly he took great pleasure in artistic 'sleuthing', and I have more than once heard his little cry of triumph when he stumbled upon a clue that established the accuracy of his conjecture about a picture or the untenability of a rival's theory. He always loved a challenge. I also suspect that in his early days he was at times a victim of what I have elsewhere described as 'Blunt gullibility' – something from which my brother Christopher, who inherited my mother's Scots common sense, never suffered.

I make absolutely no attempt to condone treachery, only to try

Anthony, August 1962, photographed by his nephew Simon Blunt. When this sad photograph was taken, he may already have foreseen that he would soon be forced to make a full confession. The lowering of the right eye was caused by a mild attack of Bell's palsy in the 1950s.

to *understand*; and very probably I am the worst person to attempt this because, inevitably, I have a *parti pris*. But at least I was around at the time. It is almost impossible for anyone now under the age of sixty to realise the frustration with which he and many other intelligent young men with Marxist leanings looked on as the Fascist threat grew daily and our Government buried its head in the sand. The work that Anthony agreed to do, and persuaded others to do, for a foreign power, in this case the Soviet Union ('our gallant Allies' as Churchill was soon to call them), would therefore have seemed to him the act of a patriot. He feared the take-over of his country by a Fascist party and government which, perhaps in league with other Fascist governments in western Europe, could have threatened and finally suppressed Communism.

From a conventional point of view, the very worst conceivable consequence of the betrayal of State secrets would have been the conquest of Britain by her enemies. If these 'enemies' were the Russian Communists, and Britain had as a result also become Communist, Anthony would have regarded this as a much lesser evil than her becoming Fascist. What he must have had in mind, though, was an independent, undominated Britain acting in partnership with Russia. The destruction of Fascism was an urgent necessity, and the risk of becoming a neutered 'satellite' of the USSR seemed more remote and less depressing than it does today.

A country is ruled by a particular party or alignment of interests. If, as so often, these interests run counter to the welfare of the people, is it not (Anthony would have argued) the duty of a patriot to sabotage them by any means at his disposal? Thus Stauffenberg and his fellow conspirators, who attempted to assassinate Hitler, regarded themselves as German patriots, and posterity has honoured them as such.

One further thing needs saying. Anthony, as is now public knowledge, had for many years been a practising homosexual: something that I did not know for certain, though of course I had guessed it, until some time after the war, when we exchanged confidences – curiously enough at a reception at Windsor Castle. In the 1930s, indeed until 1968, male homosexuals were treated not only as criminals by British law, but also as degenerates by the

British public. The effect of such treatment on intelligent, idealistic young men was hardly likely to encourage uncritical devotion to the Britain they were growing up in; naturally they would see the established regime as inhuman and oppressive.

In Russia, on the other hand, the legal code drawn up by Lenin for the Soviets included no penalties for homosexual practices as such. It was Stalin, much later on, becoming almost paranoid about dissident or deviant minorities, who inserted anti-homosexual laws. Traditionally, and with reason, homosexuals have been reckoned a poor security risk because of the danger of blackmail, yet that danger exists only because of the penalty that exposure may involve. (As Jonathan Sumption wrote of the fall of Commander Trestrail, he lost his job at the precise moment when he was invulnerable to blackmail because his homosexuality had become public knowledge.) But that is marginal. No regime is wise to entrust its secrets to those it abuses. Loyalty does not, or should not, come unearned.

Patriotism is, in any case, not a clear-cut concept. Though Samuel Johnson, we know, dismissed it as 'the last refuge of a scoundrel', while Dryden wrote, 'Never was patriot yet, but was a fool', these condemnations must not be taken out of context. There is, however, a passage in Rose Macaulay's *The Towers of Trebizond* which, since Anthony very much thought of himself as a (Western-classical) European, seems to be relevant here:

> 'Everyone should love his country.' Halide looked handsome and firm and patriotic, and as if she would fight for Turkey to the death.
> I asked, 'Why should they? Is it a merit to love where one happens to live, or to have been born? Should one love Birmingham if one was born there? Or Leeds? Or Kent or Surrey?' For I had never been able to see why, except that I suppose it is better to love every place or person. 'Or Moscow?' I added, to vex Halide.
> . . . I went on musing about why it was thought better and higher to love one's country than one's county, or town, or village, or house. Perhaps because it was larger. But then it would be better still to love one's continent, and best of all to love one's planet.

The term 'patriot-fool' might well be applied to the 'my-country-right-or-wrong' jingoist. I think that in 1936 Anthony genuinely believed that his country was wrong, and that he was acting in her best interests by following his 'political conscience' in betraying her secrets to Russia. A patriotic traitor? Well, in the end he paid dearly for his temerity or folly or crime (whichever you choose to call it), though some people, still thirsting for blood, felt that he did not pay dearly enough. Indeed, it cannot be denied that he was extraordinarily lucky to have escaped a long prison sentence when, in 1964, he came to make a full confession and was granted immunity from prosecution. Incidentally, was he also promised *secrecy* during his lifetime? I do not know. Yet even if this promise had been made, he must surely have realised that in such a situation it was impossible to guarantee that no leakage might occur: too many people knew too much. He admitted that there would inevitably have been posthumous disclosure.

What I am truly thankful for is that the blow did not fall, as it might so well have done, in 1974, while our mother was still alive. She had been very badly shaken by the defection, and the revelations of the sex-life, of Guy: 'I simply *can't* understand how he could have had such a friend!' Worse still, it might have fallen even earlier, thus putting a stop to so much of Anthony's outstanding post-war contribution to the establishment in Britain of art history as a serious study. Nothing would thereby have been gained, for he had ceased to be of any use to the Soviet Union – and so much would have been lost.

Although work, as everyone knows, is the best antidote to troubles of all kinds, to most of those of us whose work is intellectual rather than physical there comes a moment when the necessary concentration is no longer possible. Yet such was Anthony's strange metabolism that, even during those terrible weeks, indeed months and even years, that followed upon his public exposure in November 1979, he was able to continue with his book on Pietro da Cortona and his guide to the Baroque buildings of Rome, and to sleep and eat normally. In fact, the greater the strain, the more (he told me) he felt the compulsion and had the ability to do this. At such times he also drank fairly heavily, preferring (like myself) spirits or plonk.

When I went to see him in London, where he was virtually a prisoner in his flat, I would find him perfectly ready to talk on non-controversial subjects and showing no outward sign of his inner tensions. His study had a balcony that overlooked a derelict area with, about a hundred yards away, a number of big blocks of flats. As I had so often done in the past, I was about to step outside; but he put his hand on my arm and, without a word, drew me away from the French window. It was only then I realised that he feared the possibility of an assassination attempt.

He must have had almost superhuman strength and courage to have survived, outwardly undaunted, the last twenty years of his life, and in particular the last three or four when, stripped of his honours,[6] he found himself exposed to vicious attack on every hand. A split personality? Only a psychiatrist can hazard a guess. A man – one who was able to be of particular service to him at that time – wrote that he regarded this as 'a great privilege. Anthony withstood humiliation, hounding by the media and denigration with dignity and fortitude, without complaint and, so far as I could judge, without bitterness . . . I shall remember him always with admiration for the time I knew him.'

Anthony died, suddenly and without pain, on the morning of 25 March 1983. During breakfast with his friend, John Gaskin, in their flat in Portsea Hall, he got up to find a number in the telephone directory, then suddenly fell dead. What more merciful end could one wish for? For some years past his state of health had been worrying, and he had undergone operations for cancer of the colon and for cataract. Then came angina, for which he had latterly been given stronger drugs to counteract an increasingly irregular heartbeat. He must have been aware that death could come at any time and, very possibly, without warning, but I do not think that when he had lunched with me only three days earlier, or even when he spoke to me on the telephone the very evening before his death, he had any idea that his time had run out.

I knew that he shared my views about the rationality of suicide if circumstances warranted it, for we had often discussed the subject together; but if he did ever consider taking his own life in 1979, I think I can understand why he decided against it. He had two important books unfinished, and any writer or artist will

---

[6] The wife of a member of the House of Lords – a man who was very much an Establishment figure – told my brother Christopher that her husband was 'furious' that Anthony's KCVO, earned by years of devoted work on the royal collections, had been taken away from him.

appreciate what this means. By 1983 both his books were virtually complete. Yet there was no suggestion whatever that anything other than natural causes was responsible for his death. It is, however, possible to die (and many Orientals do) by sheer will-power. I sometimes wonder whether Anthony, accepting that his life's work as an art historian was at an end, may not simply have elected to stop living.

The cremation took place at the Putney Vale Crematorium. I had to give the address, and came very close to breaking down. The officiating priest – the vicar of my father's former parish in London, St John's, Paddington – handled things tactfully; but *why* is it necessary to have such a pantomime for one who was openly an agnostic and had no belief in an afterlife? I wish it were possible to let the dead bury their dead – those who loved them in their lifetime will not forget them. Needless to add, it proved impossible to keep the press away, but though they almost outnumbered the mourners they failed to force an entry into the chapel itself. In general, indeed, they behaved with unexpected discretion. The family brought small 'floral tributes', but there was no ostentatious massacre of the vegetable kingdom, which to me has always seemed only one degree less obnoxious than the slaughter of sheep and goats, or of slaves. There was, however, one bunch of flowers that was not 'family'. It came from a wholly unexpected sympathiser – Tom Keating, faker of the works of Samuel Palmer and other artists – and carried a card inscribed 'To Anthony with deepest respect'. I think I can guess what prompted him to send it: both men had successfully exposed the incompetence of the experts.

Anthony had left no instructions about the disposal of his ashes, but Christopher not only had the happy idea of having them scattered on the top of Martinsell, the hill near Marlborough that we all loved, but he himself, on his eightieth birthday, climbed to the top and performed this final act of brotherly affection. It was a cloudless July day.

After Anthony's exposure, and again after his death, Christopher and I received hundreds of letters. Those to me fell into several fairly clearly defined categories. By far the majority of the writers expressed deep sympathy for the family, praise of

At Anthony's cremation, March 1983.
Left to right: Judith Mustoe (niece), the author, Christopher.

Anthony's scholarship (and, in the case of former pupils, gratitude for his brilliant teaching), but pointedly avoided any reference to his treachery. A much smaller group at all events tried to understand how he came to be involved, while a handful of his oldest friends said that they had always loved Anthony and that nothing could diminish their affection for him. A few, however, still cannot accept that to love the sinner is not to condone the sin. The family stood united behind him, and, though he never referred to it, I know from others since his death that he valued our support.

One or two further questions about Anthony still remain but I am in no position to give a full answer to them. Did his treachery possibly lead, as some people allege, to the death of British soldiers or British agents? Anthony sadly admitted to a friend that it *might* have been responsible for 'some – not many', though Francis King wrote to *The Times* (20 November 1979) that it seemed highly doubtful whether what he did had 'caused more harm to this country than a single miners' or hospital workers' strike.

John Costello, in his *Love, Sex and War,*[7] makes – on what evidence we are not told – a very grave accusation. Anthony, for a large part of the war, was in charge of one of the most sensitive of all MI5's operations – the interception of the diplomatic bags of the neutral embassies in London, and (maintains Costello) 'on his own admission must therefore have passed a great deal of extremely valuable information to Moscow that would have facilitated Stalin's strategy in taking over eastern Europe and making a grab at the Balkans'. When, in the spring and autumn of 1944, Anthony was transferred to General Eisenhower's SHAEF headquarters to liaise with military intelligence,

> his involvement with the D-Day deception plans meant that Stalin was almost certainly informed well in advance of the secret that Roosevelt and Churchill were at great pains to keep from the Soviet leader – the time and place of the Normandy invasion. Stalin must have decided that it was not in Russia's military interests to inform Berlin of the vital secret which could have turned D-Day into the Allies' biggest defeat of the war. He needed the opening of the Second

---

[7] Collins, 1985, pp. 262–3. See also Richard Deacon, *The Cambridge Apostles*, Robert Royce, 1985, p. 144, for an even graver charge.

Front to draw off German reserves and accelerate the Red Army's advance westwards.

Surely Philby and Maclean – as well, no doubt, as other still unidentified agents – must have been equally in a position to betray these plans to *our ally*, Russia? And why, in any case, could Russia ever have wanted to pass on this information to the Germans?

As to Anthony's scholarship, was it as impeccable as many of his admirers have maintained? Godfrey Barker's article, 'Cracks in a Painted Image' (*Daily Telegraph*, 4 April 1983), and the correspondence it provoked, deserve to be studied by those better qualified than I am to judge the validity of the evidence adduced. Very probably, as Barker alleges, some of the views put forward by Anthony in articles in the *Spectator* and elsewhere in the thirties were subsequently proved untenable, and no doubt later he also sometimes formed too precipitate, and therefore incorrect, judgements. Is that surprising? Who does not? The backbiting so prevalent in all branches of higher scholarship constantly makes me thankful that I never pretended to be anything but an amateur in any field.

Yet I was always sorry that Anthony so despised the amateur, who I feel does also have a contribution to make. I am sure he did not mean to be wounding when, on receiving from me a copy of my 'popular' biography of Watts, together with a short line saying that if he did not want to keep it he could pass it on to the Courtauld Library, he replied how glad he was that he might do this, since his own shelves were already overcrowded. It was, to him, a plain statement of fact. His close friendship in early days with John Betjeman later fell apart because he felt that John, who had the makings of a scholar, elected – as Anthony saw it – to prostitute his talents by popularising what he could have directed into serious study. Even Kenneth Clark – whose arrogance, admittedly, always jarred – seemed to him not to have made full use of his potential, and I recall Anthony quoting, with obvious relish, a line from a parody about the Clarks that was at one time current: 'Jane and Sir K. in all around I see.'

It was only to be expected that Anthony, after all he had

endured, should have become almost obsessed with the vindictiveness and inaccuracy of much of the reporting by the press, to which he well knew it would be folly to attempt to reply. It was, however, inevitable that an Establishment scandal of such magnitude should have invited innumerable articles in papers of every kind, and that many of them would be scurrilous. It was equally inevitable that, in the absence of hard facts, there must be guesswork and speculation – some of it wrong. But a few of the better papers did do their best, though Anthony could not bring himself to admit it.

No less savagely condemned was, of course, Andrew Boyle's *The Climate of Treason*, which had been largely responsible for his exposure. Yet, when I try to look again impartially at the book (which is not easy), it seems to me that Boyle had not deliberately been unjust, though doubtless he had got a lot wrong. Surely Anthony's rage was that of a man who has been found out, against the man who found him out. Had the book helped – say – to expose the forgeries of Van Meegeren, would he not have been among the first to applaud it?

Godfrey Barker's article, even if sound in substance, was certainly hostile in tone. After Anthony's death, the *Burlington Magazine*, as one would expect, produced a long and balanced account by André Chastel in its September 1983 issue. There was also, rather surprisingly, an admirable piece entitled 'An Incredible Career: Anthony Blunt, 1907–1983', written jointly by Andrew Lumsden and Nicholas Cann (a former Courtauld student), which appeared in *Gay News* (14 April 1983). This dealt, honestly and generously, with his private life, his espionage, and his artistic achievement. Almost more improbable was a very stimulating article by Anthony Burgess in an American periodical – *Rolling Stone* (26 May 1983).

By contrast, the ravings of the less reputable papers were beyond belief. It was claimed that Anthony's 'royal connection' (we are distant relations of the Queen Mother)[8] was responsible for his being given charge of the royal collections. One paper even suggested that Anthony was a natural son of King George V,

---

[8] In fact third cousins, having in common a great-great-grandfather bearing the not unusual name of George Smith, MP for Wendover from 1806 to 1830 and subsequently of Midhurst.

photographs of George VI and himself being reproduced side by side to demonstrate an alleged resemblance! Even a highly respected Sunday newspaper carried a long, conspicuously placed and sensational article of the 'I can now reveal' brand, claiming that Anthony had been in the Dutch SOE and thus probably responsible for the loss of many British and Allied lives. The following week, in smallest print at the very bottom of a page, came a brief and miserable apology: the author had got the wrong man! How many, one wonders, of those who read the former chanced to see the latter?

But it was the BBC which perpetrated the most perfect howler: Blunt, a newsreader announced, had been universally recognised as the world's leading authority on the famous French artist – *Poisson*. Fowl mistaken for fish – for Anthony's *magnum opus* had been his three-volume work on Nicolas Poussin. How Anthony would have laughed at that. I remember his amusement at being introduced, by the Director of the Louvre before a lecture there, as 'Le plus grand Poussiniste du monde'.

Rebecca and Eliezer *by Nicolas Poussin (Fitzwilliam Museum).
Anthony discovered this picture for sale in 1932 for £300 –
a sum far beyond his means. His friend Victor Rothschild,
learning of this, succeeded in buying it for £100 and gave it to him.*

I fear it will be many years before Anthony is allowed to rest in peace. Though probably there is little, other than wild surmise, that can be added until the release of State papers in thirty years' time, biographies are already on the stocks and at least two television documentaries are being prepared. All involved hasten to assure the family, as they beg for interviews and titbits, that their approach will of course be completely free from muck-raking. But will it be? In my opinion, all that can be sensibly written at this stage is a full and scholarly assessment of Anthony's contribution as an art historian – nothing more. However, there seems to be no eagerness to produce such a work: the public does not want to know about Poussin or even Poisson; it wants scandal and espionage and sex.

When I think of Anthony – which is often, and always with affection – there are innumerable little episodes that come to mind that I am reluctant to leave unrecorded, but for which I could find no place in the account I have written above. I therefore propose to append one or two of them here. But first I will quote an impression of him as he appeared to a young student, Cecil Gould, who had recently arrived at the Courtauld Institute where my brother had just been appointed Deputy Director:

> Anthony Blunt was glamour personified. The combination of the very tall, thin figure, the sensitive horse-face, the light-brown wavy hair which he threw back from time to time with an impulsive gesture when it threatened to obscure his vision, and the singularly beautiful speaking voice was striking enough. His general elegance, and what the Italians call *sprezzatura* – the air of effortless superiority – together with great charm increased the effect, which his obvious intellectual distinction completed. His mind responded instantly and lucidly to any idea that was put to it. His lectures on Roman Baroque and on Poussin left an impression on my mind which I have no doubt is still there.

All Anthony's students agreed that he was a brilliant lecturer, either in English or French. If one heard him speak twice on the same subject, the two talks would be substantially different: it was as though he each time drew, as the spirit moved him, a fresh draught from a seemingly inexhaustible well of knowledge. I am sorry only that he had picked up the irritating mannerism, at that

Anthony in his room at the Courtauld Institute

time I think chiefly current at Cambridge though now sadly universal, of emphasising prepositions: 'This picture, *by* Guercino, painted *for* . . .', and so on. His favourite and rather overworked adjective of approval was 'extr*ao*rdinary' – with the second syllable strongly emphasised.

I cannot sufficiently stress his modesty, and his reluctance ever to push himself forward or use his distinguished position to his own advantage; but he was always ready to use it to help others, and then nothing was too much trouble. When the big Van Gogh exhibition was held at the Tate some years ago, a friend of his asked him whether he had seen it yet. 'Yes,' Anthony replied; 'after waiting in the queue for an hour.' The friend was amazed: 'I went past the queue to the entrance and said, "I am a friend of Sir Anthony Blunt", and they let me straight in!'

He was also entirely without snobbery. He had accepted the position of Surveyor of the King's Pictures purely because it gave him the opportunity to work on the Royal Collections, and in particular to organise the cataloguing of the drawings at Windsor. He was no courtier, and as far as possible avoided all royal occasions. In April 1948 we were together in Holland, looking at pictures, when he was suddenly summoned to Windsor to show some Scandinavian monarch round, and his satisfaction when he managed to wriggle out of it (because he was giving a lecture on the King's pictures) was undisguised. He had, however, a great personal regard for the Queen Mother, who also once spoke to me very warmly of him.

Anthony was terrified of flying (which I was not), and I remember how tense he always became on taking off and on landing. It was a phobia, and though of course he often had to fly he never really overcame it. Yet something else that scared *me* apparently left *him* quite unmoved. At a time during the war when the flying bombs were at their worst, we were visiting together a London art-dealer who occupied a top-floor studio with a vast plate-glass window. Bomb after bomb came over, and each time I heard one 'cut out' I took cover, as did the dealer, in a corner of the room well away from that window. But Anthony, absorbed in a little Flemish panel picture, never stirred. He needed the light; unmindful of any danger, he had thoughts only for the painting. It was this ability to concentrate absolutely on the matter in hand that enabled him to continue working through his darkest hours.

During our visit to the Netherlands Anthony took me to have a drink with a multi-millionaire industrialist and art collector called Van Beuningen, who had recently purchased, for what at that time was the fantastic sum of £240,000, Jan van Eyck's *The Three Marys at the Sepulchre* from the Cook collection. He lived on a heath, miles from anywhere in the north-east of Holland, and sent his car to collect us from (I think) Utrecht. The light in the house was not too good, and our host said, 'Let's bring the picture out into the garden' – and, climbing on a chair, unhooked it and cried to me, 'Catch!' Luckily I did. After we had studied it, Van Beuningen leaned it up against a tree and drinks were brought out. An hour later we returned to the house, leaving the picture where he had put it. 'Aren't you going to bring the van Eyck in?' I said. He had completely forgotten about it.

During the war a story was current that Anthony had once driven from Buckingham Palace to Windsor with the King. As they passed Runnymede, the King had (allegedly) said, 'You know, Blunt, that's where all the trouble began!' I asked Anthony whether the story was true, and he answered, 'No.' Yet I now wonder. Might it not have been that this *had* indeed happened, and that in an unguarded moment he had repeated a remark which, though harmless enough, as a member of the Royal Household he ought perhaps to have kept to himself? Anthony did, however, occasionally tell me innocent titbits of Palace gossip: for example, there was a much-loved elderly courtier who one Christmas had dared to kiss Queen Mary under the royal mistletoe. This same man had, it was related, once said to King George V, 'Sir, I have served you loyally all my life. Would it be possible for me, in my old age, to occupy one of the grace-and-favour apartments at Hampton Court?' 'Perfectly easy,' replied the King. 'All you have to do is to become the widow of a distinguished public person.' And though failing to achieve this qualification, in due course he was given one.

I have said that Anthony was never snobbish, but I suddenly recall a remark of his which might, I suppose, just conceivably have been so described. I was dining with him one evening at the Courtauld, and he had produced a delicious steak for me (he was a very competent cook). I noticed that he himself ate little. 'I imagine you had a good lunch,' I said. 'Where were you?' 'At the Palace.' Then came a throw-away line that surely nobody could have resisted: 'It was rather a strain; I was put between two Queens.'

Index

264

The sitters for the leaving photographs on p. 74 are:
top left: Peer (Lord Sudeley)
top right: Field Marshal (Sir Edwin Bramall)
bottom left: Publisher (Crispin Fisher)
bottom right: Ambassador (Hon Humphrey Maud)